P. H. Omtzigt, M. K. Tozman, A. Tyndall (eds.)

The Slow Disappearance of the Syriacs from Turkey
And of the Grounds of the Mor Gabriel Monastery

The Slow Disappearance of the Syriacs from Turkey
And of the Grounds of the Mor Gabriel Monastery

edited by

P. H. Omtzigt, M. K. Tozman and A. Tyndall

LIT

Gedruckt auf alterungsbeständigem Werkdruckpapier entsprechend
ANSI Z3948 DIN ISO 9706

Bibliographic information published by the Deutsche Nationalbibliothek
The Deutsche Nationalbibliothek lists this publication in the Deutsche
Nationalbibliografie; detailed bibliographic data are available in the Internet at
http://dnb.d-nb.de.

ISBN 978-3-643-90268-9

A catalogue record for this book is available from the British Library

©LIT VERLAG GmbH & Co. KG Wien,
Zweigniederlassung Zürich 2012
Klosbachstr. 107
CH-8032 Zürich
Tel. +41 (0) 44-251 75 05
Fax +41 (0) 44-251 75 06
e-Mail: zuerich@lit-verlag.ch
http://www.lit-verlag.ch

LIT VERLAG Dr. W. Hopf
Berlin 2012
Fresnostr. 2
D-48159 Münster
Tel. +49 (0) 2 51-620 320
Fax +49 (0) 2 51-23 19 72
e-Mail: lit@lit-verlag.de
http://www.lit-verlag.de

Distribution:
In Germany: LIT Verlag Fresnostr. 2, D-48159 Münster
Tel. +49 (0) 2 51-620 32 22, Fax +49 (0) 2 51-922 60 99, e-mail: vertrieb@lit-verlag.de

In Austria: Medienlogistik Pichler-ÖBZ, e-mail: mlo@medien-logistik.at

In Switzerland: B + M Buch- und Medienvertrieb, e-mail: order@buch-medien.ch

In the UK: Global Book Marketing, e-mail: mo@centralbooks.com

Acknowledgements and general remarks

We would like to thank Horst Oberkampf, Sébastien de Courtois, Yakup Bilge, Gabriel Gülten, Mehmet Suer and the Mor Gabriel Monastery warmly for providing us with the photographs for this book.

Moreover, we are thankful for the donations of Markus Inan, Paul C. Heule, Fahmi Yigit, ondernemersvereniging SIBO and the Kahraman family in Rijssen. Furthermore, we thank the Stichting Ondersteuning Mor Gabrielklooster (Enschede) and many other generous donors. Without their financial support, we would not have been able to print this book.

Naturally, the authors of this book deserve many compliments and our gratefulness for their profound and well researched articles.

In this book the authors of the different chapters made their own choice regarding the use of the names Suryoye, Syriacs, Syrians, Assyrians, Arameans, Syrian Orthodox, Syriac Orthodox, Syrian Catholics, Syrian Protestants, Chaldean and others. The different names should be read against the background of changes in the context of living, different ideas about the historical past of the same group of people and in the context of different opinions regarding the best name to be used.

Pieter Omtzigt (Member of Parliament, Tweede Kamer der Staten-Generaal)
Markus Tozman (Johns Hopkins University)
Andrea Tyndall (University of Maastricht)

Table of Contents

Foreword 1
(*Dr. Pieter Omtzigt, Dutch MP*)

Introduction 7
(*William Dalrymple*)

Part 1: The Syriacs

The Collapse of the Ottoman Empire and the 'Seyfo' against the
Syrians. 15
(*Prof. Martin Tamcke*)

The Lausanne Treaty: High Aspirations, Highly Neglected 25
(*Alan Hurst*)

Who are the Syriacs? 47
(*Prof. Herman Teule*)

The Syrian Orthodox Church. 57
(*Jens Nieper*)

Living Between the Fronts: The Turkish-Kurdish Conflict and the
Assyrians 63
(*Dr. Aryo Makko*)

Turkey: Secularism with an Islamic Flavour and Persisting Obstacles
to Religious Freedom 73
(*Dennis Pastoor*)

Minority Rights in Turkey: Quo Vadis, Assyrians? 99
(*Soner Onder*)

Almost a Miracle – Syriacs are Returning to their Homelands 121
(*Horst Oberkampf*)

Cadastral Registration of Lands and Preservation Orders in Turkey's
South-East: Subtle Forms of Discrimination? 139
(*Markus Tozman*)

The Role of Religious Freedom in the Context of the Accession
Negotiations between the European Union and Turkey – The
Example of the Arameans 157
(*Dr. Renate Sommer, MEP*)

Table of Contents

Persecution of Christians in Turkey 171
(*Ingrid Fischbach, German MP*)

Part 2: The Mor Gabriel Monastery

The Monastery of Mor Gabriel: A Historical Overview and its Wider
Significance Today. 181
(*Dr. Sebastian Brock*)

Reconciled by Mor Gabriel 201
(*Prof. Baskin Oran*)

The Saint Gabriel Monastery Trust. 209
(*Yakup Bilge*)

St. Gabriel and Religious Freedom in Turkey. 219
(*Gus Bilirakis, US Congress Member*)

Mor Gabriel: A Symbol of how the Turkish State Deals with its
Religious Minorities 227
(*Ute Granold, German MP*)

United for the Sake of the Mor Gabriel Monastery 231
(*Dr. Naures Atto*)

Interview with Sébastien de Courtois. 243
(*Dr. Pieter Omtzigt, Dutch MP*)

Appendix 1: Initiative Policy Document: The Alarming Situation of
the Monastery of Mor Gabriel and the Aramaic-speaking Christians
in Turkey – The Syriacs 249
(*Dr. Pieter Omtzigt, Dutch MP*)

Appendix 2: The Disappeared Documents from St. Gabriel
Monastery's Case File 261
(*Prof. Baskin Oran*)

Foto Index 265

Foreword

By Pieter Omtzigt

Dr. Pieter Omtzigt is a Member of Parliament for the Christian Democratic Party in the Netherlands and in the Parliamentary Assembly of the Council of Europe he is vice-chairman of the monitoring committee, which is responsible for verifying that Member States are in compliance with the European Convention on Human Rights.

1. A short history of the issues in this book

The Mor Gabriel monastery (AD 397) has had a rough history. Tucked away in the southeastern corner of Turkey, close to Syria and Iraq, it is not located in the quietest spot on earth. Throughout its history, it has lived through many invasions, like the Mongols', who in the 14th century killed 40 monks and around 400 Christians hiding in the monastery. Yet it has survived numerous attacks and the community has proven resilient.

The Syrian Orthodox church uses Aramaic as its liturgical language and the Mor Gabriel monastery is unique in educating young people in that language, the language Jesus Christ spoke. It has done so for more than 16 centuries, with only very short interruptions. It is one of the oldest functioning monasteries in the world.[1]

For more than three years now the monastery has faced a number of court cases. Three of those cases have been brought against the monastery by institutions of the Turkish State. So a secular state brings multiple lawsuits against the Mor Gabriel monastery and even pursues these cases to the highest legal level, as the local courts often rule in favor of the monastery.

Mor Gabriel has now lost large plots of land on which it has regularly paid its property taxes since the 1930s. This has been proven in a case brought by the Turkish Treasury. Yet the appeals court has mysteriously lost the proof of such payments, which was accepted by the Midyat court.

Moreover, it has lost land that it had turned from barren wasteland into forest with great care. But forestland, according to the state, belongs to the state. The Forestry Directorate brought this case against the monastery. Mor Gabriel has lodged a complaint on the forestry case at the European Court of Human Rights in Strasbourg.

---

[1] To my knowledge only St. Anthony's in Egypt (356 AD) was founded before Mor Gabriel.

Over the centuries, invasions, war and unrest did not manage to bring the community and the monastery to its knees. The present situation, however, may be different. Over the last century the number of Syriacs in the region declined rapidly due to the Seyfo during the First World War and large migration, caused by the violence between the Kurdish PKK and the Turkish army. Today my region of Twente has a larger Syriac population than the whole south east of Turkey, where only a few thousand Syriacs remain. The members of the church are moving ever more into a Diaspora, as the only sizeable community left in the Middle East, in Syria, just over the border from Mor Gabriel, is now under intense pressure in the civil war. The Diaspora community does feel that the monastery is part of its heritage and the number of visitors from the Diaspora, as well as Turkish visitors and tourists, has increased steadily over the years. Yet for the monastery to survive it is important that it is protected in its entirety and continues to function as a place of worship.

2. Treaties and political reactions to the Mor Gabriel case

Turkey is party to a number of treaties that protect religious minorities. It suffices to mention the Lausanne Treaty (1923), which defines the Turkish state after its war of independence and has a special section on non-Muslim minorities, or the European Convention on Human Rights.

Turkey became a Member of the Council of Europe in its founding year 1949 by ratifying the European Convention on Human Rights. Under that convention, every individual or legal entity now has the right to lodge a complaint at the European Court of Human Rights when they feel that one of the Member States has violated the fundamental rights and guarantees in the convention. A complaint can only be lodged when all domestic remedies have been exhausted.

Turkey has an awful track record at the European Court of Human Rights. Year after year[2] it has the largest number of convictions going against it of all the 47 Member States. It is one of the few Member States that is found to violate the right of freedom of thought, conscience and religion (article 9 of the Convention).

The Parliamentary Assembly of the Council of Europe, whose Members are parliamentarians of the 47 Member States, has taken the exceptional step to approve a resolution on "Freedom of religion and other human rights for non-Muslim minorities in Turkey and for the Muslim minority in Thrace (Eastern Greece)[3]" in January 2010. It states:

---

[2] Annual report of the European Court of Human Rights 2011, 2010, 2009, 2008, 2007.
[3] Resolution 1704/2010.

Foreword

Specifically concerning Turkey, the Assembly urges the Turkish authorities to:

19.6. ensure that the Orthodox Syriac monastery of Mor Gabriel, one of the oldest Christian monasteries in the world, founded in 397 ad, is not deprived of its lands, and that it is protected in its entirety. The Assembly expresses equal concern about the current status of the unlawful appropriation of significant amounts of land historically and legally belonging to a multitude of other ancient Syriac monasteries, churches and proprietors in south-east Turkey;

19.7. recognise, promote and protect the Syriac people as a minority, which is indigenous to south-east Turkey, in conformity with the Lausanne Treaty and related international conventions which guarantee their fundamental human rights and dignity; this shall include, but shall not be limited to, officially developing their education and carrying out religious services in their native language, Aramaic;

20. The Assembly asks the governments of Greece and Turkey to report back on the progress made on each point in paragraphs 16, 18 and 19 of the present resolution by February 2011.

Despite numerous reminders, the Turkish authorities have chosen not to provide any answer at all, to ignore the international community and have instead stubbornly continued their cases against the monastery. Its case has caught the attention of the European Parliament, as Turkey is a candidate Member of the European Union. It has also been raised in the parliaments of Germany, the Netherlands, Switzerland, France and Austria.

In the Annual Report of the United States Commission on International Religious Freedom (a committee of the US Congress) in March 2012, the recommendations regarding Turkey are:

"The United States regards Turkey as an important strategic partner and continues to support Turkey's European Union accession process. By designating Turkey as a "country of particular concern", U.S. policy should urge Turkey to comply with its international commitments regarding freedom of religion or belief by ending its longstanding denial of full legal recognition for religious communities and permitting religious minorities to train religious clergy in Turkey, including reopening the Greek Orthodox Theological Seminary of Halki and returning the entire territory of the Mor Gabriel Syrian Orthodox monastery."[4]

Turkey is designated as a "country of particular concern" and is thus listed among

---

[4] This is the whole recommendation on Turkey. The other priority recommendations concern Northern Cyprus.

the 15 worst offenders on religious liberty by this committee,[5] together with countries like North Korea, Burma, Iraq and Iran.

In another part of its policy, Turkey likes religious liberty. It actively uses the liberty available in the Western world to send imams, paid by the powerful state ministry Diyanet, to many Western countries. It funds new mosques abroad and it protested powerfully when Switzerland introduced a ban on the building of new minarets.

3. Content of this book

A number of NGOs have written detailed reports on the court cases against Mor Gabriel, and also on other human rights issues. Specifically the annual reports by the "Aramaic Movement for Human Rights" and reports by the "World Council of Arameans (Syriacs)"[6] provide detailed information. Yet an overview of the issues at stake has been missing thus far.

The aim of this book is to shed light on the history of the Syriac people and of the Mor Gabriel monastery and to present some of the historical and legal issues involved in the court cases against the monastery. The chapters can be read individually and in any order.

In the introduction William Dalrymple places the Mor Gabriel case in the perspective of the rapidly diminishing Christian communities in the Middle East.

Part 1 of the book contains an introduction to the history of the Syriac people. Martin Tamcke describes the collapse of the Ottoman Empire, which culminated in the First World War, the Armenian genocide and the contemporaneous Seyfo, the mass killing of Syriacs. Alan Hurst discusses the Lausanne Treaty (1923), which founded modern Turkey and should protect religious minorities.

Herman Teule describes the long history of the Syriacs in the Middle East and Jens Nieper takes on the present descriptions of the Syriacs, who now live largely in a Diaspora.

Aryo Makko describes how Syriacs were caught in the middle of the Kurdish-Turkish conflict. Then Dennis Pastoor describes what factors determine the low ranking for freedom of religion in Turkey in an international comparison.

---

[5] The committee did so with a 5–4 split vote. The minority 4 would have maintained Turkey on the Watch List.
[6] Formerly known as the Syriac Universal Alliance.

Soner Onder continues with a chapter on minority rights with special attention given to the law of foundations, which has severely hampered minority communities' ownership of property.

Horst Oberkampf describes a relatively recent phenomenon: a number of Syriacs returning from the Diaspora to their homeland. Markus Tozman then describes how the cadastral registration process, which ironically is wanted by the EU, leads to the large-scale expropriation of Syriac properties.

Renate Sommer describes the role of religious freedom in the accession process of Turkey to the EU, with a particular focus on the Syriac community, while Ingrid Fischbach describes the situation and gives recommendations as to what Germany could and should do.

Part 2 focuses on the Mor Gabriel case. Sebastian Brock gives a beautiful historical overview of the significance of the Mor Gabriel monastery. Baskin Oran describes very clearly and in great detail how Turkish laws and the Turkish court system works to the disadvantage of the Mor Gabriel monastery, with a special focus on the forestry case and the treasury case. Yakup Bilge gives an account of the way in which, throughout the ages, the monastery has owned the land through the Saint Gabriel Monastery Trust.

Gus Bilirakis describes how the Syriac community is being targeted and mentions the Greek Orthodox Halki seminary, which the Turkish government closed in 1971 and which, despite massive international pressure, remains closed until today. Ute Granold describes how the German Bundestag follows the Mor Gabriel cases and how international cooperation is slowly being established. Naures Atto shows how the Mor Gabriel case is uniting the fragmented and dispersed Syriac Diaspora into action. An interview with Sébastien de Courtois, who wrote a book on the Seyfo, *The Forgotten Genocide*, constitutes the last chapter.

The initiative policy document on the Mor Gabriel monastery, which was discussed and approved in the Dutch parliament in June 2012, is added as an appendix.

Finally, a very interesting and short article by Baskin Oran on the mysteriously lost documents of the treasury case at their latest appeal is attached.

Introduction

By William Dalrymple

William Dalrymple is an award winning historian and writer, as well as a broadcaster, critic and art historian who has studied history at the Trinity College in Cambridge. His list of publications is long and contains several bestsellers amongst which his famous book "From the Holy Mountain". In this book he describes his journey through the remnants of the Christian Levant in the middle of the 90s, in which he became witness of the situation of the Christians in Tur Abdin as well.

The monastery chapel of Mar Gabriel in the Tur Abdin, the Mountain of the Servants (of God), near Mardin in south-eastern Turkey is arguably the oldest functioning church in the Middle East. The monastery was built by the Emperor Anastasius in 512 – before Haghia Sophia, before Ravenna, before Mount Sinai. It was already eighty years old by the time St Augustine landed in Thanet to bring Christianity to Anglo Saxon England. Yet some parts of the monastery date back even earlier, to the monastery's original foundation in 397 A.D.

There are only a handful of churches anywhere in the world that old. It is incredible that it has survived at all, but that it has survived intact and still practising when Persians, Arabs, Timurid and Mongol hordes have all come and gone, Constantinople has fallen to the Turks and Asia Minor has been completely cleared of Greeks and Armenians – that is nothing short of a miracle.

To the first-time visitor, the monasteries of the Tur Abdin seem like timeless islands of Byzantium. With their bells and black robes and candle-lit processions, the monasteries are still occupied with elderly monks whose heavily whiskered faces mirror those of the saints in the ancient manuscripts in the monastery library. The monk's vestments remain unchanged since the time of the early church; the same icons are painted in the same way. Even the superstitions remain unchanged: relics are still venerated by local villagers who come to pray at the shrine of the monastery's patron saint and, indeed, many of the faithful take dust from the tomb to give both to their animals and children to keep them healthy during epidemics. More remarkable still, Muslim women queue up with their Christian neighbours to drink water from the skull of a local saint named St. John the Arab, which they believe will help barren women have children. Today, sitting under the candlelit mosaics, listening to plainchant still sung in the language of Jesus, it is still – just –

possible to forget the intervening millennia and feel that the lifeline of tones and syllables, fears and hopes linking us with the early church is still intact.

The Annunciation of Archangel Gabriel to the Mother of God; image from a Syriac Bible, Deir El-Zaafaran, 1250, Collection Leroy, EPHE, Paris. (S. de Courtois)

Until the First World War, the sister monastery of Mor Gabriel, Deir el-Zaferan was the headquarters of the Syrian Orthodox Church, the ancient Church of Antioch. The Syrian Orthodox split off from the Byzantine mainstream because they refused to accept the theological decisions of the Council of Chalcedon in 451 A.D. The divorce took place, however, along an already established linguistic fault-line, separating the Greek-speaking Byzantines of Western Anatolia from those to the East who still spoke Aramaic, the language of Christ. Severely persecuted as heretical Monophysites by the Byzantine Emperors, the Syrian Orthodox church hierarchy retreated into the inaccessible shelter of the barren hills of the Tur Abdin. There, far from the centres of power, three hundred Syrian Orthodox monasteries successfully maintained the ancient Antiochene liturgies in the original Aramaic. But remoteness led to marginalisation, and the church steadily dwindled both in numbers and in importance. By the end of the 19th century, only 200,000 Süryani remained in the Middle East, most of them concentrated around the Patriarchal seat at Deir el-Zaferan.

The 20th century proved as cataclysmic for the Süryani as it had been for the Armenians. During the First World War death throes of the Ottoman Empire, starvation, deportation and massacre decimated the already dwindling Süryani population. Then in 1924, Ataturk decapitated the remnants of the community by expelling the Syrian Orthodox Patriarch. He took with him the ancient library of Deir el-Zaferan, and eventually settled with them in Damascus. Finally, in 1978, the Turkish authorities sealed the community's fate by summarily closing the monastery's Aramaic school.

From 200,000 in the last century, by 1920, the size of the community fell to around 70,000. By 1990 there were barely four thousand Süryani living in the entire region. Now there are approximately two thousands and four hundred, plus approximately a dozen monks and a dozen nuns, spread across the five extant monasteries. One village with an astonishing 17 churches now only has one inhabitant: its elderly priest. In Deir el-Zaferan two monks rattle around in the echoing expanse of 6th century buildings, more like caretakers of a religious relic than fragments of a living monastic community.

The fate of the Christians in the region is part of a wider exodus of Christians from all over the Middle East. For several hundred years under the capricious thumb of the Ottoman Sultan, the various faiths of the Ottoman empire lived, if not in complete harmony, then at least in a kind of pluralist equilibrium. Islam has traditionally been tolerant of religious minorities, and the relatively benign treatment of Christians and Jews under Muslim rule contrasts with the fate of Christendom's one distinct religious minority, the relentlessly ill-treated European Jews. As recently as the 17th century, Huguenot exiles escaping religious persecution in Europe wrote admiringly of the Ottoman policy of religious tolerance – as M de la Motraye put it, "there is no country on earth where the exercise of all religions is more free and less subject to being troubled than in Turkey". The same broad pluralism that had given homes to the Jews expelled by the bigoted Catholic kings from Spain and Portugal protected the Eastern Christians in their ancient homelands. A century ago, a quarter of the population of the Levant was still Christian. In Istanbul, that proportion rose to almost half.

But with the collapse of the Ottoman Empire in the early 20th century, its fringes – the Balkans, Cyprus, eastern Anatolia, the Levant – have suffered decades of bloodletting. Everywhere pluralism has been replaced with a savage polarisation. Religious minorities have fled to places where they can be majorities, and those too few to do even that have abandoned the region altogether, seeking out places less heavy with history, such as America or Australia. Today the Christians are a small minority of 12 million, struggling to keep afloat amid 180 million non-Christians, with their numbers shrinking annually. In the past 20 years, at least 4 million have left to make new lives for themselves in the West. Now more Jerusalem-born Christians are living in Sydney than in Jerusalem itself, those that remain could be flown out in just nine jumbo jets.

The monastery of Mor Malke in Tur Abdin with monk Yeshu. (H. Oberkampf)

The worst catastrophe has been that which has recently displaced most of the Christians of Iraq, just over the border from the Tur Abdin. Although Iraq's 750,000 Christians only made up about 7 % of the population of pre-war Iraq, they were a prosperous minority under Saddam; a fact symbolised by the high profile of Tariq Aziz, Saddam's Christian Foreign Minister. Highly educated and overwhelmingly middle class, the Christians were heavily concentrated in Mosul, Basra and especially Baghdad, which prior to the war had the largest Christian population of any town in the Middle East. Now at least half of these Christians – approximately 350,000 people – have fled the new Iraq, unable to remain in the

Introduction

face of violence, mass-abductions and economic meltdown. Wherever you go in Syria you keep running into them: bank managers and engineers, pharmacists and scientists, garage owners and businessman, all living with their extended families in one-room flats on what remained of their savings, and assisted by the charity of the various churches.

Today their situation is more precarious than ever. The Arab Spring and the Syrian Civil War has brought still more anxiety and uncertainty and the situation of the Copts of Egypt and the Christians of Syria – until recently two of the more secure minorities – now looks profoundly uncertain. It is not impossible that both could suffer the fate of their Iraq neighbours. The fate of the Palestinian Christians, caught between Israeli settlements and the Islamists of Hamas, is little more enviable. Most of the young Christians you meet in Gaza or the West Bank already have their immigration papers in with some embassy. Being on the whole middle-class professionals, they find it easier to leave, have the money and the skills to start again and find their applications receiving preferential treatment from embassies. Canada is now the current destination of choice, the US now being perceived as too Arabaphobic for even Christian Arabs.

The exodus of the Arab Christians will radically change the plural character of the region. The Christian Arabs are a bulwark protecting the Arab World from Islamism. Since the 19th century, they have played a vital role in defining a secular Arab identity: men like Michel Aflaq, founder of the Ba'ath Party, and George Antonius who wrote *The Arab Awakening* were both Christian. Edward Said, the Arab World's most influential contemporary intellectual, was a Palestinian Christian. If they continue to emigrate, the Arabs will find it much harder to defend themselves against radical Islamism.

According to the historian Professor Kamal Salibi, the Christians have simply had enough: "There is a feeling of *fin de race* among Christians all over the Middle East", he told me in Beirut. "It's a feeling that 14 centuries of having all the time to be smart, to be ahead of the others, is long enough. The Middle Eastern Christians tend to be intelligent, well-qualified, highly educated people. Now they just want to go somewhere else".

This matters. Christianity is not a Western religion. It was not founded in Brussels or in Rome. It was born in Jerusalem and received its intellectual superstructure in Antioch, Damascus, Constantinople and Alexandria. At the Council of Nicea, where the words of the Christian Creed were thrashed out in 325 A.D., there were more Bishops from Mesopotamia and India than there were from Western Europe. Those Eastern Christians who are now leaving the Middle East preserve many of the most ancient liturgies, superstitions and traditions which hold the key to understanding early Christianity, and without which we can never really understand the roots of our own Christian-based culture. Without the local Christian population, the most important and the most ancient shrines in the Christian world will be left as museum pieces, preserved only for the curiosity of tourists. Christianity will no longer exist in the Holy Land as living faith; a vast vacuum will lie in the very heart of Christendom.

The European Community has a good record of supporting the Middle Eastern Christians, but before more can be done, their situation has first to be understood. A book like this is an invaluable tool to help understand one of the most important and interesting Christian minorities in the entire region and the editors are to be congratulated for pulling together such a remarkable group of pieces by such a distinguished group of authorities on the subject. I very much hope it will be widely distributed and avidly read.

William Dalrymple
London, June 2012

Part 1:

The Syriacs

The Collapse of the Ottoman Empire and the 'Seyfo' against the Syrians

By Martin Tamcke

Martin Tamcke is professor for ecumenics and oriental church history at the University of Göttingen and is internationally acknowledged as specialist particularly on the history and contemporary situation of the Syriac speaking Christian communities all over the world. He is the director of the conference of German speaking Syriac Scholars.

1. Decline and reforms as the political framework of the event

The religious policy of the Ottoman Empire in the 19th century repeatedly experienced course corrections. Selim III (1789–1807) initially reformed the army after the loss of the position as Great Power as well as the constant losses against Russia.[1] However, already in 1821 Greek freedom fighters had seized the Peloponnese region; in 1827 the Triple Alliance (Russia, England and France) destroyed the Ottoman-Egyptian fleet; in 1829 Greek independence was declared in the Treaty of London; France annexed Algeria in 1830; Serbia became autonomous in the same year; and Egyptian troops entered Asia Minor via Syria in 1832. This advancing decay was to be stopped by means of reforms (known as the *Tanzimat*) begun by Mahmut II (1808–1839) and announced on 3 November 1839 by his son Abdülmecit I (1839–1861). Along with securing private property and the introduction of public jurisdiction, the main goal of these reforms was to engender equality among believers of different religious communities. They were to be Ottoman citizens without restrictions. A general military duty for the army was introduced (before, only Muslims were allowed to serve in the army). The special role of the Muslim religion was underlined to make concessions to religious forces. By permitting Christians to be citizens, the reforms were not to be taken as an excuse for interventions of foreign powers on Turkish soil. The Convention of London of 1849 took these reforms into account as Great Britain, Austria, Prussia and Russia banded together against France and Egypt to preserve the Ottoman Empire.

In 1845 the University of Constantinople was founded as a visible symbol of further reforms, including in the cultural domain. The intervention of British

---

[1] This brief survey is based on Matuz, 1985; Kreiser, 2001; Kreiser and Neumann, 2003; Tamcke, 2005a.

and French troops did indeed save the Ottomans from a crushing defeat during the Crimean War. The Treaty of Paris (1856) secured the survival of the Ottoman Empire and also confirmed the reform policies. At the same time, however, the first wave of severe persecution of Christian minorities took place.

By that time the threat of hardships and more intense pogroms against Syrian Christians had been looming for some time. Two events in particular intensified the international political interest to a degree never seen before. The first was the massacre of the East Syrian Christians and the destruction of their Patriarchal See in 1848 as the result of a local unrest in this region, in which the Patriarch of the Church of the East played a prominent role. The second was the brutal massacre of Maronites – who had inhabited the Syrian region since 1858 – as a result of conflicts between Maronites and Druzes. At the same time, uprisings aimed at forcing separation continued: the uprising on Crete in 1866–1869 was only just put down; Turks and Muslims left Serbia; Bulgaria entered in a state of revolt in 1876; and, in the end, the Balkan Crisis with the victory of the Ottoman troops against the Serbs had merely a retarding effect on the decline. Sultan Abdulhamit II (1876–1909) responded by enacting a new constitution and introduced a parliamentary system. He re-enacted the contents of the reforms, but also declared Islam as the state religion. Jews and Christians were permitted to enter public office, as long as they spoke Turkish. Conservative opponents were interned and progressives were forced to emigrate. Another Russian-Ottoman War in 1877 brought Russian troops almost to the capital. The Congress of Berlin and the resulting peace treaty of 13 July 1878 declared independence for Romania, Serbia and Montenegro; Bulgaria obtained a prince who was tributary to the Ottomans; and the Armenians in the Ottoman eastern provinces were granted self-administration. Cyprus was given to Great Britain; Bosnia-Herzegovina was given to Austria-Hungary; Thessaly was given to Greece; and Batumi, Kars and Ardahan were all given to Russia. Abdulhamit responded in 1878 by dissolving the parliament, but initially retained the reforms and pursued pan-Islamic goals and the Ottomanism by which he sought to overcome the national self-interest of people. After England bought the Suez Canal in 1875, Tunisia was passed to France in 1881.

Pushing for the implementation of the promised reforms, the Armenians increasingly found themselves in opposition to the state. The sultan used the Kurds for brutal encroachments against the Armenians, but Syrians had also already been made victims of this violence at that point. The sultan ordered his troops to fire on protesting Armenians in Constantinople, while a counter-protest devolved into a deadly hunt for Armenians. The raid by Armenian activists on an Ottoman bank in 1896 aggravated the already tense situation. The attempted assassination of the sultan in 1905 was used to justify cruel revenge. Due to the national bankruptcy and the pressure by the Young Turks, Abdulhamit reinstated the constitution in 1908. At the same time, Crete declared its annexation to Greece and Bulgaria declared its independence. As a result, a counter-revolution in 1909 was able to bring the sultan back to power, whereupon troops of the 'Committee of Union and Progress' marched into the capital, deposed the sultan and declared his brother, Mehmed V (1909–1918), the new sultan, although by now the sultan had become largely a figurehead. Still the decline continued: Libya was lost to Italy during the Italo-Turkish War 1911–1912; Turkish forces were defeated during the First Balkan War; and the reclamation of Edirne during the Second Balkan War was also merely an outcome of a hasty attack by the Bulgarians.

In 1913 the 'Three Pashas' (Enver, Talaat and Cemal) assumed power. They were committed to Laicism and pushed strongly for reforms, abolished the Madrasah and placed the religious courts under the control of the Ministry of Justice. Civil law gradually replaced religious legislation. Polygamy was abolished. Schools for girls were introduced. Pan-Turkism became the ideological basis that intended for the other nationalities in the empire to become Turkish. However, by that point, Turkey had already entered World War One on the side of the Germans.

Preparations for the genocide of the Armenians, which are now well documented in numerous scholarly works, had already been completed by the spring of 1915.[2] With the aim of creating an ethnically and religiously homogenous state, not only were Armenians eliminated in the shadow of the World War, but Syrians were also victims of the same attacks by which the Young Turks sought to rid themselves of allegedly disloyal minorities. A story in its own right is the annihilation of the members of the Church of the East (Assyrians/Nestorians), which officially declared war on Turkey in an assembly of tribes. Their suffering is very much in parallel with the tale of woe of the other Syrian Christians who did not belong to this church.[3] For those affected, today's sufferings are of course a prosecution of similar events that befell them in the centuries before.[4] The Young Turks responsible believed that they could save their own state from disintegrating by exterminating those peoples who sought autonomy or independence.

---

[2] See, for instance, the profound account in Kieser, 2000.
[3] If I may refer to my own studies, see Tamcke 2009a, 2008a, 2006, 2005c, 2005d and 2004b.
[4] See for example: Tamcke, 2011. For general and fundamental information, see Tamcke, 2008b.

The village of Kafro Eleito (Arica). Until the 80s it was still inhabited by Syriacs and Kurds. Today, there are no Syriac families left. (M. Tozman)

2. Seyfo

In the period after World War One and in the context of the peace negotiations, Bishop Severos Ephrem, later Patriarch Mar Ignatius Ephrem I Barsaum (1887–1957), took action.[5] The hierarch was born in Mosul and initially entered the Deir ul-Zafaran monastery as a monk. In 1918, Ephrem was ordained metropolitan of Lebanon and Syria, with his see in Homs. He espoused supporting measures for refugees from Turkey and Syria. In 1919 he participated in the Peace Conference in Paris where he was sent by the Syrian Orthodox Patriarchate to represent the interests of the Syrian-Orthodox believers in the negotiations. At the conference, when given the opportunity to address the conference, Ephrem began his speech with the biblical words, "Blessed are the peacemakers", followed by a description of the poverty, hunger and tragedy of his people. Sadly, Ephrem felt that his words had gone unheard. A second opportunity to address the conference had similar results.

---

[5] Cf. Tamcke, 2009, esp. pp. 71–97.

His written petitions have been preserved. In a memorandum, Severos Ephrem addressed the Peace Conference on 16 January 1919 and in February 1919 to plead for the future national and religious safety of his people. He also protested against the planned autonomous Kurdish government in East Turkey. However, the intermittent Syrian plan for a Syrian nation was ignored in the peace negotiations and instead, the formation of a Kurdish state was negotiated. Article 62 of the Treaty of Sèvres held out the prospect of an autonomous Kurdistan that would provide an assurance for the protection of the 'Assyro-Chaldeans'. Those who primarily would pay the blood tax in Turkey took this as pure cynicism, as they still remembered the experiences of the barbaric, oppressive, persecuting, and murdering Kurds. What hope could they have that the willing enforcers of the annihilation would now become tolerant guardians of minorities and human rights? Ephrem Barsaum protested insistently that the concerns of the Syrians were being ignored at the conference. Moreover, the massacres were being termed 'Armenian' massacres, despite the other Christian communities that had been no less affected. It might even have been the case, he argued, that the Syrians had paid an even higher blood tax, and half his people had been murdered. Ephrem sought international help for the accommodation of widows and orphans and the rebuilding of the churches.

View on the church Mor Had Bshabo in Ciwardo (Gülgöze), one of the few centres of successful resistance of the Syriacs against the genocide. (M. Tozman)

To this day, the papers and documents regarding the Seyfo have not been studied in detail. In addition to the first testimonials of the oral tradition, which were published by Helmut Ritter, Otto Jastrow and Julius Cicek, there is, for example, the collection of interviews in David Gaunt's book *Massacres, Resistance, Protectors: Muslim-Christian Relations in Eastern Anatolia during World War I*.[6] Three other works have been published that gather accounts of the events from those affected: a book by a Malfono from Qarabasch; a book by a Syrian Catholic archpriest, who gathered his information from the reports of refugees from the Mardin region and published their experiences anonymously in 1919 in Lebanon; and a book by an archpriest who had collected reports from villages.[7]

Regarding the East Syrians, it was Rudolf Strothman who reported doggedly on their plight starting as early as 1936.[8] Gabriele Yonan's collection continued his work[9]. Members of the Church of the East published accounts of their sufferings early on, including in Western languages. However, the following explications focus only on the Syrian Christians outside of the tradition of the Church of the East, thus the Syriac-Orthodox Church and those Syrians maintaining communion with Rome.

In the following, some extracts from official dossiers shall suffice to recall the events. As early as 19 June 1915, the German consul of Mosul, vice consul Holstein, noted that the state of affairs in the region of Mardin and Amid [present-day Diyarbakir] was "turning into a real persecution of Christians".[10] By that point the Germans were aware of what the Turks were planning. A month later the German ambassador interceded in Istanbul with the Interior Minister Talaat Bey in the extermination programmes targeting Christians. At this point, it had become unmistakably clear that the actions in Mardin did not affect the Armenians alone. By order of the Wāli of Diyarbakir, Rechid Bey, gendarmes from Diyarbakir gathered in Mardin, where they arrested the Armenian bishop and numerous Armenians and other Christians ("et d'autres chrétiens"). In all, seventy people were arrested, all of whom were slaughtered like sheep the next night ("égorgé comme des moutons"). The German ambassador stated that the death toll of these massacres was 2,000 people. He summarized the intention of the Turkish Wāli as: "un massacre général de tous les habitants chrétiens". The Syrian Christians were de-

---

[6] See Gaunt, 2006; on the previous accounts and the oral tradition, see Tamcke, 2009, esp. pp. 90–97.
[7] First orientation: Tamcke, 2009b and 2009c (and related entries).
[8] See Strothmann, 1936.
[9] Yonan, 1989.
[10] All quotations according to Tamcke, 2004a, 2005b, and 2009, esp. pp. 78–89.

ported or fled. As vice consul Holstein said on 21 July 1915, the Syrian refugees in Mosul suffered inexpressible misery. The inhuman actions of the Wāli [Turkish name for governor] did not go unanswered. The persecuted Christians offered resistance. The German consul reported on 28 July that in their desperation the Syrian Christians in the area of Mardin and Midyat had revolted in response to the extreme methods employed by the Wāli of Diyarbakir against the Christians. Worried families now fled Se'ert as Turkish troops drew nearer joined by armed Kurds. Three days later, on 31 July 1915, the German ambassador in Istanbul, Prince Hohenlohe-Langenburg, reported to the chancellor of the German Reich: "As of early this month the Wāli of Diyarbakir, Rechid Bey, has commenced the systematic extermination of the Christian population in his administration district, without distinction of race or confession. This affected, among others, the Catholic Armenians of Mardin and Tell Ermen and the Chaldean Christians and the non-Uniat Syrians of the districts of Midyat, Djeziret ibn Omar and Nisibin."

In a misjudgement of their capabilities, the German Ministry of Foreign Affairs commanded the German ambassador to resolve the "resulting difficulties" – which was how he termed the brutal events – "in an amicable way". The ambassador then sent the – actually very shocking – notification on 14 February 1916 that: "The resulting difficulties between the Syrian Christians at Mardin and Midyat and the Turkish authorities are now corrected." Numerous reports confirm, with the usual distance of outsiders, what the oral tradition of those affected by the persecution gives account: the systematic annihilation of the Syrian Christian population of the Ottoman Empire.

The Councillor of Radowitz, intermittently working as chargé d'affairs of the German embassy in Constantinople, sent an article from a newspaper controlled by the Young Turks to the German chancellery. As this article noted, the original idea of a melding of the various elements of the population "went bankrupt", and instead a "cleansing" of the Empire of Christian elements was targeted. These ideas had already been partially implemented with the expulsion of the Assyrian Christians living in the Eastern borderlands (9 October 1916). As this article demonstrates, the extermination programmes were executed quite publicly.

A concluding assessment of the 'Seyfo' (as the Syrians referred to the genocide; 'Seyfo' or 'sword' being the abbreviation of 'year of the sword, as the year 1915 was termed) is not to be attempted here. However, because both the relocation of many Syrian Orthodox Christians to Syria and the fundamental altering of the area of settlement in South East Turkey are consequences of the Seyfo, blinding out the Seyfo in a book about Suryoye/Arameans/Assyrians would leave later events incomprehensible. The experience of Seyfo is at the foundation of the

Mount Izlo from the South, where first ermits came from Egypt and Syria. (S. de Courtois)

Syriac sense of insecurity to this day and reinforced, for example, the willingness to emigrate to Europe half a century ago.

References

Gaunt, David, *Massacres, Resistance, Protectors: Muslim-Christian relations in eastern Anatolia During World War I* (2006), Piscataway/NJ: Gorgias.

Kieser, Hans-Lukas, *Der verpasste Friede. Mission, Ethnie und Staat in den Ostprovinzen der Türkei 1839–1938* (2000), Zurich: Chronos.

Kreiser, Klaus, *Der Osmanische Staat 1300–1922* (2001), Munich: Oldenbourg.

Kreiser, Klaus and Neumann, Christoph K., *Kleine Geschichte der Türkei* (2003), Stuttgart: Reclam.

Matuz, Josef, *Das Osmanische Reich. Grundlinien seiner Geschichte* (1985), Darmstadt: Primus.

Strothmann, Rudolf, "Heutiges Orientchristentum und das Schicksal der Assyrer", in *Zeitschrift für Kirchengeschichte* 55 (1936), pp. 17–82.

Tamcke, Martin, "Das Schicksal des syrisch-aramäischen Volkes unter türkischer Herrschaft (part 1)", in *Mardutho d-Suryoye* 16, 47 (2004a), pp. 19–21.

Tamcke, Martin, "Der Genozid an den Assyrern/Nestorianern (Ostsyrische Christen)", in Hofmann, Tessa (Ed.), *Verfolgung, Vertreibung und Vernichtung der Christen im Osmanischen Reich 1912–1922* (2004b), pp. 95–110, Münster: Lit.

Tamcke, Martin, "Türkei", in *Religion in Geschichte und Gegenwart,* Vol. 8 (2005a), pp. 662–666, Tübingen: Mohr Siebeck.

Tamcke, Martin, "Das Schicksal des syrisch-aramäischen Volkes unter türkischer Herrschaft (part 2)", in *Mardutho d-Suryoye* 17, 48 (2005b), pp. 19–22.

Tamcke, Martin, "Die Vernichtung der Ostsyrischen Christen im Osmanischen Reich und den osmanisch besetzten Gebieten des Iran", in *Der Völkermord an den Armeniern und syrischen Christen, epd Dokumentation 17/18* (2005c), pp. 28–48, Frankfurt: Evangelischer Pressedienst.

Tamcke, Martin, "Ein Brief des Lazarus Jaure aus dem Frühjahr 1916 zu den Geschehnissen in Urmia", in Tamcke, Martin & Heinz, Andreas (Eds.), *Die Suryoye und ihre Umwelt. 4. deutsches Syrologen-Symposium in Trier 2004. Festgabe Wolfgang Hage zum 70. Geburtstag* (2005d), pp. 59–72. Munster: Lit.

Tamcke, Martin, "Die Zerstörung der ostsyrischen Gemeinde in Wasirabad im Kontext von religiöser Konkurrenz, Weltkrieg und ökonomischer Not", in Walter Beltz & Jürgen Tubach (Eds.), *Expansion und Destruktion in lokalen und regionalen Systemen koexistierender Religionsgemeinschaften* (2006), pp. 191–202, Halle: Hallesche Beiträge zur Orientwissenschaft.

Tamcke, Martin, "Theologische Deutungen der Verfolgungen der ostsyrischen Christen aus ostsyrisch-lutherischen Berichten während des Ersten Weltkrieges", in Tamcke, Martin (Ed.), *Christliche Gotteslehre im Orient seit dem Aufkommen des Islams bis zur Gegenwar* (2008a), pp. 203–212, Würzburg: Ergon.

Tamcke, Martin, *Christen in der islamischen Welt. Von Mohammed bis zur Gegenwart* (2008b), Munich: Beck.

Tamcke, Martin, "World War I and the Assyrians", in Hunter, Erica C.D. (Ed.), *The Christian Heritage of Iraq. Collected papers from the Christianity of Iraq* (2009a), pp. 203–220, Piscataway/NJ: Gorgias.

Tamcke, Martin, "Sleman de Beth Henno: Gunhe d-Tur 'Abdin (Die Verfolgung und Vernichtung der Syro-Aramäer im Tur Abdin 1915)", in *Kindlers Literaturlexikon*, Vol. 15, 3 (2009b), p. 274, Stuttgart/Weimar: J.B. Metzler.

Tamcke, Martin, "Malfono Abed Mschiho Naman von Qarabasch", in *Kindlers Literaturlexikon,* Vol. 10, 3 (2009c), p. 571, Stuttgart/Weimar: J.B. Metzler.

Tamcke, Martin, *Die Christen vom Tur Abdin. Hinführung zur Syrisch-Orthodoxen Kirche* (2009d), Frankfurt: Lembeck.

Tamcke, Martin, *Bedrängte Existenz. Ein historisch-exemplarischer Streifzug zum irakischen Christentum* (2011), Berlin: Aphorisma.

Yonan, Gabriele, *Ein vergessener Holocaust. Die Vernichtung der christlichen Assyrer in der Türkei* (1989), Göttingen: Gesellschaft für Bedrohte Völker.

The Lausanne Treaty: High Aspirations, Highly Neglected

By Alan Hurst, The Becket Fund

The Becket Fund for Religious Liberty is a non-profit, public-interest, legal and educational institute that protects the free expression of all faiths. It is based in Washington D.C. The Becket Fund exists to vindicate a simple but frequently neglected principle: that because the religious impulse is natural to human beings, religious expression is natural to human culture. It advances that principle in three arenas – the courts of law, the court of public opinion, and the academy – both in the United States and abroad.

1. Introduction

From a Western European or American perspective, the St Gabriel Monastery controversy might look like a mere technical legal matter – just a set of lawsuits between a monastery, its neighbours and the Turkish government over ownership of land.[1] Although the monastery alleges violations of its religious freedoms, the Turkish government insists that the entire affair is nothing more than a routine dispute under Turkish property law.[2] Outside observers can evaluate each side's arguments only with difficulty, as the relevant facts and legal materials are largely local in nature, and few have been translated from the original Turkish.

In fact, regardless of the legal merits, the St Gabriel case neatly illustrates the precarious place of religious minorities in Turkey. In principle, the groups' religious freedom is protected by both national and international law, but in practice, numerous legal and extralegal obstacles interfere with their religious life. They have a right to religious foundations and schools, but the state makes it difficult to establish and operate them. They have a right to preach and to proselytize, but they face harassment and violence when they do so. They have a right to worship, but when they try to maintain places of worship, the state refuses to recognize them, or finds convenient ways to deny that they actually own the land.

Religious freedom and minority rights are the most volatile issues in Turkish politics, and most religious minorities are too small and powerless to avoid being caught in the maelstrom – all of Turkey's non-Muslim minorities put together add up to only 0.2 % of the population, and the smallest groups have only a few thousand members in a country of more than 70 million inhabitants. Worse still,

---
[1] Economist, 2010.
[2] Turkey's FM, 2011.

Turkey is still animated by strong nationalist ideals[3] and allowing real religious differences can seem like a dangerous concession to foreign powers, and thus potentially at odds with the goal of Turkish unity.

This apparent conflict ignores the fact that the roots of religious freedom in Turkey are as much Turkish as they are foreign. Turkey's oldest religious freedom law, the Lausanne Treaty of 1923, is the agreement through which the new Turkish regime gained international recognition after its triumphant war of independence. The Treaty was negotiated by Turkish hero Ismet İnönü and signed mere months before Atatürk and the Grand National Assembly declared the establishment of the Turkish Republic. Even the Treaty's religious freedom provisions were not truly foreign. True, they were based on the other minority protection agreements being signed in the aftermath of World War I, but to these general provisions the Lausanne Treaty adds further protections based on the Ottoman Empire's indigenously developed *millet* system. Part II of this chapter will describe these historical circumstances in more detail.

The Treaty has its failings, as Part III's summary of its religious freedom protections will make clear. Most importantly, the majority of its provisions do not cover all religious minority groups. Most clauses apply only to 'non-Moslem minorities' – a phrase the Turkish government has wrongfully interpreted as applying to only a few of its many non-Muslim religions. The Treaty, therefore, has limited usefulness to Turkey's Muslim religious minorities, such as the Alevis and other Shias, who are orders of magnitude more populous than the non-Muslim groups.

Still worse, as Part IV will discuss, the Turkish government has routinely failed to respect the Lausanne rights of even the few recognized Lausanne minorities. Despite these failings, however, the Lausanne Treaty represents a robust, workable and uniquely Turkish approach to protecting religious freedom – one the Turkish government would do well to follow.

2. Historical context

The Treaty of Lausanne marked the beginning of modern Turkey, and its religious freedom provisions attempted to deal with a basic problem of the new Turkish Republic. Turkey's predecessor, the Ottoman Empire, had been a multinational state governing many ethnic groups and religions, but Turkey itself would be a re-

---

[3] For example, "damaging the indivisible unity of the state with its territory and nation" was one of the goals prohibited by Turkey's terrorism statute until 2003, and political parties can still be banned for encouraging minority groups to believe that they should receive official recognition and minority rights (Oran, 2007, pp. 45–46).

ligiously homogeneous state, founded on an explicitly nationalist ideal of Turkish unity. How would minorities be treated when their presence in the state was no longer the norm but an aberration?

The Ottoman Empire had managed its internal diversity with its so-called *millet* system. Under this system, individual religious groups were treated as separate *millets* or 'nations' inside the Empire. *Millet* status gave a group official recognition as an autonomous religious and legal community. Though *millet* leaders could be dismissed by the Sultan, they were chosen by their community, and they served simultaneously both as officers of the Ottoman government and as their religions' representatives to the Sultan. In private matters such as family law and inheritance, the *millets* governed themselves, resolving disputes under their own laws.[4]

The *millet* system had its flaws. The Ottoman Empire was explicitly Islamic, and its Sultan was also Caliph, religious and political successor to Muhammad. As a result, Muslim law could take priority over any other *millet*'s law, members of non-Muslim *millets* were usually subjected to heavier taxes, and non-Muslims' right to serve in government and the military was severely restricted. Another problem was that the power to incorporate a *millet* rested with the sultan, and any group seeking to separate itself from an existing *millet* and start a new one could only do so with the sultan's permission. Muslim minorities like the Shias were governed by the Sunni majority whether they wished to be or not. For most of Ottoman history, smaller Christian minorities were assigned to the larger Greek Orthodox or Armenian *millets* by the Sultan's whim, though the difficulties of long-distance administration granted them significant de facto independence. By the end of the Empire, however, most of these groups had been granted official *millet* status.[5]

Nevertheless, the non-Muslim *millets* had sufficient liberty and autonomy to establish churches, worship according to their beliefs, educate their children in their native languages at their own schools and operate their own hospitals and other charitable institutions. Flawed though it was, the *millet* system was impressive for its time, and by and large it allowed religious minorities to coexist and flourish in a diverse Islamic empire.[6]

In the 19th century, however, rising nationalist sentiments and declining Ottoman power turned the *millet* system's strengths into weaknesses. The religious identities it recognized and legitimated became a major basis for the nationalist

---

[4] For a brief introduction to the *millet* system, see McCarthy, pp. 127–132, and Aral, pp. 454–482.
[5] McCarthy, 1997, p. 132.
[6] Aral, 2004, p. 475; and Barkley, 2005, pp. 5–19.

Collapsed monastery of Mor Abhay close to the abandoned village of Beth Man'im. Tradition goes that the monastery had 365 rooms, for each day of the year one. (M. Tozman)

identities that ultimately split the Empire apart. Further, shared religious identity became one of the justifications for foreign powers to intervene in Ottoman affairs, as when Russia claimed responsibility for the Empire's Christian subjects. Though 19th-century reforms attempted to ease tensions by declaring religious equality, the regime's tolerance toward the religious minorities likely made it easier for nationalist movements to form and grow, and hindered the development of an Ottoman identity.[7]

Eventually, nationalism bulldozed the religious geography the *millet* system had governed. New nationalist states broke the Empire apart and then usually made themselves religiously homogeneous through migration, ethnic cleansing and even genocide. They became 'nations', as nationalists understood the word, and their legitimacy rested on shared nationality as expressed in ethnicity, language, culture and religion.

Turkey itself was no exception. A Turkish nationalist movement gained influ-

---

[7] McCarthy, 1997, pp. 205–207.

ence in the last decades of the Ottoman Empire, bringing about nationalist policies ranging from the benign – e.g., mandatory instruction in Turkish – to the horrific, like the mass deportation and murder of Ottoman Armenians, Aramean Christians (Syriac Orthodox) and others during World War I. The exact number of dead is highly controversial, as is the question of whether the Ottoman government's actions constituted genocide. Most historians agree that it was in fact genocide, while Turkey and sympathetic historians argue it was an undeclared war in which both sides suffered atrocities.

When the Allies partitioned the Empire, Turkish nationalists led a war of independence, regained the Empire's lost Anatolian territory and abolished the Ottoman Sultanate. As the new Turkish government negotiated a new peace treaty with the Allies at Lausanne, it also concluded a population transfer agreement with Greece and began denaturalizing and deporting its hundreds of thousands of Greek Orthodox residents. Very few Greek Orthodox – mostly those in Istanbul, the seat of the Ecumenical Patriarchate – retained their citizenship and were permitted to stay.[8] About two million people lost either Greek or Turkish citizenship through this arrangement.

As a result, the provisions of the Treaty of Lausanne governing treatment of non-Muslim minorities dealt with both a smaller and a much larger problem than the *millet* system had been designed to manage. On the one hand, there were only a tiny fraction as many non-Muslims as in the old Empire – ironically, the officially secular Turkish Republic was much more uniformly Muslim than its explicitly Islamic predecessor. But on the other hand, this handful of non-Muslim citizens was now an aberration: citizens of an explicitly nationalist Turkey who were neither ethnically nor linguistically Turkish, nor shared the religion of their overwhelmingly Muslim neighbours. Though religion was legally irrelevant to Turkish citizenship, the circumstances made it inevitable that being Muslim would come to be seen as part of being Turkish, while other religions would inevitably be seen as non-Turkish and foreign. And how does one protect un-Turkish religions in a Turkish nationalist state?

3. The Lausanne Treaty compared with other human rights instruments

The Lausanne Treaty attempted to solve this problem by including Turkey in a new international minority protection regime administered by the League of Na-

---

[8] Convention, 1923.

"Önce Vatan" – "(My) fatherland first". Nationalistic dictums in Turkish public to stir nationalist sentiments. This picture was taken close to Midyat. (M. Tozman)

tions, the predecessor to the United Nations.[9] In Section III of the Treaty, Turkey committed to recognize a number of religious freedom provisions "as fundamental laws", promising that "no law, no regulation nor official action shall conflict or interfere with these stipulations, nor shall any law, regulation nor official action prevail over them".[10] It further agreed that it could not modify the Treaty's protections for non-Muslim minorities without consent of the League Council.[11] Though the dissolution of the League of Nations ended this minority protection regime, an early report by the United Nations Economic and Social Council concluded that Turkey's obligations under the Treaty were still in force[12], and Turkey still considers itself bound by Lausanne.[13]

This section of the paper will explain Turkey's obligations under the Lausanne Treaty and briefly compare them with the other human rights instruments Turkey has signed, specifically the Universal Declaration of Human Rights (Universal Declaration), the International Covenant on Civil and Political Rights (ICCPR) and the European Convention on Human Rights (ECHR). In making these com-

---

[9] For a succinct description of the League of Nations' minority rights regime, see Fink, 1995.
[10] Treaty of Peace, 1923, Art. 37.
[11] Treaty of Peace, 1923, Art. 44.
[12] U.N., 1950, pp. 56–67.
[13] According to Baskin Oran, Turkey has implemented Lausanne through Law No. 340, and its 1982 constitution does not permit courts to find Lausanne or other treaties unconstitutional (2007, p. 37).

parisons I will focus on the ways in which the Lausanne Treaty commits Turkey to do more for its religious minorities than its other international obligations require.

The protections of the Lausanne Treaty can be classified in two categories: individual rights for members of minority groups, which resemble the other minority protection treaties signed among many states at the end of World War I, and group rights, which echo the privileges afforded minority religions under the *millet* system.

3.1. Individual rights

The Lausanne Treaty contains protections for individual rights that resemble those of other major human rights instruments but go beyond them, adding important specifics to their aspirational general language.

3.1.1. Free exercise of religion

Lausanne Treaty, Article 38: All inhabitants of Turkey shall be entitled to free exercise, whether in public or private, of any creed, religion or belief, the observance of which shall not be incompatible with public order and good morals.

Universal Declaration, Article 18: Everyone has the right to freedom of thought, conscience and religion; this right includes freedom to change his religion or belief, and freedom, either alone or in community with others and in public or private, to manifest his religion or belief in teaching, practice, worship and observance. [The ICCPR's Article 18 and the ECHR's Article 9 echo this language; the differences are not relevant here.]

The language of the instruments is different: the Universal Declaration, ICCPR, and ECHR all use the expressions "freedom of religion" and "freedom to manifest one's religion", while the Lausanne Treaty uses the Unites States Constitution's phrase "free exercise of religion". Nevertheless, the chief implications of both phrasings are clear: the documents protect all individuals' freedom both to believe in and to practice their religion, both in public and in private. In one respect, the Lausanne Treaty is stricter. It permits the state to restrict religious observance only when it is "incompatible with public order and good morals"; the ICCPR and ECHR add "public safety", "public health" and "protection of the fundamental rights of others" to the list.[14]

---

[14] ICCPR Art. 18; ECHR Art. 9.

In addition to these general protections for all Turkish citizens, which are some of the very few promises of the Lausanne Treaty made to Muslims as well as non-Muslims, the Treaty of Lausanne makes a more specific promise to Turkey's non-Muslim minorities:

Lausanne Treaty, Article 43: Turkish nationals belonging to non-Moslem minorities shall not be compelled to perform any act which constitutes a violation of their faith or religious observances, and shall not be placed under any disability by reason of their refusal to attend Courts of Law or to perform any legal business on their weekly day of rest.

Here the Treaty of Lausanne shows again that it was ahead of its time, promising accommodations for religious individuals that are not universal even today. For comparison, the United States Supreme Court currently recognizes no right for religious minorities to be exempted from neutral and generally applicable laws[15], whether or not those laws compel believers to "perform [an] act which constitutes a violation of their faith or religious observances".[16] Yet, Turkey has promised to provide just such a right, and the circumstances in which this right may be circumscribed are narrower than with the more general provisions above, allowing exceptions only for obligations "imposed upon all other Turkish nationals for the preservation of public order".

Additionally, it should be noted that the Treaty of Lausanne, unlike the Universal Declaration and the ECHR, does not provide for a right to change one's religion. This omission has little importance, however, as Turkey has recognized that right by ratifying the ECHR.

3.1.2. Non-discrimination

Lausanne Treaty, Articles 38–39: The Turkish Government undertakes to assure full and complete protection of life and liberty to all inhabitants of Turkey without distinction of birth, nationality, language, race or religion.... Turkish nationals belonging to non-Moslem minorities will enjoy the same civil and political rights as Moslems. All the inhabitants of Turkey, without distinction of religion, shall be equal before the law.

ICCPR, Article 26: All persons are equal before the law and are entitled without any discrimination to the equal protection of the law. In this respect, the

---

[15] Employment Division v. Smith, 1990.
[16] Treaty of Peace, 1923, Art. 43.

law shall prohibit any discrimination and guarantee to all persons equal and effective protection against discrimination on any ground such as race, colour, sex, language, religion, political or other opinion, national or social origin, property, birth or other status.

Again Lausanne and the modern treaty most nearly on point provide similar, if very general protections. In this case Lausanne's general provision is somewhat less thorough than its analogue, as it does not require Turkey to take any measures against private discrimination, but like the ICCPR (and unlike most of the Lausanne Treaty), it applies to all Turkish citizens and not merely to non-Muslims.[17] Non-Muslim minorities also benefit from two more specific non-discrimination clauses:

Lausanne Treaty, Article 38: Religious minorities must have "full freedom of movement and emigration", subject to the same terms as all other citizens.

Lausanne Treaty, Article 39: Differences of religion "shall not prejudice any Turkish national in matters relating to the enjoyment of civil or political rights, as, for instance, admission to public employments, functions and honours, or the exercise of professions and industries".

I repeat for emphasis: these protections obligate Turkey to provide additional freedoms to its religious minorities, above and beyond what the ICCPR and ECHR require. If Turkey complied with the ICCPR and the ECHR without protecting these freedoms, it would still be in violation of its international obligations.

3.2. *Group rights*

As we have seen, the Lausanne Treaty promises substantial protections for individual religious freedom, usually matching the general provisions of modern human rights treaties and adding more specific requirements on top of them. But the treaty's most impressive protections are those it promises to religious minorities as groups, what legal jargon refers to as *corporate rights*. Modern defenders of human rights did not begin to focus on the rights of minorities as groups until the 1980s[18], but thanks in part to ideas inherited from the *millet* system, Turkey already committed itself to protect its religious minorities in 1923.

---

[17] Again, this deficiency is unimportant because Turkey has ratified the ICCPR. Turkey has also ratified the International Covenant on Economic, Social, and Cultural rights, which promises to protect a wide variety of economic and other rights "without discrimination of any kind as to ... religion" (1966, Art. 2).

[18] Karimova & Deverell, 2001.

A group of Süryanis after the church service in the village of Bsorino. (S. de Courtois)

The corporate rights provisions in the Treaty of Lausanne have two primary concerns: religious minorities' right to use and propagate their native languages, and their right to form and act through religious institutions. The Treaty devotes much more text to these provisions than to the individual rights provisions; measured by word count (in English), over 60 % of the Treaty deals with group rights, and nearly 40 % with institutional issues alone. Space requires that I summarize more than quote.

3.2.1. Language rights

Three articles of the Lausanne Treaty protect religious minorities' language rights. Article 39 guarantees that 'no restrictions shall be imposed' on the use of any language in public or in private, including in publications and public meetings. It further guarantees Turkey will allow non-Turkish-speaking citizens to use their own language orally in court. These two protections are not limited to Turkey's non-Muslim minorities but instead apply to all Turkish citizens.

Non-Muslim minorities possess further language rights. Article 40 guarantees that their religious and charitable organizations may use their own languages, and Article 41 promises that in towns and districts with "a considerable portion of non-Muslim nationals", the Turkish government itself will grant "adequate facilities for ensuring" that non-Muslim children receive primary school instruction "through the medium of their own language". Though Turkey has not signed the European Charter for Regional and Minority Languages, the Lausanne Treaty already commits it to some of the Charter's most important stipulations.

3.2.2. Institutional rights

Though modern human rights instruments protect religious institutions as part of their general idea of freedom of religion, the Lausanne Treaty describes its promises to religious institutions in much more detail. Three provisions are particularly important.

First, non-Muslim minorities are guaranteed "an equal right to establish, manage and control at their own expense, any charitable, religious and social institutions, any schools and other establishments for instruction and education".[19]

Second, Turkey promised "full protection to the churches, synagogues, cemeteries and other religious establishments of the [non-Muslim] minorities", including "any of the necessary facilities which are guaranteed to other private institutions of that nature". This promise applies both to the foundations existing when the Treaty was ratified and to foundations the non-Muslim minorities have since founded.[20]

Third, "where there is a considerable proportion of Turkish nationals belonging to non-Moslem minorities, these minorities shall be assured an equitable share" of state funds provided "for educational, religious or charitable purposes".[21]

Finally, retaining a key aspect of the old *millet* system, the Treaty of Lausanne promises that Turkey will allow religious minorities to settle matters of "family law or personal status ... in accordance with the customs of those minorities".[22]

In short, although Turkey has not signed the Council of Europe's Framework Convention for the Protection of National Minorities, the Lausanne Treaty already commits it to do much toward "promot[ing] the conditions necessary for persons belonging to national minorities to maintain and develop their culture, and to preserve the essential elements of their identity, namely their religion, language, traditions and cultural heritage".[23]

---

[19] Treaty of Peace, 1923, Art. 40.
[20] Treaty of Peace, Art. 42.
[21] Treaty of Peace, Art. 41.
[22] Treaty of Peace, Art. 42.
[23] Framework Convention, Art. 5.

3.3. Summary and evaluation

In short, even by modern standards the religious freedom protections promised by this ninety-year-old treaty are very robust, much more so than those of the most important international human rights instruments. Indeed, some of the provisions go beyond what many liberal democracies would support. In particular, the promise to apply religious family law would make many advocates of liberal democracy uncomfortable, though some liberal democracies in fact permit the use of religious family law through the means of arbitration agreements.[24]

But as an instrument intended to allow diverse religious communities to coexist and flourish, the Lausanne Treaty has only two serious deficiencies. First, most of its provisions apply only to Turkey's non-Muslim minorities; the only provisions that do apply to Muslims are the 'free exercise of religion' clause in Article 38 and most of the non-discrimination promises of Articles 38 and 39. Further, according to Oran, the protections provided to Muslims are not under international guarantee.[25] In a country in which only two people in a thousand are not Muslim but approximately one in four belong to Muslim minority groups, the failure to protect Muslim religious minorities is an exception that dwarfs the rule.

Second, Lausanne has not been complied with. Neither Turkey nor the other parties to the Treaty have had the necessary political will to see that it was actually implemented.

4. Turkish compliance (and non-compliance) with the Treaty

That Turkey has not complied perfectly with the Treaty is hardly surprising. It has long struggled to meet its human rights obligations, though most observers agree that it has slowly made progress.[26] Further, it faces special challenges in dealing with religious minorities. Because of the ongoing conflict between Kemalist secularists and Islamic political movements, religion policy can be explosively controversial. And because of the sometimes violent conflict between Turkish nationalism and Kurdish separatism, policies regarding minorities are also dangerous. The politically powerless Lausanne minorities thus find themselves caught in the vortex of the two most volatile issues in Turkish politics. Nevertheless, Turkey's

---

[24] For further information on religious arbitration as a way of implementing religious family law, see Helfand, 2011, and Shachar, 2008. My conversations with activists on behalf of Turkish minority groups have suggested that they are currently too focused on other religious freedom issues to assert their right to use religious law in matters of family and personal status. Under Lausanne, however, they retain the right to do so.

[25] Oran, 2007, pp. 40–42.

[26] European Commission, 2010; and European Commission, 2005.

history of non-compliance goes beyond what could be explained by the political difficulties it faces.

Because the other chapters in this volume cover Turkey's treatment of its religious minorities in much more detail, I will not attempt a complete assessment of Turkey's compliance with its obligations under Lausanne.[27] Instead, I will give a quick overview of the protections Turkey has in fact extended to the minorities covered by the Lausanne Treaty and the most important ways in which it has neglected its obligations.

4.1. Bright spots of compliance

The Turkish government does not flout the Lausanne Treaty entirely; it does provide some protection for the minorities it recognizes as covered by Lausanne, and even those it refuses to recognize enjoy many basic protections that should not be undervalued.

Non-Muslims in today's Turkey do not generally live in fear for their lives, and the Turkish government has made at least some effort to prosecute private religious violence. It permits non-Muslim minorities to worship, allows them to publish their own materials, does not ban proselytism or conversion and does not have blasphemy laws of the sort some Muslim-majority states have used to punish non-Muslim religious expression.[28]

None of these protections are as robust as they seem, in large part because lawless behaviour by government officials often thwarts laws that should protect minorities. The government does prosecute religious hate crimes, but the police sometimes fail to cooperate with the prosecution.[29] Non-Muslim minorities are permitted to worship at state-recognized places of worship, but officials make it very difficult to obtain state recognition and then molest unrecognized congregations. Bureaucrats harass converts who wish to change the religious affiliation on their identity cards. Although proselytism is technically legal, it is often met with official harassment and private violence. Although there are no blasphemy laws, prosecutions for "insulting Turkishness" serve the same purpose of suppressing unpopular religious speech.

Nevertheless, the protection provided to non-Muslim minorities is sufficient that the U.S. Department of State's annual religious freedom report on Turkey can

---

[27] For more information on this topic, see Pastoor's article in this book.
[28] Most of the information in this section on compliance comes from U.S. State Department Bureau of Democracy, Human Rights, and Labour, 2011. Where I have used other sources, I will cite them.
[29] Bos, 2009; and Dogan, 2012.

Mor Gabriel's outer wall. Parts of it will have to be demolished after the judgement by the Turkish court, expropriation lands of the monastery. (H. Oberkampf)

begin, "The constitution protects religious freedom, and, in practice, the government generally enforced these protections".[30]

The three minorities to which Turkey has officially extended Lausanne protections – Greek Orthodox, Armenian Orthodox and Jews – have some limited additional freedoms.[31] As promised in the Treaty, they are permitted to pay for and run their own schools, in which their own religious beliefs and languages are taught. Like the more basic rights above, this right is not complete. Non-Muslim minorities' schools are under tight supervision by the education authorities, who appoint some of the administration and faculty of each institution.[32] Further, the government has not respected this right in the context of higher education. Since 1971, the only Greek Orthodox seminary in Turkey has been closed because the gov-

---

[30] U.S., 2011, p. 1.
[31] Sources disagree as to whether Turkey recognizes three or four Lausanne minorities. The U.S. religious freedom report on Turkey lists only these three, as does Baskin Oran (2007, p. 38), while Dr. Otmar Oehring of Missio adds Bulgarian Orthodox (2002, p. 21).
[32] Oehring, 2002, p. 29.

ernment insists on controlling all post-secondary education in the country. Since Turkish law requires Greek Orthodox leaders to be Turkish citizens, this threatens the viability of the Ecumenical Patriarchate and makes Turkey's Greek Orthodox dependent on the government's willingness to grant citizenship to priests brought in from other countries.

In short, Turkey has partially – but only partially – complied with the most important provisions of the Treaty of Lausanne, specifically the "free exercise of religion" and the "full protection of life and liberty" provisions of Article 38. Further, I have found no complaints that Turkey has violated many of the more specific provisions, like the full freedom of movement and emigration provision in Article 38 (note that emigration is only the right to leave Turkey, not to immigrate into it). But Turkey has clearly violated some other provisions of the Lausanne Treaty, and the effect of these violations on its religious minorities has been serious.

4.2. Non-compliance

As stated above, given the challenges Turkey faces in dealing with religion issues and minority issues, it would be miraculous if its record on religious freedom were perfect. But unfortunately, Turkey has violated religious minorities' rights in a number of ways that its political difficulties neither explain nor excuse. Its record shows lingering prejudice against religious minorities, often expressed as a fear that they are not really Turkish but rather foreigners fomenting separatism. Turkey's Constitutional Court, for example, has banned political parties for the supposed crime of telling minorities that they deserve official recognition and rights, and it has concluded that "demands for the recognition of cultural identities ... will in time incline toward a break from the whole".[33] This fear may be understandable, considering the Ottoman Empire's painful dissection at the hands of nationalist movements, but it is hardly rational, especially with so few non-Muslims left in Turkey.

Turkey fails to comply with the Lausanne Treaty in at least seven important ways. First, as explained above, it recognizes only a few of its many non-Muslim groups as protected minorities under the Lausanne Treaty. According to Baskin Oran, the official justification for this interpretation of the Treaty is not clear, though as a practical matter it may have come about because the unrecognized

---

[33] Oran, p. 49. Baskin Oran calls this paranoia 'Sevres syndrome', after the post-World War I treaty that partitioned the Ottoman Empire, and gives many examples of the oppressive measures it has been used to justify: property confiscation, treatment of non-Muslims as foreigners, and of course widespread denial of minority rights. See ibid., pp. 44–53.

minorities lacked a 'kin-state' to advocate for their rights.[34] Otmar Oehring recounts rumours that in order to show their loyalty, leaders of the unrecognized groups supposedly asked the Turkish government not to recognize them under the Lausanne Treaty. Neither his report nor my research has been able to find any evidence for these rumours.[35] I have seen some indication that Turkey might believe it is recognizing only those minorities that were recognized at the time Lausanne was signed, but this justification is also implausible, as the Ottoman Empire gave *millet* status to both Catholics and Arameans, two groups that Turkey currently refuses to recognise.

In contrast, the text of Treaty itself does not single out particular religions for special treatment, other than its general exclusion of Muslims from protection, nor does it contain any indication that it applies only to those non-Muslim groups that were present in Turkey when it was signed. Its language states only 'non-Moslem minorities', the natural meaning of which would imply that the Treaty applies to all non-Muslim religious groups in Turkey, regardless of when they arrived there. At the very least, it must apply to all of the many non-Muslim groups that were present in Turkey in 1923.[36]

Moreover, the Treaty gives no reason to suppose that Turkey's non-Muslim minorities could relinquish protection under Lausanne even if they were inclined to do so. The Treaty is an agreement among states, and the minorities themselves are not parties to the Treaty but merely its promised beneficiaries under international law. At the time when the Arameans and other groups supposedly abandoned their Lausanne rights, the League of Nations still guaranteed the Treaty, and changes to the Treaty would have required approval by the League Council. The League Council never gave such approval, nor have the other state parties given Turkey permission to narrow the Treaty's scope. Therefore, though some minority groups may be too intimidated to assert their rights under Lausanne, they have no power to renounce them.

Because Turkey fails to give the words "non-Muslim minorities" their natural meaning, non-Muslim religions in Turkey other than the Greek Orthodox, Armenians and Jews are usually not permitted to use their buildings for educational purposes and have difficulty even training their clergy, to say nothing of educating their children in the faith. This is true whether they arrived in Turkey after the Lausanne Treaty or, like the Arameans, were recognized as a *millet* in the Ottoman

---

[34] Oran, 2007, p. 10.
[35] Oehring, 2002, p. 32.
[36] Oehring, 2002, pp. 31–32.

Empire[37], and have actually been practicing their faith in Anatolia since centuries before Muhammad's birth.

Second, and ironically, Turkey has failed worst in providing the type of protection that the Lausanne Treaty discusses the most, the one most firmly embedded in the Ottoman *millet* system: institutional rights. I will not go into detail because other chapters will focus on this issue[38], but the problems Turkey's associations laws pose for non-Muslim minorities are substantial. Turkey does not recognize non-Muslim minorities' religious leaders, nor does it give the religious groups' hierarchies the legal identities they need in order to own property or raise money on their own. Instead, it recognizes only the individual foundations that run congregations, schools or charities.

Turkey closely regulates the foundations, often causing problems. For example, all religious leaders must be Turkish citizens, even if not enough Turkish citizens are qualified. Turkish law and discrimination by Turkish officials make it difficult to organize new foundations, and it has historically been impossible to organize foundations for explicitly religious purposes. As is discussed elsewhere in this volume, Turkish foundations law has been reformed repeatedly in recent years, often with these problems in mind, but whether the reforms will actually increase minority religions' institutional freedom remains to be seen.

The inflexibility the foundations laws have typically displayed ties religious groups to the foundations and governance structures they already have, which may not be ideally tailored to their changing demographics. The foundations are not allowed to pool or transfer their resources, leading to situations where some foundations have unused funds while others face financial difficulties. The government's traditional unwillingness to give foundations more freedom has had much to do with its attempts to keep Islam in the country under control and its fear that unregulated foundations could become a tool of Islamist movements. But while disfavoured variants of Islam have enough supporters to flourish despite these restrictions, the rules have been almost crippling for the tiny non-Muslim minorities.[39]

Third, the Turkish government has long failed to recognize non-Muslim minority groups' property rights. This is one of the hardest issues for outsiders to evaluate properly, as the cases tend to involve issues of Turkish property law and evidence in Turkish about specific pieces of real estate, but the overall pattern clearly indicates a sustained program of legal and extralegal confiscation – some-

---

[37] Taylor, 2006, p. 76.
[38] For more information on this topic, see Onder's article in this book.
[39] Oehring, 2002, pp. 24–27.

times legally justified by the absurd claim that the non-Muslim minority foundations are foreign, rather than Turkish, and thus cannot own property. Turkey has begun to make promises of restitution, but it remains to be seen how effectively they will be implemented.[40] In the past, the government has sometimes promised restitution for confiscated real estate, paid it into special state bank accounts, and then refused to let the religious foundations access it.[41]

Children receiving class in Syriac village of Midun. (S. de Courtois)

Fourth, although I have found no indication that Turkey has banned the private use of non-Muslim minorities' languages, the government has certainly made it difficult to use these languages in public, for example in the broadcast media. Much of its fear of allowing linguistic diversity derives from the problem of Kurdish separatism, but as with its strict foundations laws, non-Muslim minorities are injured at least as much as the intended targets.[42]

Fifth, Turkey has not legally barred non-Muslims from public employment, but informal discrimination has made it very difficult for non-Muslims to be hired. This problem, like some others on this list, may be improving somewhat,

---

[40] Yildirim, 2011.
[41] Oehring, 2002, pp. 33–34.
[42] Smith/Kocamahhul, 2001.

as Turkey has recently elected its first non-Muslim Member of Parliament.[43] Nevertheless, to the extent non-Muslims are discriminated against in obtaining public employment, Turkey is in violation of Article 39.

Sixth, despite its promises in Articles 40 and 41, Turkey has not funded the provision of primary education in non-Muslim minorities' native languages nor given non-Muslim minorities any share of the funds it makes available to Muslims for religious, educational and charitable purposes.

Seventh and finally, Turkey imprisons non-Muslim conscientious objectors like Jehovah's Witness Yunus Erçep in violation of its promise in Article 43 not to compel non-Muslim minorities to commit acts violating their religious beliefs.[44] Turkey may plausibly argue that compulsory military service comes under the "public order" exception to this clause, but it is unlikely that prosecuting the handful of non-Muslim conscientious objectors endangers public order in any meaningful sense. This violation may soon be remedied, however, as international pressure and repeated defeats before the European Court of Human Rights have led Turkey to consider legislation legalizing conscientious objection to military service.[45]

Both religion and minority rights are explosive issues in Turkey, so it is not surprising that politically powerless non-Muslim religious minorities should find themselves collateral victims of much larger conflicts. Further, it is not surprising that they would face prejudice and informal discrimination, since both sides of Turkey's unique political spectrum are uncomfortable with them: Islamists because they are not Muslim; secular nationalists because their linguistic, ethnic, and religious distinctiveness make them appear un-Turkish. The government sometimes treats them as if it fears they will turn separatist and ally with foreign powers – a fear roughly 90 years out of date.

But to a surprising degree, the authors of the Lausanne Treaty seem to have anticipated these problems and designed the Treaty to protect religious minorities from the difficult circumstances in which they find themselves. Their work combined corporate rights inspired by the Ottoman *millet* system with more modern individual rights to create a regime that, if realized, would have allowed Turkish minorities to maintain their religious communities and participate in Turkish society as equals.

Instead, Turkey has pursued policies from which some have inferred a desire to encourage the remaining Jews and Christians to emigrate voluntarily – to fin-

---

[43] Cagaptay, 2011.
[44] Jehovah's Witnesses, 2011.
[45] Jones, 2011; and "Turkey May Decriminalize", 2011.

ish what 1923's population transfer started and create a religiously homogeneous state. If this was in fact Turkey's goal, its program has been effective, and non-Muslim populations have declined until some may no longer be viable. But if Turkey wishes to depart from this goal, and create a state that truly respects religious freedom, keeping the promises it made in the Lausanne Treaty would be a good place to start.

References

Aral, B., 'The idea of human rights as perceived in the Ottoman Empire', in *Human Rights Quarterly,* (2004) 26, 454–482.
Barkley, K., 'Islam and toleration: Studying the Ottoman imperial model', in *International Journal of Politics, Culture, and Society*, (2005) 19, 5–19.
Bos, S.J., 'Turkey Christians fear no justice for killers of publishers', in *BosNewsLife* (26 July 2009). Retrieved from: http://www.bosnewslife.com/8466-turkey-christians-fear-no-justice-for-killers-of-publishers.
Cagaptay, S., 'Turkey's "first Christian"', CNN.com (6 July 2011). Retrieved from: http://globalpublicsquare.blogs.cnn.com/2011/07/06/turkey%E2%80%99s-%E2%80%9Cfirst-christian%E2%80%9D/.
'Convention concerning the exchange of Greek and Turkish populations, and protocol' (signed 30 January 1923), *League of Nations Treaty Series*, 32, 75 (1925). Retrieved from: http://treaties.un.org/doc/publication/unts/lon/volume%2032/v32.pdf.
Dogan, Y.P., 'Murders of Turkey's non-Muslims await illumination', in *Today's Zaman* (22 January 2012). Retrieved from: http://www.sundayszaman.com/sunday/newsDetail_getNewsById.action?newsId=269215.
Employment Division v. Smith, 494 U.S. 872 (1990).
European Commission (2005). Turkey: 2005 progress report. *European Commission*, COM (2005) 561 final.
European Commission (2010). Turkey: 2010 progress report. *European Commission*, COM(2010) 660. Retrieved from: http://ec.europa.eu/enlargement/pdf/key_documents/2010/package/tr_rapport_2010_en.pdf.
European convention on human rights (signed 4 November 1950). *European Treaty Series*, 5.
Framework Convention for the Protection of National Minorities (signed 1 February 1995). *European Treaty Series*, 157.
Fink, C., 'The League of Nations and the minorities question', in *World Affairs*, (1995) 157, 197–205.
Helfand, M.A., 'Religious arbitration and the new multiculturalism: Negotiating conflicting legal orders', in *New York University Law Review*, 86, (2011) 1231–1305.
International covenant on civil and political rights (signed 16 December 1966). *United Nations Treaty Series*, 999, 171 (1976).

Jehovah's Witnesses Official Media Web Site, 'European court protects rights of conscientious objectors in Turkey' (23 November 2011). Retrieved from: http://www.jw-media.org/tur/20111123.htm.

Jones, D., 'Turkey considers allowing conscientious objection to military service', in *Voice of America News* (23 November 2011). Retrieved from: http://www.voanews.com/english/news/middle-east/Turkey-Considers-Allowing-Conscientious-Objection-to-Military-Service-134408028.html.

Karimova, N. & Deverell, E., *Minorities in Turkey*. Stockholm: Utrikespolitiska institutet (Swedish Institute of International Affairs), 2001).

McCarthy, J., *The Ottoman Turks: An introductory history to 1923*. New York: Longman (1997).

Oehring, O., 'Human rights in Turkey – Secularism = religious freedom?' in *Aachen: missio* (2002).

Oran, B., 'The minority concept and rights in Turkey: The Lausanne peace treaty and current issues', in Z. F. Kabaskal Arat (Ed.), *Human Rights in Turkey* (35–56), Philadelphia: University of Pennsylvania Press (2007).

Shachar, A., 'Privatizing diversity: A cautionary tale from religious arbitration in family law', in *Theoretical Inquiries in Law*, 9, (2008) 573–607.

Smith/Kocamahhul, J., 'In the shadow of Kurdish: The silence of other ethnolinguistic minorities in Turkey', *Middle East Report*, 219, (2001) 45–47.

Taylor, W.H., *Antioch and Canterbury: The Syrian Orthodox church and the Church of England*, (2006) Piscataway, N.J.: Gorgias Press.

Treaty of peace (signed 24 July 1923). *League of Nations Treaty Series*, 8, 701 (1924). Retrieved from: http://treaties.un.org/doc/publication/unts/lon/volume%2028/v28.pdf.

'Turkey's FM visits Orthodox and Syriac churches in Germany' (Dec. 5, 2011), *World Bulletin*. Retrieved from: http://www.worldbulletin.net/?aType=haber&ArticleID=82546.

'Turkey may decriminalize conscientious objection to military service', in *Today's Zaman* (15 November 2011). Retrieved from: http://www.todayszaman.com/news-262701-turkey-may-decriminalize-conscientious-objection-to-military-service.html.

U.N. Economic and Social Council, Commission on Human Rights (7 April 1950). *Study of the legal validity of the undertakings concerning minorities*. U.N. Doc. E/CN.4/367.

U.S. State Department Bureau of Democracy, Human Rights, and Labor (2011). July–December 2010 international religious freedom report on Turkey. Retrieved from: http://www.state.gov/documents/organization/171727.pdf.

'Wooing Christians: Some, but not all, want to improve the lot of Christians in Turkey', in *The Economist* (2 December 2010). Retrieved from: http://www.economist.com/node/17632939.

Yildirim, M., 'Turkey: What does Turkey's Restitution Decree Mean?', in *F18News* (6 October 2011). Retrieved from: http://www.forum18.org/Archive.php?article_id=1621.

Who are the Syriacs?

By Herman Teule

Herman Teule is the head of the Institute of Eastern Christian Studies and a professor in the Faculty of Philosophy, Theology and Religious Studies at Radboud University Nijmegen, and a professor extraordinarus in the Faculty of Theology and Religious Studies at the Catholic University of Leuven. His field of research is, amongst others, the interaction between the religious and cultural world of Middle Eastern Christianity and Islam; more specifically in the period of the so-called Syriac Renaissance (12th-14th centuries) as well as the modern developments within the present-day Churches of the Middle East. He is a consultor of the Congregation of the Eastern Churches in Rome and of the Foundation Pro Oriente (Vienna), as well as a member of the editorial board of several international scholarly periodicals and series in the field of Eastern Christianity.

1. Introduction

In this volume, 'Syriac' is the somewhat unusual term used to designate the Christians of the Tur Abdin region in south east Turkey. Normally, 'Syriac' refers to a language: the form of Aramaic spoken in Edessa (Urhōy, today Şanlı-Urfa) at the beginning of the Christian Era which developed into an important literary language used by various Christian communities. In this volume, Syriac, the translation of Suryōyō (plural: Suryōyē), is used to designate a community that has traditionally defined itself as Syrian Orthodox, or sometimes Syriac Orthodox. The advantage of the term Syriac as the designation of a community is that it clearly distinguishes the Suryoye from other ethnic groups, such as the Kurds, the Armenians or the Turks; an important distinction to make in the present-day discussions in Turkey or other countries regarding the recognition of specific cultural, ethnic or linguistic rights. The disadvantage of the term, however, is that it tends to obliterate the fact that the primary identity marker for many Suryoye is their membership in the Syrian Orthodox Church. Moreover, the term Suryoye is broader, strictly speaking, than the Syrian Orthodox community, and may also include other communities that use the Syriac language, such as Syrian Catholics, the Chaldeans and members of the ('Assyrian') Church of the East. To indicate this supra-denominational character, some people and associations – among them a number of Syrian Orthodox – prefer the term 'Assyrian'. However, due to the close association of this label with one specific ecclesiastical community, the Church of the East which also has 'Assyrian' in its official title, the term is less acceptable to some members of the Syrian Orthodox community. Hence, the introduction of the term 'Syriac' reflects a discussion on identity (ethnic, supra-denominational or ecclesiastical) – an issue that is hotly debated both in the Diaspora and in the Middle East.

In this article, I use 'Syriac' or 'Suryoye' as synonymous with Syrian Orthodox, the predominant Christian community in Tur Abdin, which has specific religious and ethnic characteristics.

2. The beginning

Two centres, both situated within Turkey, are important to understanding the early history of the Suryoye: Edessa (Urfa) and Antioch (Antakya). According to a venerable tradition, it was Addai, one of the seventy-two disciples mentioned in the New Testament, who Jesus promised would bring Christianity to Edessa and later to Nisibis (Nüsaybin). The story of the conversion of the King of Edessa Abgar by Addai can be found in two legendary accounts: the 4th century Ecclesiastical History of Eusebius of Caesarea and an apocryphal work from the 5th century called the *Doctrine of Addai*. This legend gives Christianity in Edessa an apostolic origin and even relates it to the person and the land of Jesus himself. Many of the Syrian Orthodox faithful today are proud that their Syriac (Aramaic) language is the language of Jesus and the Apostles. Modern scholars are more sober in their description of the beginning of Christianity in Edessa and refer to the so-called *Chronicle of Edessa* (6th century), which mentions a Christian temple destroyed at the beginning of the 3rd century – a fact that presupposes an established Christian community in the course of the 2nd century.

According to the *Doctrine of Addai*, one of Addai's successors, Palut, was ordained as the new leader of the community by Serapion, the Bishop of Antioch. Antioch was the most important ecclesiastical centre of the region, where according to tradition Christianity had been introduced by the Apostle Peter himself.

The theological developments in the 4th and 5th centuries are characterized by a reflection on the mystery of Jesus Christ being a man, and at the same time the son of God or God. In the 5th century, the Bishop of Alexandria, Cyril, defended the formula of 'One Nature (in Greek: *mia fysis*) of God the Word becoming Incarnate'. For Cyril, it was important to emphasise the unity of Christ's humanity and divinity.

This was a reaction against Nestorius, the Bishop of Constantinople who, in order to safeguard God's transcendence, preferred to emphasize the distinction between Christ's humanity and divinity so that Christ's human actions would only

A Syriac Bible with a cover made of gold and silver. The Syriacs are well known for their fine goldsmithery. (M. Tozman)

be ascribed to his human nature. A compromise was reached at the Council of Chalcedon in 451 A.D., where the Fathers did not recognize Cyril's One Nature formula, but preferred to speak of two distinct natures, albeit without entirely following Nestorius. This rejection of the one nature doctrine was unacceptable to the majority of Christians in Egypt (the Copts), but also to many Christians in Syria and Mesopotamia, who consequently split into two communities: those who accepted the resolutions of the Council of Chalcedon (the Chalcedonians) and those who adhered to Cyril's formula of one nature, designated by modern theologians as the *Miaphysites*. The Chalcedonian party had the support of the Emperor and considered the Miaphysites to be heretics. Bishops suspected of Miaphysite sympathies were removed from their positions or, as was the case for Patriarch Severus of Antioch (d. 538), one of the most important theologians of the Syrian Orthodox Church, were forced to leave the country.

In the 6th century, the Byzantine Empress Theodora, herself of Syrian origin and married to Emperor Justinian, arranged the episcopal ordination of Jacob, a monk from the region between Mardin and Edessa, who himself nurtured Miaphysite convictions. Following his ordination, Jacob crossed Syria and neighbouring lands, ordaining (according to the sources) thousands of deacons and priests, as well as 89 Bishops. While these figures are no doubt highly exaggerated, the fact remains that Jacob can rightly be considered to be the organiser of a strong Miaphysite movement in Syria, and provided it with a solid ecclesiastical structure. It is in his honour that the Syrian Orthodox Church is sometimes referred to as the Jacobite Church, however, this term is no longer used so as to avoid the suggestion that the Syrian Orthodox Church would only have started with this Jacob. Jacob's surname, Baradaeus (the Latinized form of the original Syriac Burd'ono or Burd'oyo), is an allusion to his habit of wearing clothes made from saddle blankets, which he wore to mislead the imperial agents sent to pursue him. Both Severus and Jacob (d. 578) are considered Saints by the Suryoye.

By the end of Jacob's term as bishop, Miaphysite missionaries had already crossed the borders of the Persian Empire and made Tikrit, situated in present-day Iraq, the centre of their activities.

3. The Islamic Period

The arrival of Islam in Syria and the Persian Empire in the first half of the 7th century in no way precluded the end of Syrian Orthodox Christianity. On the contrary, liberated from Byzantine and Persian pressure and persecution, the Church was able to reorganize itself and to adapt to the new political situation. Not long after the Islamic conquest of Syria, the newly appointed governor of Homs invited the Syrian Orthodox Patriarch to give a presentation of the Christian faith – one of the earliest religious encounters between Christians and Muslims. In this period, the Patriarch generally resided in a monastery in the region of Antioch. From the 11th century onwards, the Patriarch resided in the Monastery of Mar Barsaumo in the region of Malatya.

When, in the 8th century, Baghdad became the capital of the Islamic world, the position of the Bishop of Tikrit grew in importance. The Bishop was responsible for representing his Patriarch vis-à-vis the authorities and received far-reaching competences such as the right to appoint bishops for the region under his authority. For this reason, he would receive the honorary title of Maphrian, the 'consecrator'.

In the first Abbasid period (750–950 A.D.), several Syriac Orthodox scholars adopted Arabic for their writings and thus were able, thanks to their knowledge of Greek and Syriac philosophy, to contribute to the development of Muslim scholarship. They realized the importance of explaining their Christian belief in Trinity (answering the question of how can God be one and three? A basic question addressed to them by contemporary Muslims) and Incarnation (the question how can the man Jesus Christ, son of Mary, be called Son of God?) in terms understandable to a Muslim public. Yahya ibn Adi (d. 974 A.D.), a member of the famous School of Philosophers in Baghdad and the Syriac Orthodox teacher of many Muslim students, was much appreciated for his scientific, philosophical approach to these types of theological problems.

In spite of this atmosphere of interreligious dialogue, this was also a period that saw the first conversions to Islam. As early as the 9th century, the theologian Abu Ra'ita had already reflected on what would motivate people to accept a particular religion, which he found to include career, material advantages and family. While not mentioning it specifically, he certainly had conversions to Islam in mind. Many of these conversions, he felt, were undoubtedly the result of a number of discriminatory measures issued by the authorities.

4. Crusaders and later developments

By the end of the 11th century, the Crusaders had established themselves in the Middle East, partly in the heartland of Syrian Orthodox Christianity, including in Edessa and parts of Syria. Generally speaking, the relations with these European Christians were cordial. In the case of the Syrian Orthodox, these cordial relations can be explained by the fact that a number of their theologians in the 12th and 13th centuries had developed original forms of ecumenical thinking, considering the former Christological dissensions to be merely verbal quibbles and no longer a true cause for divisions. These centuries represented an interesting intellectual period, with major authors such as the Maphrian Bar Ebroyo, who enjoyed good relations with Muslim scholars, or Patriarch Michael the Syrian, the author of a great universal *Chronicle* with important information on political and ecclesiastical developments.

The new political circumstances, however, brought this intellectual renaissance to a standstill. In 1258, the Islamic capital Baghdad was destroyed by the Mongols, who, despite some flirtation with Christianity, adopted Islam by the end of the century, in the same period that the Crusaders were forced to surrender their final stronghold in the Middle East. In Anatolia, Turkish rulers managed to establish a number of local emirates. At the start of the 15th century, the devastating campaigns of Timurlane destroyed much of the infrastructure of the Church, including in the Tur Abdin region.

This political instability was also not without consequences for the Syrian Orthodox Church. In 1293, the Patriarch moved his residence to the Monastery of Deir al-Za'farân, near the city of Mardin. In the mid 14th century, however, a rival patriarchate, one recognised by the local Muslim authorities, was established in the Tur Abdin region. Despite some earlier attempts at reconciliation, the schism was only healed in 1839.

In 1453, Constantinople (present-day Istanbul) became the new capital of the Ottoman Empire. As a result of the change, the Syrian Orthodox now found themselves in one of the marginal provinces of the Empire. For their relations with the authorities and the payment of taxes, they had to rely on the personal relations of Patriarchs and Bishops with local (often tribal) rulers. At the highest level, it was the Armenian Patriarch in Istanbul who was considered to be the defender of their interests – a system that did not always function in the best interests of the Syrian Orthodox. Not until 1883 was the Syrian Orthodox Church recognized as an independent millet, which allowed the Patriarch to obtain an official position within the Ottoman state system.

Despite this situation, it would be wrong to think of the Syrian Orthodox Church as only a self-centred community with only limited contact with the external world. Although the Tur Abdin was the centre of the Church, the Patriarch supervised an extensive network of dioceses throughout the Middle East, including in Syria, Iraq, Lebanon and Jerusalem. In the 17th century, a substantial group of Christians in Southern India (who trace the beginnings of their Christian beliefs back to the Apostle Thomas and had always maintained contacts with the Christian world of the Middle East) accepted the authority of the Syrian Orthodox

Patriarch. This resulted in intensive contacts between both communities, which led to regular visits by Syrian Orthodox Prelates to India.

Starting in the 17th century, and continuing in the centuries that followed, Roman Catholic missionaries were active across the Middle East. The missionaries managed to convince a number of members of the Syriac Orthodox Church to enter into a union with Rome – the precondition, of course, being the acceptance of the authority of the Pope and the abjuration of their Miaphysite Christology, still considered by Rome to be a heresy condemned at the Council of Chalcedon. On the other hand, they were permitted to keep their oriental liturgical and spiritual traditions, as well as their own ecclesiastical structure. This led to the creation of a Syrian (Syriac) Catholic Church, which also attracted a number of Syriac Orthodox faithful from Mardin. In the 19th century, Mardin even became the residence of the Syriac Catholic Patriarchate, with an influx of Roman Catholic missionaries in the region. In response, the Syrian Orthodox began to establish contacts with the Anglican Church and the Archbishop of Canterbury, with Church hierarchs paying visits to London and official agreements being signed between the Churches.

5. Recent developments

In 1895, the Ottomans ordered a series of attacks directed mainly against the Armenian Christians of Eastern Anatolia. Regrettably these attacks would only be the prelude to the massacres of 1915, which were indiscriminately directed against all Christians in the Empire.[1] The Syriac Orthodox of the Tur Abdin were not spared. Many of their villages, churches and monasteries were destroyed, and thousands of people – including men, women and children alike – were murdered. They remember this year as the 'Year of the Sword', or the 'Shato d-Seyfo'.

When in 1923, standing atop the ruins of the Ottoman Empire, Mustafa Pasha Kemal Atatürk proclaimed the new Turkish Republic, a *modus vivendi* had to be sought with its Christian subjects who had survived or had not been expelled. Articles 37 through 44 of the Lausanne Peace Treaty, concluded in 1923, are devoted to the non-Muslim minorities, who are granted full protection, equality before the law, free exercise of religion and the right to organize their own charitable, religious, social and educational institutions where they are permitted to speak and to teach their own languages. The Treaty does not mention any specific community, but only speaks of non-Muslim minorities or nationals in a general sense. As a matter of fact, according to the current Turkish interpretation, the treaty applied

---

[1] For more information on the genocide against the Syriacs, see Tamcke's article in this book.

(and applies) only to the Greek (and Bulgarian) Orthodox, the Armenian Orthodox and the Jewish community. The Syriac Orthodox Patriarch Elias III declared (or was forced to declare) that the members of his community were merely ordinary Turkish citizens, which implied that the Syrian Orthodox were not entitled to the special cultural protection as defined in the Lausanne Treaty. This overture towards the Turkish Republic did not change the fact that he *de facto* no longer resided in the monastery of Deir al-Za'farân, but rather outside of Turkey. His successor, Ephrem Barsaum, who as bishop had participated in the peace negotiations in Paris at the end of World War I (1919), where he became an advocate for the Arabic cause, officially transferred the See of the patriarchate to the city of Homs in 1933. In fact, he was simply following the path of many Syrian Orthodox who, as a result of all that they had experienced in the Year of the Sword, did not see any future for themselves or their children in Turkey and decided to migrate to other countries in the Middle East. Others also moved to the United Sates. In the 1960s, the great majority of the remaining Suryoye of Tur Abdin left their homeland and settled in Germany, Sweden and the Netherlands as foreign workers.

In 1959, the See of the Patriarchate was again moved, this time from Homs to Damascus. In recent years, the Syrian capital has developed into the true centre of the Syrian Orthodox Church, particularly since a new theological academy was opened in Ma'arret Seydnaya, in the neighbourhood of Damascus, which offers the opportunity for thorough training in the classical Syriac language to (future) priests or deacons, as well as to those who will work in the Diaspora. Nevertheless for many Syrian Orthodox in Europe the Tur Abdin remains their true homeland.

Despite this centralizing initiative, for the present, the reality is that there are more of the Syrian Orthodox faithful living outside the Middle East than in their original lands – a fact that raises an entire set of identity-related questions.

6. Diaspora and identity

A first question is that of Christian identity: How do you impart Christian values to youngsters who grow up in secularized European societies in which religion plays only a marginal role?

Since, as we have seen in the introduction, religious identity cannot be separated from ethnic identity, the transmission of religious values also involves the question of fidelity to the linguistic and cultural tradition of the homelands. The question is: which tradition? Is it important for the second and third generations to learn the classical Syriac language used in the liturgy, or rather the spoken language of the Tur Abdin? Is it possible to make adaptations to the liturgy and

Apse of the church Mor Dodo in Basibrin (Haberli). (M. Tozman)

to the teachings of the Church to cope with the new reality of the Diaspora, or should Church leaders content themselves with translating the classical religious handbooks also used in the East?

A second set of questions relates to the relationship with the homeland. Despite some initiatives by a number of Syriac Orthodox families to return to the homeland (the village of Kafro Tahtayto, for example, was rebuilt entirely by Suryoye who, disillusioned with life in the Diaspora, saw greater opportunities for their children to preserve their religio-ethnic identity in the Middle East than in Europe[2]), it seems realistic to consider the Diaspora to be a permanent reality. The majority of the Suryoye do not wish to return, with the exception of a holiday or a crash course in Syriac for their children in one of the monasteries. Nevertheless, the homeland continues to mark the identity of the Suryoye abroad. One could even say that the disappearance of a Suryoyo presence in the Tur Abdin would mean the end of a Suryoyo identity. How, then, should the Suryoye relate to the homeland? By sending financial help and thus enabling the few remaining Christians to survive? By trying to influence local political developments? By lobbying the international community to demand Turkish recognition for the genocide of 1915 as a precondition for entering the European Union? Or by cooperating with the recent developments within the Turkish academic and political world, which is gradually discovering the importance of the Syriac language and the cultural heritage of the Suryoye?

7. Conclusion

The Suryoye developed from a Middle Eastern Church with specific ethnic and linguistic characteristics to become a global, transnational community, the identity of which (is it primarily ethnic or religious?) is not so easy to define. The emergence of a secular, non-religious leadership along with the traditional ecclesiastical authority appears to be the real challenge for the future. The way in which lay and church leaders begin to interact with one another will determine the identity of the Suryoye in the forthcoming years.

---

[2] For more information on the resettlement of the village of Kafro, see Oberkampf's article in this book.

The Syrian Orthodox Church

The Aramean Community as an Ecumenical Entity in a Transnational Dimension

By Jens Nieper

Jens Nieper is senior church staff member (Oberkirchenrat) and chair of the Desk "Near and Middle East and Foundations in the Holy Land" of Evangelical Church in Germany (EKD).

The Arameans are one of the ethnic and religious groups that suffer restrictions and discrimination in Turkey. In order to adequately reflect the situation of the Arameans in Turkey, we must understand that the Arameans are not restricted to the territory of the modern Republic of Turkey. We also must consider not only a far wider geographical context, but also a long historical perspective, which goes back at least to the times of the Early Church. It is important to relate both the current geopolitical situation, as well as the situation for Aramean religious minorities in the Muslim setting of Turkey with these aspects.

The Arameans of today identify themselves as the continuation of an eponymous population, which can be demonstrated to have lived in that part of the Middle East known as 'Greater Syria' since the Bronze Age. Hence they are commonly referred to as 'Syrian' ('Suryoye' in Aramaic). The precise extent of Greater Syria is difficult to determine, but is believed to have ranged from the Levant to Mesopotamia and from the Arabian desert to Anatolia. It influenced its neighbours and traded and corresponded with other regions. Significantly, the Aramaic language – which is technically a collective term and not a single language – became the *lingua franca* in the Near East, for example, under Assyrian and Achaemenid rule. In the time of Christ, even the Jewish population in the region spoke Aramaic as well as Koine Greek in their daily lives – a fact that is borne out by Aramaic expressions in the New Testament, and also by Jewish documents of the time written in Aramaic (such as targumim and the Jerusalem Talmud).

As a result of the Aramean presence and Aramaic influence both within the empires of Rome and Byzantium, as well as beyond the eastern borders of the empire, the conversion and church histories of the 'Syrians' are both varied and diverse. Accordingly several Syrian or 'Syriac' denominations remain in existence to this day. Roman-Byzantine efforts to construct a uniform imperial church and confrontation with other religions drove Syrian Christianity to identify itself as an oppressed community from its earliest days.

For the sake of presenting a complete picture, it must be mentioned that not all Arameans are Christians. The Mandeans, for example, also belong to the Aramaic people and in Syria we can find Muslims speaking Aramaic.

Church service during the Holy Week in Midyat. The Archbishop of Tur Abdin Samuel Aktas, together with now deceased Monk Yaqub, Deacon Isa Gares and several acolytes. (S. de Courtois)

Today's "Syrian" Churches are the product of a long and complex series of developments in dogmatic and ecclesiastical history and belong to several Church traditions. Accordingly their theologies can be close, distant or even in opposition to each other. What they more or less have in common is that they use Aramaic languages in their liturgies and writings, and, to some extent, even as everyday language – for example Turoyo, Hertevin and Kaldaya or the Ma'alula dialect. Furthermore modern Syrian Churches consider themselves to be descendents of the ancient Arameans, which is why they refuse to be defined as a minority. Rather, they consider themselves to be the remainder of the former – that is, pre-Islamic or pre-Arabic – traditional population. It is no surprise then that some of today's Arameans refer to themselves for example as Assyrians or Chaldeans. In addition representatives of these Churches at times describe the Muslim population in the region – both Arabs and Kurds – as Christians who were converted to Islam long ago.

Along with the Syrian Orthodox Church, the largest of the Aramaic churches in Turkey, there are the Chaldean and the Syrian Catholic Church (both united with the Roman Church), the Assyrian Apostolic Church of the East and the Ancient Church of the East, which was established in 1968 following a dispute within the Assyrian Church on the church calendar and dogmatic issues. The Maronites – generally residing in Lebanon and, again, united with the Roman Catholic Church – are also considered to be a Syrian church. The Greek Catholic Melkites and the Rum Orthodox Church are rooted in the "Greater Syria" region as well, but both evolved away from the Aramaic culture and are therefore generally no longer considered to be 'Syriac'. A distinct Protestant branch, as can be found in the related Armenian and Coptic churches, is missing among the Syriacs. However, Protestant Aramaic congregations can be found, for example, the Syrians of Hassana, who were converted by American missionaries and who today live mainly in the Netherlands and Eastern Westphalia.

In Western Europe two types of church are dominant: the Roman Catholic model, which considers itself to be global and multi-national, and the Protestant model, which is usually considered national with respect to modern political borders (such as the Church of Sweden, the PKN in the Netherlands and the EKD, the communion of Evangelical regional churches in Germany ('Landeskirchen')). With the Syrian Churches we experience a model that defines itself nationally, but in an ethnic sense. For this reason, political borders – particularly the mostly artificial modern borders in the Middle East – have no real meaning for the ecclesiastical structure of the various Aramaic denominations. This means that each of these denominations operates trans-nationally in the territorial sense whilst being predominantly homogenous in its language, culture and character. The Syrian Orthodox Church, for example, can be found not only in Turkey, but also in modern Syria, Lebanon, Iraq, Jordan and the Palestinian Territories – hence the concept of the historic "Greater Syria". The presence of 1,600 year old church buildings and monasteries demonstrates that this church is at home and deeply rooted in most of these countries. The same is also true for other Syriac churches.

It makes sense, therefore, that there are hardly any fully developed ecumenical organizations at the national level in the Middle East, and only a single regional ecumenical organization (REO): the Middle East Council of Churches (MECC). Founded in 1974, the MECC operates trans-nationally with regard to its member churches and church families. There are hardly any national church bodies at all in the Middle East. Due to the structure of the various denominations, no state church has been formed in the region in modern times. Because nearly all Churches in the Middle East are present in several states, it is difficult for any individual state to exploit a church for political ends, especially foreign policy, because they would be confronted in neighbouring countries by not only fellow-believers in general (Christians of other traditions, cultures and languages), but also members of their own specific church. This fact has given the churches a strong connective aspect. This aspect, however, should not be overestimated, considering the marginalized position of Christians and the socio-political mechanisms in the countries of the Middle East. Nevertheless it should be taken into account as a development opportunity.

The Syrian Orthodox Church in Turkey is linked to other groups of that denomination and is an integral part of that entire Church. Despite this fact, the Church should not be seen as a foreign body within Turkey. That would be an incorrect understanding of the case, particularly if you draw the conclusion that such an element must be removed and expelled. Rather, this Church represents an integrative and connective element, which enriches Turkey, as long as Turkey is not limited to a politically defined "Turkdom".

We must bear in mind the fact that the Syrian Orthodox Church – like all other Churches in the Middle East – is no longer limited to the Orient for several reasons. Emigration and flight have created a significant Diaspora, especially in Western and Northern Europe as well as in Northern America and Australia. The 'mother Church' in the Middle East is linked to all these parts of this Church; the native region and the Diaspora each have an effect on the other. The Church members in the Diaspora hold diverse citizenships, originally mainly Turkish and Lebanese, Iraqi and Syrian, while others are citizens of their new home land (this is especially valid for the younger generation, already born in the Diaspora), but they still all belong to the same Church. An estimated 300,000 Syrian Orthodox Christians live in Europe, with the largest community in Sweden.

In Germany, for example, Syrian Orthodox congregations have been founded in several cities and have an estimated 100,000 combined members. Emigrants, foreign workers and refugees all meet there. The congregations are structured within a diocese (or patriarchal vicariate) with the monastery of St Jacob of Sarug in Warburg at its centre.

Meanwhile the Syrian Orthodox congregations are integrated into the German ecumenical landscape and this integration is still in progress. The Syrian Orthodox Church, as well as other Churches of non-German origin and language, is no longer an exotic and bizarre guest: it is involved and contributes to German society.

View on the Monastery Church of the Holy Virgin of Hah, with its foundation going back as far as the first century, one of the oldest churches in Tur Abdin. Tradition goes that the Three Wise Men founded it after they had given their presents to Jesus Christ in Bethlehem. (M. Tozman)

Questions remain about how this integration process in the Diaspora impacts the 'motherland' of the Syrian Orthodox Church. How, for example, can the Syrian Orthodox Church support other congregations and churches that do not originate from the Middle East, but are present there today, to integrate and to become naturalized? How can the widespread traditional concept of a 'canonic' territory (the sole claim of a denomination on a specific area) – which was never the reality in the Orient – be replaced with a new, more ecumenical model? Is the Syrian Orthodox Church able to support Christian expatriate congregations of Western origin as well as congregations of African and Asian foreign workers and migrants to integrate? In the Middle East and in Turkey these non-Oriental Christian congregations already exist, but are frequently marginalized and ignored by the Middle Eastern churches. At best they are recognized as guests.

These questions seem unfitting for a church which itself struggles to be accepted in Turkey and suffers discrimination. Perhaps an integrative and connective power may arise as a result of their experience – a power that will help to improve the situation of Christians in general in Turkey in all their diversity and plurality. Such an improvement would also benefit the Syrian Orthodox Church.

A review of the Arameans in Turkey which takes their international linkage into consideration clarifies the choices facing this community – for itself, but also for the Republic of Turkey.

Living Between the Fronts:
The Turkish-Kurdish Conflict and the Assyrians

By Aryo Makko

Dr. Aryo Makko earned his doctoral degree in History at Stockholm University in 2012. Makko has been a Research Fellow at the Graduate Institute of International and Development Studies in Geneva (IHEID) and has taught at Stockholm University and Worcester College, University of Oxford. He has recently been elected as member of Wolfson College, University of Oxford and is also a founder and board member of the Modern Assyrian Research Archive (MARA) in partnership with the Faculty of Asian and Middle Eastern Studies, University of Cambridge.

1. Introduction

Recent years have seen the appearance of an increasing body of literature on the conflict between the Turkish state and the Kurdistan Workers' Party (PKK, *Partiya Karkerên Kurdistan*).[1] Yet, very little has been written about other ethnic and religious minorities living in the area in question – minorities that have been caught in the middle of a conflict that has dominated their lives since the first massive Kurdish uprisings of the 1920s.[2] Thus, important questions remain to be asked. For example, how have the ethnic minorities been affected by the conflict between the Turkish state and what some have called Kurdish 'rebels' and others 'liberation fighters'? This article seeks some introductory answers to the question by examining the effects of the Turkish-Kurdish conflict on the Assyrians, who are an indigenous people of south eastern Turkey and neighbouring areas in Iraq, Iran and Syria. It will give a short historical background and an equally concise description of the current situation, continue with examples of the most eminent effects of the Turkish-Kurdish conflict and conclude with a brief outlook on future scenarios.

---

[1] See, for example, Parts II and III in Casier & Jongerden, 2011; Mango, 2005; and Ibrahim & Gürbey, 2000. The issue also receives increasing attention in the broader literature on terrorism. See White (ed.), 2012.

[2] As pointed out by Martin Bruinessen, 'Kurdistan never was the land of the Kurds alone; its population was ethnically and religiously highly heterogeneous'. See http://igitur-archive.library.uu.nl/let/2007-0313-202741/bruinessen_00_transnational_aspectsKurds.pdf.

2. The century of violence and the invention of 'Turkishness'

Throughout much of the 20th century, south eastern Anatolia was the scene of large-scale violence. Following the genocidal extinction of large portions of the local Christian population in the years of the First World War[3], a process of social engineering was unleashed by the power holders in the new capital of Ankara.[4] During the decades that followed the events of the war and its aftermath, the Turkish state propagated and forcibly implemented a homogenous identity based on 'one state, one nation and one flag' as current Prime Minister Erdogan phrased it as late as in 2005.[5] While the Turkish state faced the challenge of severe transitions from empire to nation state and from one-party state to democracy, until the 1950s, its minorities continued their existence in neglect. Their legal situation – or rather the inexistence of it – had been formalized in the 1923 Treaty of Lausanne.[6] To the Assyrians, the vast majority of whom maintained simple and apolitical village lives in the mountainous areas of Tur Abdin and Hakkari, these decades were a renewed era of oppression, violence and exodus.[7] *Seyfo* ('The Sword'), the genocide, was followed by several outbursts of violence. In the shadow of the ongoing controversy between Great Britain, the mandatory power of the newly formed Iraqi state and Turkey in 1924–25, Assyrian attempts to resettle in their native areas of Hakkari were answered with severe violence by the Turkish military.[8] During the Istanbul riots of September 1955 and in the aftermath of the Turkish invasion of Northern Cyprus in July 1974, Assyrian citizens were targeted by their Muslim neighbours in Istanbul, Midyat and elsewhere.[9] Such recurring outbursts of violence caused by domestic and international political conflicts added to the daily socio-cultural tension that characterized their life in modern Turkey.[10]

With earlier contacts with Western churches and attempts at political involvement in the diplomatic aftermath of World War I at the Paris and San Remo conferences proving to be of little help in improving their situation, the Assyrians now preferred to remain outside of any political controversy. Their earliest reappearance on the political stage was a result of the end of isolation caused by the em-

---

[3] Gaunt, 2006; Yonan, 1989; Travis, 2006.
[4] Üngör, 2011.
[5] Duran, 2008. For more information on the identity policies of the Turkish state, see Onder's chapter.
[6] For a broader background, see Zürcher, 2004, or Hurst's article in this book.
[7] See Beth-Sawoce and BarAbraham, in Fikret Başkaya & Sait Çetinoglu (eds.), 2009.
[8] Donef, 2009; and Makko, 2010.
[9] Güven, 2012; and Travis, in Lemarchand (ed.), 2011.
[10] For more information on this topic, see Onder's article in this book.

igration of labour migrants (*Gastarbeiter*) to Germany and other West European countries in the second half of the 1960s which complemented the simultaneously growing integration into public life in Syria where many of them had settled in search of labour and greater freedom. With these processes came the rise of a small group of educated Assyrian elites and politically interested Assyrian workers. Establishing a new form of social and cultural, but also political, activism, they would respond to cases of oppression and murder against their community. These groups also participated in or responded to Turkish political life, in and outside of Turkey, and most often as sympathisers of the new Turkish Left. As a result of this development, there was a fertile soil for politicization of the Assyrian minority for the first time in more than half a century. Naturally, the rise of the Kurdish Workers' Party provoked a response.[11]

The origins of the PKK can be traced back to the student days of its founding member and long-time leader Abdullah Öcalan at the University of Ankara. Öcalan arrived in the capital in 1966 to study political science during a time that saw the "quiet growth of a defiant Kurdish identity in the big cities" as one scholar has put it.[12] Similar to many other youngsters with a minority background, Öcalan initially turned to the Turkish left for political orientation. In 1974, however, together with a circle of likeminded friends, he decided to unite his perception of socialism with his ethnic background. Roughly two years later, the core of the new organisation, originally known as Apocus, moved to the south eastern provinces. Within short time, the PKK launched attacks against the Turkish military and such groups and individuals who were thought to collaborate with the state. Among these were Kurdish tribes but also members of other minority groups. By the late 1970s, assassinations and counterattacks became almost daily routine. To the Assyrians of the Tur Abdin region, the rise of the Kurdish struggle primarily meant unwelcome additional attention of the state towardstheir area as the authorities responded with a number of measures, most notably the establishment of a system of "village guards", the so-called korucu. With this, the state forced villagers to take side in the conflict, a fact that held potential risks as became apparent within short time.[13]

---

[11] Oral history or fragments of the narrative spread out in publications which deal with the bigger picture are often the only available sources. Much of the information on the politicization of the Assyrians remains shattered as very little research has been carried out on the topic.
[12] On the origins of the PKK, see Marcus, 2007.
[13] Niehaus, 2010.

3. Caught in the middle: The rise of the PKK, the *Korucu* system and the Assyrians

Due to the similarities in settlement and legal status, Kurdish and Assyrian affairs in Anatolia have long been intertwined. Thus, the rise of the Kurdish political movement highly affected the Assyrians who themselves had traditionally maintained their political anonymity with Church leaders as their political representatives and religion as their centre of gravity. In this section, the following three areas, which have been affected by the conflict, are identified. Firstly, the social relationships between the Assyrians, their Kurdish neighbours and the state; secondly, the emerging Assyrian political arena; and thirdly, identity politics and the *'otherisation'*[14] of the Assyrians in Turkey. All three together are considered as reasons behind the marginalization of the minority discussed in this volume.

Christian graveyard at Mor Abrohom monastery in Midyat. This graveyard and other Christian tombs have frequently been defiled during the 80s and 90s. (M. Tozman)

---

[14] For an example of social arrangements into 'we' and 'them', see Kamali, 2009.

As mentioned above, the Turkish state established a system of village guards as a reaction to the positive response of the Kurdish population to the rise of the PKK.[15] With this, it sought the alliance of the influential Kurdish tribal leaders (*aghas*) opposed to the nationalist movement and the PKK. In every village, one or several loyal individuals were given the task of 'protecting' the village by maintaining close ties with the nearest available military unit. From an Assyrian perspective, this new immediate presence of the state contributed further to the already worsening situation as they were pressured ever more to take sides in a conflict that offered nothing to them but punishment from one party or the other.

Assyrian villagers quickly became caught in the middle of the conflict between the Turkish state and PKK fighters as both sides demanded loyalty from them denying a position as neutral bystanders. Whereas the former expected information on the actions of the PKK and report on the immediate sight of the appearance of members of the organization, the latter most often demanded shelter, silence and money. Quickly, both sides used force to demonstrate their determination. With this, the conflict between the two major ethnic groups in Turkey prolonged the ongoing exodus which saw the Assyrian population dwindling to about 500 families in the original settlement areas. In the early 1990s, the tension reached its climax with several cases of murder carried out by masked gunmen and state authorities against Assyrian villagers.[16] According to Martin van Bruinessen, these crimes were committed by Kurds collaborating with the state:

Another exception [from the otherwise friendly attitude of (nationalistic) Kurds towards minorities] may have to be made for the violent Kurdish Islamist movement Hizbullah [Hezbollah], which not only appears to have carried out assassinations of personalities considered as pro-PKK but also of prominent Christian personalities, in both cases in part for ideological reasons. The PKK, on the other hand, has at least verbally come to the defence of the threatened minorities (and in a few cases "punished" Kurdish oppressors of the Christian minority). Perhaps in order to distance itself from the assimilationist policies of Kemalist Turkey, the PKK has at least verbally been a consistent advocate of an ethnically pluralistic Kurdistan and of minority rights.[17]

One concrete example in the Assyrian case is the village of Marbobo in Tur Abdin which was abandoned in 1995 due to the continuous attacks carried out by Hezbollah.[18]

---

[15] Secer, 2006.
[16] Yonan, Hermes & Wiessner, www.gfbv.de/inhaltsDok.php?id=91.
[17] Van Bruinessen, 1999, available online at www.hum.uu.nl/medewerkers/m.vanbruinessen/publications/Violence.htm.
[18] I owe Markus Tozman thanks for drawing my attention to this example.

With this, life-threatening danger was added to other *push* factors that lay behind the process of migration such as social tension, legal neglect and economic deprivation. Essentially, thousands of Assyrians left Turkey due to the immediate threat directed against them by the state and the PKK. The foremost example of the destructive effect of the conflict on the Assyrians was the destruction of the village of Hassana by the Turkish military in 1993. It resulted in the relocation of the village to Europe, more concretely to the city of Mechelen, Belgium, in its entirety.[19]

Turkey's Assyrians were left untouched by the emergence of Assyrian political movements in other Middle Eastern countries and the Western Diaspora. Neither the Assyrian Democratic Organisation (Syria) nor the Assyrian Democratic Movement (Iraq), the two most notable political parties based in the area, attempted to establish themselves in Turkey. Little research has been carried out on the reasons behind the absence of the transnationalisation of such parties but most likely, their decisions were based on historical experience and, at a later stage, on the outbreak of the Turkish-Kurdish conflict. At the same time, there were sentiments among the local Assyrian youth to fill the political vacuum by establishing an Assyrian branch of the PKK. From these considerations arose the GHB (*Gabo d'hirutho Bethnahrin*, the Mesopotamian Freedom Party). Propagating violent resistance, they quickly rose to popularity among Assyrians in the European Diaspora by the late 1990s. Due to the strong anti-Kurdish sentiment among their own people, however, they quickly disassociated themselves from the PKK institutionally. The similar Marxist-Leninist ideology and general sympathy towards the Kurdish struggle however survived the separation for roughly another decade. Regardless of this, the influence of the GHB on the situation in Turkey was rather insignificant. Again, the lack of research or serious investigative journalism leaves much of the narrative in uncertainty and it remains a task for future research what approach to the Assyrians the PKK was planning to take during that period. What is obvious is that there has been a recent shift in the politics of the GHB with a friendlier attitude towards the Turkish state adopted.

The conflict, together with accusations of historical betrayal, also fuelled the targeting of the Assyrians as the 'other' in Turkish society[20]. Together with claims of alliance with the state's enemies during the First World War, suspicions about collaboration with the PKK pushed anti-Assyrian animosity in Ankara. At the

---

[19] The story arose the interest of a Belgian scholar who came to document it in book form and on a website, see www.shlama.be (accessed on 12 May 2012) and Thiry, 2001. Another example is that of the village of Sare which was 'evacuated' by Village Guards in a similar fashion.

[20] See also Onder's chapter.

Living Between the Fronts: The Turkish-Kurdish Conflict and the Assyrians

Sunset above Tur Abdin, close to Mor Yaqub monastery. (M. Tozman)

same time, this did not improve their position with respect to the Kurdish minority as can be seen from recent examples such as recurring tension in a number of villages or the legal battle against the Mor Gabriel monastery which has been going since 2008.[21] Today, in spite of the constructive reforms carried out since 2005 by the AKP as part of Turkey's convergence with the Copenhagen criteria, the Assyrians still appear as the social, legal, cultural and religious 'others' in Turkey. It may be argued that the tension caused by the conflict between the state and the PKK contributed to the absence of a shift in social engineering towards greater emphasis of Turkey as a mosaic of peoples, cultures and religions.

4. Outlook

Due to the pending permanent solution to the Kurdish-Turkish conflict, the Assyrians of Turkey are left in a state of uncertainty. On the one hand, their situation in south eastern Turkey has improved over the past decade in terms of economic

---

[21] *The Economist*, 2 December 2010.

well-being and general conditions of life. As a consequence, a growing number of retirees as well as a smaller number of families consider the possibility of returning to Turkey. In this regard, Turkey's aspirations to enter the EU and meet the Copenhagen criteria have played a significant role. On the other hand, Assyrians still have to deal with considerable pressure exerted by both Kurdish neighbours and the Turkish authorities. They are yet to receive their legal recognition as an indigenous minority and much remains to be done for them to be accepted as equal Turkish citizens. With Turkey's EU membership aspirations increasingly replaced by considerations which have been called a 'Neo-Ottoman' *Ostpolitik*, the role of the West, and in consequence that of the Assyrian Diaspora in Europe and other Western countries, might diminish in the future. Whether or not conservative democracy à*la* AKP will facilitate permanent representation of the minorities in the country remains to be seen. The same can be said for the will of Ankara to push for the reintegration of the Assyrians into Turkish society regardless of the development of its own conflict with the PKK.

References

Beth-Sawoce, J. and BarAbraham, A., "Repression, Discrimination, Assimilation and Displacement of East and West Assyrians in the Turkish Republic", in Fikret Başkaya and Sait Çetinoglu (eds.), *Minorities in Turkey*, 2009 (Resmi Tarih tartismalari: Özgür Universite Kitapligi, Ankara).
Casier, M. & Jongerden, J., *Nationalisms and Politics in Turkey: Political Islam, Kemalism and the Kurdish Issue*, 2011 (Milton Park; New York: Routledge).
Donef, R., *Massacres and Deportation of Assyrians in Northern Mesopotamia: Ethnic Cleansing by Turkey 1924–25*, 2009 (Stockholm: Nsibin).
Duran, B., "The Justice and Development Party's 'New politics': Steering toward conservative democracy, a revised Islamic agenda or management of new crises?", in Ümit Cizre (ed.), *Secular and Islamic Politics in Turkey: The Making of the Justice and Development Party*, 2008 (Milton Park; New York: Routledge).
Economist, The, "Turkey and Religious Freedom: Wooing Christians", 2 December 2010. Retrieved on 17 May 2012 from: www.economist.com/node/17632939.
Gaunt, D., *Massacres, Resistance, Protectors: Muslim-Christian Relations in Eastern Anatolia during World War I*, 2006 (Piscataway, NJ: Gorgias Press).
Güven, D., *Nationalismus und Minderheiten: Die Ausschreitungen gegen die Christen und Juden der Türkei vom September 1955*, 2012 (München: Oldenbourg).
Ibrahim, F., & Gürbey, G. (eds.), *The Kurdish Conflict in Turkey: Obstacles and Chances for Peace and Democracy*, 2000 (Münster: LIT).
Kamali, M., *Racial Discrimination: Institutional Patterns and Politics*, 2009 (Milton Park; New York: Routledge).

Makko, A., "Arbitrator in a World of Wars: The League of Nations and the Mosul Dispute", *Diplomacy & Statecraft*, Vol. 21(4), 2010.
Mango, A., *Turkey and the War on Terror: For Forty Years We Fought Alone*, 2005 (London: Routledge).
Marcus, A., *Blood and Belief: The PKK and the Kurdish Fight for Independence*, 2007 (New York: New York University Press).
Niehaus, L., *Der türkische Staat und die Kurden – Strategien ziviler Konfliktbearbeitung*, 2010 (München: GRIN Verlag).
Secer, E., *Die Türkei und der Minderheitenschutz: Perspektiven der kurdisch-türkischen Konflikte*, 2006 (München: GRIN Verlag).
Thiry, A., *Mechelen aan de Tigris: Het verhaal van een dorp en een wereld*, 2001 (Mechelen: CIMIC/Emo).
Travis, H., "Native Christians Massacred: The Ottoman Genocide of the Assyrians during World War I", in *Genocide Studies and Prevention*, Vol. 1(3), 2006.
Travis, H., "The Assyrian Genocide: A Tale of Oblivion and Denial", in René Lemarchand (ed.), *Forgotten Genocides: Oblivion, Denial, and Memory*, 2011 (Philadelphia, PA: University of Pennsylvania Press).
Üngör, U.U., *The Making of Modern Turkey: Nation and State in Eastern Anatolia, 1913–1950*, 2011 (Oxford: Oxford University Press).
Van Bruinessen, M., "Transnational aspects of the Kurdish question",
  retrieved from www.igitur-archive.library.uu.nl/let/2007-0313-202741/bruinessen_00_transnational_aspectsKurds.pdf.
Van Bruinessen, M., "The Nature and Uses of Violence in the Kurdish Conflict", paper presented at the International Colloquium *Ethnic Construction and Political Violence* (Cortona, 1999), retrieved 14 June 2012 from www.hum.uu.nl/medewerkers/m.vanbruinessen/publications/Violence.htm.
White, J.R. (ed.), *Terrorism and Homeland Security*, 2012 (Belmont, CA: Wadsworth Cengage Learning).
Yonan, G., *Ein vergessener Holocaust: die Vernichtung der christlichen Assyrer in der Türkei*, 1989 (Göttingen: Gesellschaft für bedrohte Völker).
Yonan, S., Hermes, A. & Wiessner, G., "Assyrer", Document prepared for the Society for Threatened Peoples. Retrieved 12 May 2012 from www.gfbv.de/inhaltsDok.php?id=91.
Zürcher, E.J., *Turkey: A Modern History*, 2004 (London: Tauris).

Turkey: Secularism with an Islamic Flavour and Persisting Obstacles to Religious Freedom

By Dennis Pastoor, Open Doors

Open Doors is non-denominational Christian mission supporting persecuted Christians in more than 50 countries where Christianity is socially or legally discouraged or oppressed; its work focuses upon field work and the direct support of Christian minorities.

Turkey and the World Watch List

Each year, Open Doors[1] produces the World Watch List (WWL)[2], which ranks 50 countries according to the intensity of persecution Christians face for their faith. The 2012 WWL covers the period from 1 November 2010 through 31 October 2011.

The WWL is based on a questionnaire[3] developed by Open Doors to gauge the level of persecution in over 60 countries. The questionnaires are completed by Open Doors field personnel working in the countries, as well as by external experts, to arrive at a quantitative score for each country. Countries are then ranked according to the points received. A country's position on the list is not an indication of persecution worsening or improving in the country. In some cases a country's score will be higher than in the previous year, and yet the country might

---

[1] www.opendoors.org
[2] www.worldwatchlist.us
[3] The questionnaire that Open Doors uses is currently being revised. Until 2012, the countries on the WWL were scored and ranked based on a questionnaire that was divided into six blocks: (1) Legal status of Christians (Is religious freedom guaranteed by the Constitution or comparable laws, and applied in court?); (2) Position of state toward Christians (What is the attitude of the state towards Christians and churches?); (3) Church organization (Can churches function freely?); (4) Role of the Church in society (Is it possible for Christians to express their faith in public life, not only evangelization?); (5A) Situation of individual Christians (part A) (What are the persecution incidents: killings; (arbitrary) arrests; kidnappings; physical harassment; houses or meeting places attacked; Christians forced to flee); (5B) Situation of individual Christians (part B) (What are the persecution incidents at a bit more generic level: discrimination at school or work (in general, with the authorities); hindrance in travelling; fines, threats or obstruction; pressure to change or renounce their faith); (6) Other Factors limiting the life of churches and believers (Are other groups/organizations besides the state monitoring or restricting the activities of Christians or churches?).

have a lower position on the list because ranking is determined in relation to what has happened in other countries.

Table 1: Open Doors' World Watch List 2011–2012

Ranking 2012	Country	Points 2012	Ranking 2011	Points 2011
1.	North Korea	88	1.	90.5
2.	Afghanistan	67.5	3.	66
3.	Saudi Arabia	67.5	4.	64.5
4.	Somalia	66.5	5.	64
5.	Iran	66	2.	67.5
6.	Maldives	63	6.	63
7.	Uzbekistan	61	9.	57.5
8.	Yemen	58.5	7.	60
9.	Iraq	57	8.	58.5
10.	Pakistan	56.5	11.	55.5
11.	Eritrea	56	12.	55
12.	Laos	55.5	10.	56
13.	Northern Nigeria	55	23.	44
14.	Mauritania	54	13.	53.5
15.	Egypt	53.5	19.	47.5
16.	Sudan	53.5	35.	37
17.	Bhutan	51	14.	53.5
18.	Turkmenistan	50.5	15.	51.5
19.	Vietnam	49.5	18.	48
20.	Chechnya	49.5	20.	47
21.	China	48.5	16.	48.5
22.	Qatar	47	17.	48.5
23.	Algeria	46.5	22.	45
24.	Comoros	45.5	21.	46.5
25.	Azerbaijan	45.5	24.	43.5
26.	Libya	42	25.	41
27.	Oman	42	26.	41
28.	Brunei	42	29.	39.5
29.	Morocco	41	31.	39.5
30.	Kuwait	40.5	28.	40
31.	**Turkey**	**40.5**	**30.**	**39.5**

Table 1 cont.

Ranking 2012	Country	Points 2012	Ranking 2011	Points 2011
32.	India	40.5	32.	39
33.	Burma/Myanmar	39	27.	40
34.	Tajikistan	39	33.	38
35.	Tunisia	39	37.	35
36.	Syria	39	38.	34.5
37.	United Arab Emirates	38.5	34.	37.5
38.	Ethiopia	36	43.	30
39.	Djibouti	33.5	39.	33.5
40.	Jordan	33.5	40.	33.5
41.	Cuba	33.5	41.	33.5
42.	Belarus	33.5	42.	32
43.	Indonesia	31.5	48.	26.5
44.	Palestinian Territories	31	44.	29.5
45.	Kazakhstan	30.5		
46.	Bahrain	30	45.	28.5
47.	Colombia	30		
48.	Kyrgyzstan	29.5	46.	28.5
49.	Bangladesh	27.5	47.	27.5
50.	Malaysia	27	50.	22.5

Source: Open Doors International

Persecution situations are often a confusing mix of political, economic, social, ethnic and religious factors. As restrictions on religious freedom increase, the more vulnerable Christians are, particularly when persecution originates from both the government and hostile social groups.

In the case of Turkey, the combination of persistent legal restrictions and negative comments by some government officials towards Christians, social hostilities and the rise of observant Islam, has translated into a relatively high degree of persecution of Christians. Turkey ranked 31th on Open Doors World Watch List in 2012, ranking 30th in 2010 and 39th in 2009. This climb indicates that the levels of persecution of Christians have (comparatively) increased and that the situation in the country has deteriorated.[4]

Table 2: Turkey on Open Doors' World Watch List 2002–2012

	2012	2011	2010	2009	2008	2007	2006	2005	2004	2003	2002
Rank	31	30	35	39	34	35	36	39	39	34	35
Points	40.5	39.5	36.0	33.0	36.0	34.0	30.5	29.0	32.0	34.5	35.5

Source: Open Doors International

In Turkey[5], religious freedom and persecution of Christians coexist. The rights of religious minorities are respected and protected by officialdom, but a large number of government restrictions affect the religious activities of Christians. The government restrictions on religious freedom, as this article will show, are based essentially on interpretations of the secular constitution and laws of the country that are heavily biased against both non-Muslim minorities and anti-secular Islamists. These restrictions add to the persistent societal intolerance against Christians.

This article will first provide an overview of traditional persecution dynamics in Turkey, which are a combination of legal restrictions and societal hostilities deeply rooted in the country's nationalist and secular ideology. This presentation will be followed by a description of newer trends regarding Christian persecution in Turkey related to thegrowing influence of Islam in Turkish society. Finally, this article will conclude with some remarks on the future outlook for Christian persecution in Turkey.

1. Traditional persecution dynamics in Turkey: nationalism and secularism

The Turkish secularist model can be described as 'secularism with an Islamic flavour', to grasp the contradiction between the institution of a strict separation of religion and state and the actual preferential treatment for Sunni Islam. There is

---

[4] Turkey also ranks 'high' in Pew Forum's Government Restrictions Index and Social Hostilities Index, which is an alternative measure of religious freedom worldwide (Pew Forum on Religion & Public Life, *Rising Restrictions on Religion*, 2011). For the first time, Turkey was also categorized as a 'country of particular concern' by the United States Commission on International Religious Freedom in its 2012 annual report.

[5] This article will describe the situation of the Church in Turkey in general, but will not refer to the very specific problems faced by Christians within the Kurdish minority.

indeed a huge difference between the formal interpretation of the country's secular legislation and the informal practices by government officials, police officers and judges, which in fact are often discriminatory against Christians.[6]

Turkey is a secularist state in name and to a certain extent this is true in practice, but various forms of persecution of non-Muslim minorities, including Christians, subsist. Turkish secularism is in fact anti-religious.[7] No chaplains are permitted in the Turkish Army and, until recently, headscarves were forbidden in universities and in public offices.

Legal restrictions, societal hostilities and nationalism are significant sources of persecution, causing human rights violations, such as hate crimes, unfair judicial treatments, discrimination and so on. People with a Muslim background who are interested in the gospel are often victims of strong discrimination by their families. In a society as strongly patriarchal as Turkey, conversion of a family member is considered to bring shame upon the entire family. Many converted Christians are disinherited or are disowned by their families. Muslims who convert to Christianity also risk losing their jobs. The government remains passive in the face of these types of discrimination that concern only a very small minority.

The country's nationalist ideology does not provide for the protection of minorities in practice. Nationalism has led not only to persecution of Christians, but also of other minorities such as the Alevi and Kurds. The Alevi are a minority branch of Islam that is considered 'deviant' by mainstream Islam. Approximately 15–20 million Turks (20–30 % of the population) follow Alevism and are subject to persecution.

As Tozman[8] shows in his research, persecution of Kurds has almost always been at the expense of Christians. Tozman, quoting Yacoub, indicates that: "This particular form of nationalism pervades not only State institutions but society as a whole, and generally conveys a massage that leaves no room for the Christian minorities."

According to Tozman:

Turkey's nationalism is an exclusive form of nationalism aiming at assimilation or marginalization, combined with severe suppression and discrimination. Neither the Lausanne minorities nor the other minorities were protected by the Turkish state and are even today still struggling to survive.... The main obstacle to an improvement in Turkey is the ultra-nationalistic attitude condemning everybody outside the 'main group' and perceiving them as threat to the integrity of the state. If Turkey does not start distancing herself

---

[6] For examples, see Compass Direct News, 15 March 2011, 19 October 2010 and 28 May 2010.
[7] Oehring, 2008.
[8] Tozman, 2011.

from her current form of nationalism, any changes in law will continue to appear only on paper and not in reality.[9]

It is important to note that there are significant differences between ethnic minorities and converted Muslim Background Believers (MBBs). It is generally considered that "to be a Turk is to be a Muslim". For this reason, Christians may be considered citizens, but never a Turk.[10] A person in Turkey who leaves Islam for Christianity is considered a disgrace to his/her family and risks honour killing, as was reported to Open Doors.

Threats against non-Muslims create an atmosphere of pressure and diminished freedom for other religions. In general, Christians face societal suspicion and mistrust, which is accentuated by the fact that Christians are often portrayed negatively in the national media. Some TV shows even encourage attacks on Christians[11], as reported in 2012 by the Turkish Association of Protestant Churches[12], which noted a "root of intolerance" in Turkish society toward adherents of non-Islamic faiths.

The judicial system defends religious freedom in name, but in practice, beliefs other than Sunni Islam are viewed with suspicion.[13] The Judiciary[14] is not always impartial and laws are sometimes applied in discriminatory ways.[15]

– The right to distribute religious propaganda is not always respected, despite the fact that the Turkish Constitution guarantees freedom of religion and even the right to distribute religious information which has no proven political motive.
– The secular system, which was designed to definitely obstruct the implementation of an Islamic theocracy, is being used for anti-secularist purposes by prosecutors, becoming discriminatory for non-Muslim religions.[16]
– Illegal detentions and intimidations (human rights violations) of religious minorities, tourists and expatriates are not uncommon.
– Christian evangelistic activities are sometimes criminalized.

---

[9] Tozman, *ibid.*
[10] For more information on the concept of Turkish nationality and citizenship, cf. Icduygu and Soner, 2006.
[11] *Compass Direct News*, 2006.
[12] Association of Protestant Churches, 2012.
[13] United States Department of State, 2011.
[14] For an overview of recent court cases against Christians, please refer to Middle East Concern, www.meconcern.org/index.php?option=com_content&view=article&id=298:turkey-persecution-of-christians&catid=29:turkey&Itemid=9.
[15] Yildrim, 2012.
[16] For examples, refer to Compass Direct News, 2006.

Secularism with an Islamic Flavour and Persisting Obstacles to Religious Freedom

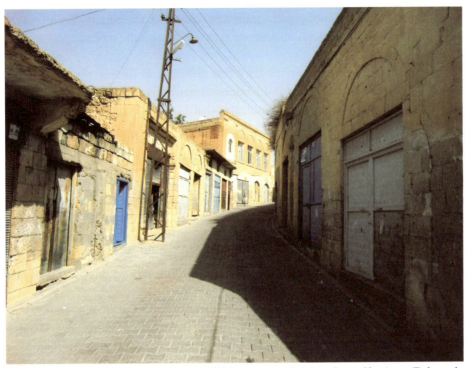

The old Christian commercial main street of Midyat; once a thriving place of business, Today only abandoned stores remain. (M. Tozman)

– Judicial investigations against Christians, whether proven or not, are included on individuals security records', making them ineligible for government employment.

The legal status of several Christian churches is not fully recognized: the only non-Muslim minorities that are formally recognized are the Armenians (Gregorian Orthodox, 60,000), the Greek Orthodox (3,500) and the Jews (25,000). For historical reasons Christian denominations such as the Syriac Orthodox (15,000) are not officially recognized but have the right to operate churches. Catholics (including Chaldean, Armenian, Greek and Syrian rites, 35,000), Bulgarian Orthodox (500) and Evangelical Protestants (3,000–3,500) do not receive formal recognition.[17]

Christian denominations are not permitted to establish universities or seminaries to train their leaders[18], therefore religious communities outside the Sunni

---

[17] The numbers used are estimations from Open Doors International Research and reflect the situation in 2011.
[18] Because the government requires all places of learning to be under the control of the Education Ministry, the Greek Orthodox and Armenian Orthodox chose not to train their clergy in the

Islamic mainstream cannot legally train new clergy in the country for eventual leadership. Faith-based social institutions (schools, hospitals, orphanages) are under official control[19].

Some Christian denominations have had difficulty in finding places to lease, buy or in which to meet.[20] In its 2011 International Religious Freedom report, the United States Department of State indicates that:

[S]ome religious groups reported difficulties opening, maintaining, and operating houses of worship. Under the law religious services may take place only in designated places of worship. Municipal codes mandated that only the government can designate a place of worship, and if a religion has no legal standing in the country, it cannot register a site. Non-Muslim religious services, especially for religious groups that did not own property recognized by the GDF [General Directorate of Foundations], often took place on diplomatic property or in private apartments. While police and prosecutors did not attempt to prevent or prosecute such gatherings, landlords were hesitant to rent to groups without confirmation that they would not be harassed by the police.[21]

Religious affiliation is listed on national identity cards but citizens can choose not to include a religion on their identity cards. Turkey is one of the few Muslim majority countries that allow their citizens to change their religious affiliation on their ID cards[22].

Although it is legal for citizens who convert from Islam to another religion to amend their religious identity on their national identification cards, local officials sometimes harass individuals who have converted from Islam to another religion when they try to do so. Some non-Muslims maintain that listing religious affiliation on the cards exposes them to discrimination and harassment. Muslims who

---

country.

[19] These limitations were one of the main reasons for the United States Commission on International Religious Freedom to categorize Turkey as a country of particular concern in its 2012 annual report, in which it criticizes Turkey for regulating non-Muslim groups by restricting how they can train clergy, offer education and own their places of worship.

[20] According to Compass Direct News (2009): *"More than half of the population of Muslim-majority Turkey opposes members of other religions holding meetings or publishing materials to explain their faith, according to a recently issued survey. Fully 59 percent of those surveyed said non-Muslims either 'should not' or 'absolutely should not' be allowed to hold open meetings where they can discuss their ideas. Fifty-four percent said non-Muslims either 'should not' or 'absolutely should not' be allowed to publish literature that describes their faith."*

[21] United States Department of State, 2011.

[22] Open Doors International World Watch List Unit.

convert to Christianity are victims of various forms of harassment by government institutions.[23]

Religious minorities are legally exempted from compulsory religious and moral instruction in primary and secondary schools. The Government has claimed that the compulsory instruction covers the range of world religions, but religious minorities[24] assert that the courses reflect Hanafi Sunni Islamic doctrine and that anti-missionary rhetoric remains in compulsory school textbooks. A few religious minorities, such as Protestants and Syriac Orthodox, have encountered difficulty in obtaining exemptions, particularly if their identification cards did not list a religion other than Islam.

Moreover, maintenance of historic religious buildings requires government approval, so religious properties can fall into government hands if specific conditions are not met, such as belonging to a recognized religious community and complying with a number of administrative requirements including zoning issues. The case of the Mor Gabriel monastery[25] belonging to the Syrian Orthodox community is a clear example of this, however there are numerous other examples that could also be mentioned[26].

Christians in Turkey also suffer from a number of social hostilities[27] from nationalist and secularist groups, inspired by misconceptions of the nature of the secular state, historical resentments or irrational fears of Christians. The intensity of these social hostilities, which range from various forms of discrimination and intolerance to the use of physical violence, varies throughout the country.

The printing and distribution of Bibles and Christian literature is permitted and a Bible translation in modern Turkish was produced in 2001. The missionary agency Operation Mobilization publicly offers a "Bible correspondence course" through the creation of a foundation that operates without restrictions.[28] Legally

---

[23] Oehring, 2009.
[24] This concern has been voiced on various occasions by all religious minorities in Turkey.
[25] Omtzigt, 2012(this initiative policy paper is added as an appendix to this volume), and Compass Direct News, 2012.
[26] For more information on this trials of the Mor Gabriel monastery, see Oran's article in this book.
[27] According to the United States Department of State, *International Religious Freedom Report 2011*: "There were reports of societal abuses and discrimination based on religious affiliation, belief, or practice. Threats against non-Muslims created an atmosphere of pressure and diminished freedom for some non-Muslim communities. Many Christians, Bahais, Jews, and Alevis faced societal suspicion and mistrust, and some elements of society continued to express anti-Semitic sentiments. Additionally persons wishing to convert from Islam sometimes experienced social harassment and violence from relatives and neighbors."
[28] www.bccturkey.org/

Christians are free to print and distribute Christian literature, but strong societal limits persist outside of the major cities.

Although religious speech and persuasion is legal, some Christians face various restrictions and occasional harassment for alleged proselytizing. Christians and their lawyers engaged in religious advocacy have occasionally been threatened or pressured by government and state officials. Proselytizing on behalf of non-Muslim religious groups is considered socially unacceptable and provocative, and at times dangerous.

Although some positive changes have been brought about at the national level, forms of discrimination may continue at local police stations or in smaller towns of Turkey. Hostility against Christians tends to be stronger in rural areas, according to reports from Open Doors.

In spite of these difficulties, the Church as a whole has grown over the past decades. The various Orthodox denominations have remained stable or have decreased in size, mostly due to immigration, but the Catholic and Protestant Turkish populations have grown. Convert Protestants have also increased in number from a few hundred in 1992 to 3,000–3,500 Evangelical Christians, whilst other denominations have remained stable.[29]

Church growth has stabilized now: "The Turkish Church has often been described as a church with a revolving door. It seems that many who came through the front door have left through the back door and therefore the faces in the church have changed but the number stayed the same," says one missionary expatriate Christian living in Turkey.

2. The growing influence of Islam in Turkish society

In addition to these nationalist and social hostilities, the growing influence of Islam in Turkish society has added to the persecution of Christians in the country. In order to properly understand the growing influence of Islam in Turkish society, it is important to bear in mind the following conceptual clarifications.

As the following sections make clear, there has undeniable been a revival of observant or conservative Islam over the last decade. Society as a whole has become more Islamic. Furthermore, without establishing a direct relation with the former, hate crimes against Christians have also increased. In some cases, these hate crimes can be linked to extremist Islamic movements, although the majority of cases are perpetrated by radical nationalist groups. Additionally, parallel

---

[29] Some reports indicate that the population of Catholics has also increased, but this could not be confirmed by independent sources.

Secularism with an Islamic Flavour and Persisting Obstacles to Religious Freedom

Image and calligraphy of the last supper from an old, handwritten Syriac Bible. (From the book by Y. Bilge)

to these major social trends, the governing AK party has progressively moved towards an Islamic agenda – political Islam.

2.1. The revival of observant Islam

Whilst traditionally persecution originated mainly in nationalism (equating Turkishness to being a Muslim), combined with a discriminatory form of secularism as described in the preceding section, some new trends can be perceived. Observant Islam is growing stronger in the country in spite of the country's secular Constitution and tradition and it can be said that parts of the country are slowly Islamising.

The country's landscape is changing rapidly. Significant numbers of mosques are being built, financed mostly through government funds. According to Forum 18, there are now about 85,000 mosques in Turkey. For comparison, in 2009, the Turkish government contributed 3,060,000 Turkish lira (the equivalent of 1,343,365 euros or 1,991,820 US Dollars) to 85 mosques for building expenses.[30]

The rise of conservative Islam in the country has added to the persecution of Christians in Turkey.[31] Police officers are present in some church services to protect churchgoers, but also to monitor the activities of Christians. This police protection began only after the deadly attacks against Christians in the past six years, following the heavily publicized Malatya murders.[32]

On the one hand, this police presence is positive because it is an indication that violence against Christians is a concern for the police. On the other hand, it is discomforting that this police protection is needed and that Islamist and nationalist movements are repeatedly using violence against Christians. However, this protection is not generalized and many church properties are vandalized. Also, the presence of police officers in church services could also be seen as a form of control or surveillance of religious activities in the country.

"Despite some promising developments, Christians in Turkey continue to suffer attacks from private citizens, discrimination by lower-level government officials and vilification in both school textbooks and news media, according to a study by a Protestant group. In its 2012 annual Report on Human Rights Violations, released in January 2012, the country's Association of Protestant Churches

---

[30] Yildrim, 2011.
[31] United States Commission on International Religious Freedom, 2012.
[32] According to the International Religious Freedom Report, 2011 from the United States Department of State: *"Several Protestant pastors, some Protestant church legal advisors, and several Protestant churches across the country received heightened police protection due to threats. Some pastors reported receiving threatening telephone calls or messages during the reporting period."*

notes mixed indicators of improvement, but notes that there is a "root of intolerance" in Turkish society toward "adherents of non-Islamic faiths".[33]

2.2. Frequent hate crimes against Christians

Hate crimes against Christians are commonplace. As noted in one of the two reports published by the Turkish Association of Protestant Churches in 2010, "Hate crimes continued to be perpetrated against Christians in 2010 and there were various attacks carried out against Protestants and their churches".[34] Religious meetings in homes are strongly discouraged in some parts of the country for fear of Muslim extremists. Church properties (including cemeteries) are frequently vandalized and are not always given protection by the police.

A military coup in 1980 put an end – temporarily – to an extended period of terrorism and violence by both far-left extremists and radical Islamic movements[35], but extremist Islam seems to be resurging once again, albeit underground and illegally. There is clear evidence that Al Qaeda is recruiting Turks for its ranks abroad and perhaps domestically, as well.[36] In addition to Al Qaeda, Turkish Hezbollah is another illegal group that has been active since its founding in 1979 aiming at imposing a Turkish Islamic state similar to Iran.[37]

Extremist Islam has existed for decades, but has never been a mass movement and has so far been contained by the country's military. In recent years, an increasing number of violent incidents by Islamic movements have been reported, some of which appear to be related to Al Qaeda and other Islamic groups. The planned attack on churches in Ankara and their clergy, the Turkish Parliament and the U.S. Embassy by 11 alleged Al Qaeda militants that was made public in December is the most recent illustration of this.[38]

Middle East Concern, a Christian human rights advocacy organization, counted 22 incidents – defined as any reported case of persecution of Christian, although not necessarily religiously motivated – in 2011, 22 in 2010, 14 in 2009 and 16 in 2008.

Between September 2011 and February 2012, the World Watch List Unit of Open Doors recorded the following incidents, based on media research only:

---

[33] Compass Direct News, 2012.
[34] Association of Protestant Churches (Turkey), Committee for Religious Freedom and Legal Affairs, 2010.
[35] For more information, refer to Laciner, 2007; Ozoren, 2004; and Levitsky, 2003.
[36] Rotella, 2009.
[37] Markus Tozman, op. cit.
[38] Compass Direct News, 2012.

Close up of the church of Mor Had Bshabo in Ciwardo (Gülgöze). During the genocide it was successfully used as fortress against Kurdish and Turkish attacks. The village offered shelter for Syriacs from all over the Tur Abdin region. (H. Oberkampf)

- A large-scale Al Qaeda plot to bomb "all of the churches in Ankara," as well as the Turkish Parliament and U.S. Embassy in the Turkish capital (9 December 2011);
- A child whose father was a Muslim religious leader who converted to Christianity, made a public profession of Christian faith at school. The child's classmates mocked and spat upon him. When the boy threatened to inform the principal, a fellow student threatened to murder him if he did so. The boy's father went to talk to the father of the aggressor, who responded by threatening the convert's life. The Christian child began to be subject to beatings with a stick, inflicted by the religion teacher at the school (17 February 2012).
- Officials from the Malatya Municipality demolished three buildings under construction in an Armenian Christian cemetery (2 February 2012).

Of course, not all of these hate crimes against Christians should be assigned to Islamic extremists, given the prevailing anti-Christian attitude in Turkish society. Extremist Islam does exist as an underground movement, but it is not a major challenge in Turkey. It is also important to underline that ultra-nationalists also often use Islam as a cover.

2.3. The institutionalization of political Islam

Perhaps the clearest expression of the growing influence of Islam in the country are the policies of the Justice and Development Party (AKP), which has been in power since 2002. The traditionally secular state, under constant protection by the national army, has in recent years become more permissive of public expressions of Islam under the Government of Prime Minister Recep Tayyip Erdoğan and President Abdullah Gül.

The ruling AK party, has – at least partially – an Islamist agenda. Although some analysts would disagree with this interpretation, the AKP Government should be evaluated based on its actions and rather than on its official discourse. Whether the AKP is simply being politically pragmatic – opportunistic – and whether this Islamist agenda is a moderate or a radical one is unclear, as clever strategists can be expected to conceal their intentions.

When looking at statements by Turkish officials, many cases of doublespeak can be found. On one occasion, Prime Minister Erdoğan stated that his goal was "to raise a religious generation", but President Gül has also declared that Muslim countries should avoid politicizing Islam. Many statements by the government are also more cosmetic than substantial. For example, the official decree issued by the government in August 2011 regarding the possibility of religious minorities to reclaim their confiscated religious properties,[39] did not apply to all religious communities nor the majority of properties appropriated in recent decades.

The ruling AK party was founded in 2001, and by the 2002 general elections the party had already obtained a two-thirds majority in Congress. The AKP describes itself as a mainstream liberal-conservative party "with no religious axis," but it is undeniable that its roots are in the Islamic tradition (the Islamist Virtue Party of which Gül was a prominent member, amongst others). Erdoğan himself was banned from his office as mayor of Istanbul and sentenced to prison in 1994 after an incident in which he read a pro-Islamist poem.

The AKP leaders may publicly deny their Islamist agenda and claim that the party has abandoned its Islamist roots, but the multiplication of issues contradicting the country's secularist tradition must not be overlooked. As one analyst consulted for this article declared, "to the AKP, Islam is more important than Kemalism". Just three examples of this development are the changes in the country's

---

[39] Compass Direct News, 2011.

foreign policy priorities, the legislation concerning minority foundations and the role that is played by the Diyanet (the presidency for religious affairs).

2.3.1. Turkey's Islamist foreign policy turn

Prime Minister Erdoğan is a charismatic leader, but his position and that of his party regarding the relation between Islam and the state is unclear. Some analysts say that the AKP promotes a moderate Islam, without renouncing the secular organization of the state and democratic values, but recent pro-Muslim shifts in Turkey's foreign policy indicate that the AKP is probably more Islamist than it confesses publicly.[40]

During its first years in government, it appeared as if the AKP had abandoned its Islamist roots. The AKP once had a pro-Western leaning (membership negotiations with the European Union, intensification of the cooperation with Israel and active collaboration with NATO); but recent developments seem to indicate a change in the country's foreign policy.[41]

The escalation of a diplomatic conflict with Israel leading to the withdrawal of the Turkish ambassador to the country (following the Gaza flotilla raid in which nine Turkish activists were killed[42]), the apparent loss of interest in EU membership and the *rapprochement* with Islamic nations such as Iran and the Palestinian Authority can be seen as elements of what could be an Arab-Muslim turn in Turkey's foreign policy.[43]

Turkey's role in the Middle East is something to monitor in the future. In the aftermath of the Arab Spring revolutions, it is likely that Turkey will seek to reinforce its leadership in the region and that the AKP will intensify its ties with Islamic parties. As the international think tank Stratfor writes in its 2012 forecast: "On the foreign policy front, Turkey will try to influence the rise of political Islamists, particularly in Egypt and Syria", noting however that, "Ankara's [domestic policy] constraints will prevent it from taking meaningful steps in that regard".[44] Erdogan's government is immensely popular mainly because of its very successful economic policy. The country's infrastructure and living conditions have considerably improved. Turkey is the fastest growing economy of Europe. Turkey's exports to Iran and the Arab world are rapidly becoming more important

---

[40] International Crisis Group, 2010.
[41] Cagaptay, 2012.
[42] Mitnick, 2010.
[43] Barkey, 2011.
[44] Stratfor, 2012.

than exports to Europe, which is probably one of the underlying explanations of the country's pivotal turn in foreign policy.[45]

For many, the fact that the Government is pro-Islam and its policies have been economically beneficial for the country, this Islamist orientation is also seen as something positive, leading to a decreasing support for secularism and increasing support for (moderate) Islam, because previous secular governments were characterized by high levels of corruption and inflation.

2.3.2. Law on Foundations[46]

In Turkey, fiscal policies heavily affect religious minority foundations. Orhan Kemal Cengiz claims that the legislation regulating minority foundations, which are foundations set up for religious minorities to allocate funds or property for charitable purposes, is being used as a means to "routinely and systematically [deprive] these vulnerable groups of their possessions and financial means".[47] Though the foundations were introduced to curve and control Islamist movements that were regarded as a threat to the secular state, in the course of time, the system came to be used mainly against minorities.[48]

Since 1949, these foundations have been granted autonomy in their administration, after having been under the governance of the General Directorate of Foundations from 1936 onwards. However, since then these minority foundations have been subject to high taxes and faced bureaucratic and judicial obstacles to acquire property.

Starting in 1936, the Turkish government seized hundreds of lands and buildings owned by its Greek, Armenian, Syriac and Jewish communities.[49] As a result, several foundations ceased to exist, because many of them had relied heavily on revenues earned from leasing out their properties.[50] In 2002, within the context of Turkey's EU membership negotiations, the Law of Foundations was amended to allow minority foundations to acquire real estate with the permission of the responsible government department, overturning a ruling in 1974 that prohibited non-Muslim communities from acquiring new property. But once again, huge bureaucratic burdens and non-compliance by civil servants impeded a palpable improvement in the situation.

---

[45] Cagaptay, 2012.
[46] For more information on this topic, see Onder's article in this book.
[47] Cengiz, 2010.
[48] Cengiz, 2003.
[49] Compass Direct News, 2011.
[50] Icduygu, A., Toktas, S. & Soner, A., 2008.

Image of a "sislo" bell symbolizing cherubim; they are used during the Eucharist service. (S. de Courtois)

Moreover, these amendments did not resolve the issue of the historic religious properties that had been confiscated by the government after 1936. As a result of pressures from the European Court of Human Rights (ECHR), recent developments involving this issues appear to be positive. In August 2011, *Compass Direct News* reported that:

> The Turkish government made a historic U-turn in state policy ... issuing an official decree inviting Turkey's Christian and Jewish communities to reclaim their long-confiscated religious properties.... The landmark decree is a significant step toward eliminating decades of unfair practices imposed by the Turkish state against its non-Muslim citizens.

Orhan Kemal Cengiz, however, warns that "appearances might be deadly deceiving in Turkey".[51] The international community should monitor the implementation of this decree closely. The scope of this decree is limited to the recognized religious minorities in Turkey only. Beyond that, a similar law had already been adapted in 2008, in which the recognized minorities were also permitted to claim their property confiscated from 1974 onwards. Of the several thousand claims submitted to date, only a tiny fraction has been returned. The majority of the requests were declined with the most arbitrary rulings by judges and by civil servants who simply did not adhere to the government's decrees.[52]

2.3.3. The Diyanet (presidency for religious affairs)

It would be premature to state that Turkey is becoming an Islamic state in disguise. Support for the secular state is still very strong in the country. However, the military, long a powerbroker in its role as watchdog of the secular state, has in the past year been subjected to civilian government controls.

Islam is more visible in society, as it becomes 'politically correct' for women to wear headscarves and people of influence to attend Friday prayers. Until recently, women attending university or in public office were not permitted to wear a headscarf. This principle has been effectively challenged by both the President and the Prime Minister, both of whose wives wear headscarves.

The Turkish state was founded on the basis that the state must control religion and carefully monitor religious groups for what it considers 'extremist messages'. However, only Sunni Islam is being protected. Shi'a Muslims and Alevis are discriminated against in a way similar to the Christian minorities.

Through the Diyanet, which is the Presidency for Religious Affairs and is funded by a separate tax, the government exerts control over religious activities:

---

[51] Orhan Kemal Cengiz, idem.
[52] *Welt Online*, 2008, and Yacoub, 2004.

imams are appointed and paid by the Department of Religious Affairs (under the responsibility of the Prime Minister) and mosques are maintained with government funds. In fact, the government actively supports the building of mosques and schools as part of its agenda to promote Islam in the country.

As Mine Yildrim writes:

The Diyanet is a massive organization with a broad mandate, large budget and vast sphere of influence. Under Law no. 633 of 1965 ("The Presidency of Religious Affairs, Its Establishment and Obligations"), its mandate is to operate affairs related to the belief, worship and moral principles of the Islamic Religion, enlighten the public about religious issues and to administer places of worship (mosques and mescit). Operating under the Prime Minister's Office and with a president appointed by the Prime Minister, the Diyanet has five main departments; the Higher Committee for Religious Affairs, an advisory council; Education, including Koran courses for children and adults; Religious Services, including services for families, discipleship, mosque services and social and cultural services with a religious content; and Publications and Public Relations. Domestic activities are carried out via muftis and religious personnel all over Turkey. Activities carried out abroad are conducted by Diyanet religious counsellors, diplomatic attachés and other personnel, with 1,350 people in 81 countries.[53]

In the same article, Yildrim notes that:

Since the Justice and Development Party (AKP) came to power in 2002, the number of Diyanet personnel has increased from 74,000 to 117,541. During this period, 2,000 Diyanet personnel have moved to positions in other state departments. Currently its budget is about 2,500,000,000 Turkish lira (1,097,538,190 Euros or 1,626,694,770 US dollars). This is a larger budget than some full government ministries.

Yildrim also notes that:

As part of the state the Diyanet plays an active role in influencing the extent to which freedom of religion or belief can be enjoyed in Turkey. One example is that the state accords a de facto authoritative status to formal Opinions from the Diyanet on religious or belief communities outside the Diyanet's structure.

As the United States Department of State claimed:

Members of recognized non-Muslim religious communities were exempted legally from compulsory religious and moral instruction in primary and secondary schools but in practice faced difficulty obtaining exemptions from the compulsory instruction, particularly if their identification cards did not list a religion other than Islam. The government claimed

---

[53] Yildrim, 2011.

The Church of Mor Quryaqus in Anhel (Yemişli). (H. Oberkampf)

the compulsory instruction covered the range of world religions, but religious groups asserted that the courses reflect Hanafi Sunni Islamic doctrine.[54]

Religious education in fourth grade should provide an introduction to various faiths, but most of the time is spent teaching Islam. As reported by the Turkish Association of Protestant Churches, the presentation of Christian faith is highly negative, presenting the Bible as a falsified document. This organization finds that some text books encourage discrimination of the country's small Christian community, despite growing international concern over increasing violence against non-Muslims in Turkey.

3. Future outlook of Christian persecution in Turkey

It is important to underscore that the traditional persecution sources – secularism and nationalism – that were described in the first section of this article, are still the main sources of persecution today. The ongoing, rising anti-Christian mindset

---

[54] United States Department of State, op. cit.

triggering violence in the recent years is rooted mainly in very ingrained nationalism which is deliberately exploiting Islam. The influence of conservative Islam in Turkey should not be ignored or underestimated, but should not be exaggerated either. Political Islam is a trend that still is in an early stage but that could develop more negatively in the future.

Understanding the general tendencies regarding religious freedom in Turkey is extremely complex. Government restrictions, social hostilities and nationalism are indeed important sources of persecution, causing severe human rights violations, such as hate crimes, unfair judicial treatments, discrimination and so on, and observant Islam is increasing.

Not all is negative, though. Following lengthy legal battles, some churches are now registered and have authorizations to organize church services or the renting of a meeting place. Other churches do not have these authorizations, but are not hindered by government in doing so.[55] For the first time in fifty years, a Christian Assyrian won a seat in the Turkish Parliament in the 2011 elections.

When Turkey was still actively negotiating its membership of the EU,[56] the country adopted a series of reforms to comply with the Copenhagen criteria, which contributed to increased religious tolerance in the country and protection for minorities. The government was determined to prevent incidents similar to the Malatya murders in 2007, which badly affected its image.

However, this process of reform, considered too slow and insufficient by many European observers, has now been halted. Enthusiasm in Turkey for EU membership has dropped from 2/3 of the population a decade ago to 1/3 today.

---

[55] In the words of Association of the Protestant Churches (Turkey), "The only way the Protestant Community can obtain legal personality is by establishing a foundation or association. Now that it is possible for churches to establish associations, gradually more and more churches are doing so. Although a small number of churches that have established an association have had a positive experience, some negative observations have also been made: many other types of associations exist for years without government inspection but Christian associations are inspected within their first year of existence. This is taken as an indication that the government views Protestants with suspicion and wants to keep them under government control. Furthermore, administrative practices are so inconsistent as to prove chaotic. Virtually every church has experienced a different set of procedures. In experience the procedures followed by the police and civil authorities have been far from predictable, transparent or consistent. Civil servants are permitted to use excessive personal discretion and they use this to restrict the religious freedom of Protestants. The Protestant Community's basic desire is that their existing congregations be recognized by the government as religious congregations and that a legal structure be created that all can understand and apply. It is believed that having legal personality will lead to acceptance in the society and significantly aid in efforts to solve other related problems".

[56] Negotiations about the membership of the European Union of Turkey have effectively stopped, although officially they are still open.

The needed reforms were not completed and whilst some improvements can be seen, the country did not succeed in eliminating the various forms of discrimination against Christians completely. Moreover, as Markus Tozman analyzes, after EU negotiations started, "open discrimination against Christians, too, decreased – but instead, subtle discrimination takes place, today".

It seems as though Turkey is taking steps backwards and steps forward at the same time as far as religious freedom is concerned. In particular there remains a constitutional vacuum concerning Christian churches, since only the Armenian and Greek Orthodox denominations are recognized. The new Constitution to be written by the end of 2012 could have a positive outcome for the Christian minorities in the country, but could also be used by the AKP to further implement their Islamist agenda.[57]

Summarizing the situation of religious freedom in Turkey, an expatriate Christian who formerly lived in Turkey says, "In Turkey, there is freedom of religion but Christians are not given any space to exert this right". The legal and constitutional protection of nationalism, together with the principle of indivisibility of the nation and the people and the deeply engrained nationalism in Turkish culture, have been the main sources of persecution of Christians in the country. The rise of violent incidents against Christians in recent years were in almost all cases perpetrated by nationalists.

The tension between secularism and (moderate) Islam at the political level, also contributes to an identity crisis at the individual level. Most Turks are nominal Muslims and are searching for their identity. Less than 33 % of the Muslims in the country would be adhering to the five pillars of their faith. The rest are nominal Muslims living secular lives. Considering that 50 % of the Turkish population is younger than 25 years of age, it is clear that most of these young people are not devout Muslims. Many Turks are very curious about Christianity and ask expatriate Christians many questions, giving them hope for a revival in Turkey. But the (recent) rise of extremist Islam can also be interpreted as a consequence of this identity crisis.

Since the AKP is in power, the situation in the country is rapidly changing. To some extent, it might be a positive change that Kemalism – nationalism – is promoted less under the AKP Government than under the previous secular governments. However, political Islam as a substitute for radical nationalism can hardly be seen as an element that will improve the situation of Christian minorities.

---

[57] For more information on the constitution drafting process, see Onder's article in this book.

References

Association of Protestant Churches (Turkey), Committee for Religious Freedom and Legal Affairs, *Report on Human Rights Violations 2010*.

Association of Protestant Churches (Turkey), Committee for Religious Freedom and Legal Affairs, *A Threat" or under Threat? Legal and social problems of Protestants in Turkey, 2010*.

Barkey, Henri J., "Turkish Foreign Policy and the Middle East", in *CERI Strategy Papers*, No. 10, 6 June 2011.

Cagaptay, Soner, "Turkey's post-EU world", *Hurriyet Daily News*, 28 February 2012. Available at: www.cagaptay.com/11266/turkey-post-eu-world.

Cagaptay, Soner, "Turkey's Foreign Policy Pivot", *Los Angeles Times*, 21 March 2012. Available at: www.cagaptay.com/11403/turkey-foreign-policy-pivot.

Cengiz, Orhan Kemal, Transcript of an oral presentation for the working-level meeting of foreign embassies organized by the Dutch Embassy in Ankara, 4 April 2003.

Cengiz, Orhan Kemal, "Minority foundations in Turkey: From past to future", in *Today's Zaman*, 6 June 2010.

Compass Direct News, "Media Bias Fans Anti-Christian Sentiment", 17 March 2006.

Compass Direct News, "Converts Subjected to Official Harassment", 3 July 2006.

Compass Direct News, "More than Half in Turkey Oppose Non-Muslim Religious Meetings", 4 December 2009.

Compass Direct News, "Trial over 'Insulting Turkishness' Again Yields No Evidence", 28 May 2010.

Compass Direct News, "Christians in Turkey Acquitted of 'Insulting Turkishness'", 19 October 2010.

Compass Direct News, "Christians in Turkey Face Harassment; Murder Trial Stalls", 15 March 2011.

Compass Direct News, "Turkey Overturns Historic Religious Property Seizures", 30 August 2011.

Compass Direct News, "Al Qaeda Cell in Turkey Accused of Planning to Bomb Churches", 9 December 2011.

Compass Direct News, "Ancient Monastery Threatened", 22 January 2012.

Compass Direct News, "Turkish Christians Subject to Discrimination, Attacks, Report Says", 14 February 2012.

Icduygu, A., & Soner, A., "Turkish Minority Rights Regime: Between Difference and Equality", in *Middle Eastern Studies, 42* (3) (2006), pp. 447–468.

Icduygu, A., Toktas, S. & Soner, A., "The politics of population in a nation-building process: Emigration of non-Muslims from Turkey", in *Ethnic and Racial Studies,* 31 (2) (2008), pp. 358–389.

International Crisis Group, "Turkey and the Middle East: Ambitions and Constraints", 7 April 2010. Available at: www.crisisgroup.org/en/regions/europe/turkey-cyprus/turkey/203-turkey-and-the-middle-east-ambitions-and-constraints.aspx.

Laciner, Sedat, "Combat against Religionist Terrorism in Turkey: Al Qaeda and Turkish Hezbollah Cases", in *Turkish Weekly*, 2 April 2007.

Levitsky, Olga, "In the Spotlight: Turkish Hezbollah". Center for Defense Information 2003.

Middle East Concern, "Turkey: Persecution of Christians. Information from Annual Survey for 2010". Available at: www.meconcern.org/index.php?option=com_content&view=article&id=298:turkey-persecution-of-christians&catid=29:turkey&Itemid=9.

Mitnick, Joshua, "Flotilla Assault Off Gaza Spurs Crisis", *The Wall Street Journal*, 1 June 2010.

Oehring, Otmar, "Turkish nationalism, Ergenekon, and denial of religious freedom" in *Forum* 18, 21 October 2008.

Oehring, Otmar, "Religious freedom survey, November 2009", in *Forum* 18, 27 November 2009.

Omtzigt, Pieter, "Initiatiefnota: De zorgwekkende situatie van het Mor Gabriel Klooster en de Aramees sprekende Christenen in Turkijke – De 'Süryoye'", 8 March 2012. Available at: www.cda.nl/Upload/Omtzigt/Initiatief_Nota_Mor_Gabriel_Pieter_Omtzigt.pdf.

Ozoren, Suleyman, "Turkish Hizballah: A Case Study of Radical Terrorism", in *Turkish Weekly*, 1 December 2004.

Rotella, Sebastian, "Turks increasingly turn to Islamic extremism", *Los Angeles Times*, 28 June 2009. Available at: www.articles.latimes.com/2009/jun/28/world/fg-turk-terror28.

Strategic Forecasting Inc. (Stratfor), *Annual Forecast 2012*. Available at: www.stratfor.com/forecast/annual-forecast-2012.

Tozman, Markus, "Turkey for the Turks: Syrian Orthodox Arameans in Southeast Anatolia", BA Paper II, Maastricht University, 2011.

United States Commission on International Religious Freedom, *Annual Report 2012*.

United States Department of State, *International Religious Freedom Report*, 2011

Welt Online, "Vorladung für Jesus Christus", 21 February 2008. Available at: www.welt.de/politik/article1706413/Vorladung-fuer-Jesus-Christus.html.

Yacoub, Jospeh, "Minorities and Religions in Europe. Case Study: The Assyro-Chaldeans of Turkey", in *European Yearbook of Minority Issues*, 4 (5) (2004), p. 29–4.

Yildrim, Mine, "The Diyanet: The elephant in Turkey's religious freedom room?", *Forum* 18, 4 May 2011.

Yildrim, Mine, "Denigrating religious values: A way to silence critics of religion?", in *Forum* 18, 15 February 2012.

Minority Rights in Turkey: Quo Vadis, Assyrians?

By Soner Onder

Soner Onder is a PhD Candidate at the Department of Political Science, University of Amsterdam. He is studying the recent changes in Turkish Foreign policy discourses towards the Middle East.

I still recall the responses of ordinary Turkish citizens twenty-five years ago when I described myself as being 'Assyrian' (in Turkish: Süryani).[1] The majority of them had never heard of Assyrians, their identity, their religion or even their existence in Turkey – it was as if this group did not exist and had not been living in this region for thousands of years. To those who did have some knowledge of other cultures in Turkey, Assyrians were either unknown or known by different names, such as 'Fellah' (Kurdish for 'Christian'), 'Gavur' (Turkish for 'infidel'), 'Armenians' (mixing their ethnicity with their religion) or by appellations such as 'Turkish Christians' or 'Turkish Süryani' (Türk Süryani). The concept of 'Süryani' as a distinctive ethnic group, therefore, was absent from the collective imaginary of the broader Turkish society. Making a group invisible can be perceived as both a strategy of 'everyday discrimination'[2] and as an outcome of a state policy. Thus, in order to explain the invisibility of Assyrians and how they have been structurally discriminated throughout the history of the Turkish Republic, we must look at Turkey's minority policies.

Turkey's minority policies are founded mainly on the 'outdated'[3] provisions of the 1923 Treaty of Lausanne. Although the treaty provides protection for all non-Muslim minorities, all Turkish governments since 1923 have interpreted the treaty in such a way as to guarantee protection only to three minority groups which have been defined as 'religious minorities': Armenian Orthodox Christians, Greek Orthodox Christians and Jews. As a result of this 'narrow definition'[4] of minorities, other non-Muslim minorities such as Assyrians have been excluded from this definition and do not enjoy the same rights as other recognized minorities. This

---

[1] The term Assyrian here refers to the group which is also known in English as 'Syriacs', 'Arameans' or, in their mother tongue, 'Suryoye'.
[2] Essed, 1991.
[3] Minority Right Group International, 2007.
[4] Oran, 2007.

'arbitrary' definition,[5] which has no legal basis in international law is one of the main sources of minority problems in Turkey.[6]

As mentioned earlier, the invisibility of Assyrians and other non-Muslim minorities is an outcome of a state policy. To highlight the components of this policy, we must look at the strategies utilised regarding minorities. The first is the strategy of *denialism*. Until recently, not only their problems, but even the very existence of minorities was denied in Turkey. Modern Turkish identity is built on the denial of the 'others'. In relation to this, since the establishment of the Turkish Republic, minorities have been systematically subjected to *assimilationist* policies aimed at homogenizing the Turkish nation, in which only Turkishness and Sunni Islam have been favoured. To start, the family and location names, the culture and language of minorities have all been 'Turkified'. In addition, minority lands have also been plundered and seized – a practice that continues to this today. *Confiscation* as a policy tool has been widely yielded against minorities in order to create a Turkish bourgeoisie and a state capital. To homogenize the population living in Turkey, *deportation* or *forced migration* have also been utilised as a strategy against minorities. Deportation of Armenians and Assyrians during the genocide of the First World War and the so-called 'population exchange' of millions of Pontus Greeks are well known examples of this policy. Those non-Muslims who survived genocide and deportations, later left the country during various periods of the Republic (i.e. after the 'Wealth Tax'[7] (*Varlık Vergisi*)[8], the 6–7 September pogroms, the Cyprus Events, the Military Coup of 1980 and during the civil war between Kurds and the state.[9]

This systematic policy has resulted in a situation in which Turkey, as a multi-ethnic and multireligious country, has been emptied of its non-Muslim minorities. Those minorities who against all odds remained in the country have now been pushed into the darkness of invisibility. And minorities have become a mysterious 'unknown'; a 'foreign' entity to the broader Turkish society.

---

[5] Cengiz, 2003.
[6] For more information on the Lausanne Treaty, see Hurst's article in this book.
[7] The Wealth Tax was imposed on non-Muslim groups in Turkey in 1942 and was an important phase in the capital accumulation from non-Muslims to the state and other third parties. As a result of the tax, the majority of non-Muslim groups lost the last remnants of their financial wealth and were forced to sell their properties to pay the arbitrary taxes. Those who could not afford to pay the tax were sent to 'working camps'. During this period 30,000 Jews left Turkey.
[8] One striking story concerns an Assyrian family that borrowed money from their Muslim neighbours to pay the tax. The family was finally able to repay the debt in the 1980s. For more information, see Özmen, 2012.
[9] For specific accounts of the emigration of Assyrians, see Deniz, 1999, and Atto, 2011.

During the EU accession process, Turkey's discriminatory approach towards minorities has been questioned and has become a salient object of criticism. Turkey has made a strong political commitment to the so-called Copenhagen Criteria, in which democracy, the rule of law, human rights and the respect for and protection of minorities have been formulated as the requirements of membership for a candidate country. Despite some positive developments in the last ten years, Turkey's protection of minority groups continues to fall considerably short of European and other international standards.[10]

1. The rediscovery of Assyrians: the objectification of a group

In contrast to the picture painted above, many people in the broader Turkish society today now have an impression of the Süryaniler. In recent years, while Turkish authorities have rediscovered Assyrians as a 'resource', awareness has increased among ordinary Turks of the existence of a group of people living in Turkey who are different from Turks and who have a different language, religion and traditions. In the transformation of the traditional denialist approach, Assyrians have been objectified in several ways. Their collective identity has been rendered 'exotic' and ready to be rediscovered and reconstructed in different ways. The new approach treats Assyrians as an object of tourism to attract both domestic and international tourists. Today Turkey's remote regions (such as Tur Abdin) and the cultures living in those areas have become an object of Turkish popular culture. In Turkish soap series the distorted image of the forgotten 'others' is generally portrayed in supporting roles as an exotic object (such as the surrealistic image of a priest), and their historical sites (such as churches, houses and ruins) are used to add depth to their superficial series or to denigrate the represented others.

In policy discourses, the category 'Süryaniler' is pointed to as evidence of the Turkish Republic's tolerance towards other cultures and religions. The approach is, as Edward Said termed it, orientalist. The reconstructed image of Süryaniler is a distorted version of the reality that fails to deal with critical and normative

---

[10] Turkey has also failed to take serious steps to become a party to the first legally binding multilateral treaty devoted to the protection of national minorities, the Framework Convention for the Protection of National Minorities, which entered into force in 1998. Similarly, Turkey has still not signed and ratified the European Charter for Regional or Minority Languages, which entered into force in 1998. As part of the EU accession process, in 2003 Turkey ratified both the International Covenant on Civil and Political Rights (ICCPR) and the International Covenant on Economic, Social and Cultural Rights (ICESCR) with some reservations, such as Article 27 of the ICCPR, which is the most widely accepted legally binding provision on minorities in international law and to Article 13, paragraph 3 and 4 of the ICESCR, regarding the right to education (see further European Commission, 2005).

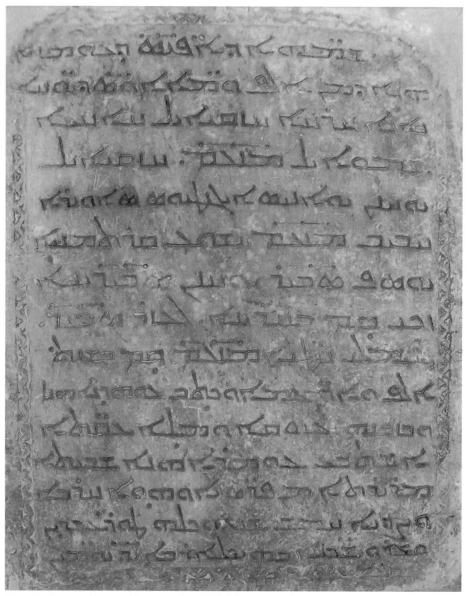

Aramaic Estrangelo carved in stone. (Mor Gabriel monastery)

questions such as: Why has this group left Turkey? What happened to them? Why do they not enjoy the same minority rights as other recognized minorities?

A recent example effectively illustrates this approach. In a public statement, an official at the Ministry of Culture and Tourism, Güven Tasbasi, stated that as the southern province of Mardin emerges as a new hub for tourism and cultural activities, the Ministry of Culture and Tourism aims to bring nearly four million Süryani to the historic city. According to Tasbasi, the move would be necessary to preserve the Assyrian presence in the city and to give Assyrians around the world the message: "Your ancestors lived in these lands, in Mardin". The Ministry is also planning to finance an Assyrian festival in Stockholm, "with the aim of attracting the attention of Assyrians". In addition Ministry intends to organise a similar festival in Midyat.[11] On the surface this plan appears to be an improvement in the approach towards minority groups. Nevertheless, there are at least three main critical points that must be mentioned. First it is ironic that, in this new Turkish approach, the Ministry treats Assyrians as a potential group of tourists that should be attracted to visit their homeland. Thus, it reduces their historical rootedness to that of modern tourists in Western countries who can bring money to the state's treasury. Secondly, this approach sidesteps the addressing the question of why the Assyrians disappeared from this region in the first place. The approach is merely instrumentalist and pragmatic, aiming to attract Assyrians as tourists. Finally, Turkish authorities are sending contradicting messages to Assyrians. While the Turkish Ministry aims to support an Assyrian festival in Sweden, at the same time, the Turkish Embassy in Stockholm enthusiastically organises lobbying activities and mobilises Turks in Sweden aiming to change the Swedish Parliament's resolution regarding the recognition of the genocide of the First World War.[12]

Objectification of Assyrians in Turkish public discourses goes hand in hand with an inaccurate understanding and use of the concept of tolerance. In Turkish media and policy reports, Assyrians are at times presented as a group 'loyal' to the state. The use of loyalty is relative, contingent and conditional. Loyalty is defined in relation to the loyalty of other groups and assumes an unwritten conditionality and the dominancy of the powerful majority groups. The hidden message which the term tolerance or loyalty assumes is that 'we' as the majority group tolerate 'you' as a subordinated group. Hence, loyalty is conditioned by the political praxis of the group: if they remain *loyal*, we will tolerate 'them'! Otherwise, they will be punished!" This concept is even employed in the history textbook used in 10th grade high school classes in Turkey that is published by the Turkish National Edu-

---

[11] Zaman, 2012.
[12] To give one example, the Turkish Youth Federation in Sweden has begun to organise a demonstration condemning the genocide resolution of the Swedish Parliament each year on the 11th of March – the date on which the Parliament passed the resolution. For more information, see: www.tuf.nu/index.php?option=com_content&task=view&id=1708&Itemid=1351&lang=en.

cation Ministry.¹³ The textbook presents distorted historical information regarding Assyrians and portrays them as traitors who rebelled against Turkey. Indirectly, the discourses aim to justify the genocide that Assyrians faced during the First World War. Reports of this distortion of history have attracted a global response. In response to the written question directed by the first Assyrian MP in the Turkish Parliament, Erol Dora[14], the Turkish Minister of Education claimed that they have never given space in school textbooks for a statement which will foster hatred against other races, cultures and religions and that they are planning to review the mentioned textbook within the general revision work of 2012.[15] Although the textbook is an obvious example of hatred against minorities, the Minister in charge continues to avoid issuing a formal apology and refuses to take immediate action to make the necessary corrections. From this statement, it is unclear whether the Ministry will correct this discriminatory description after the general review work. It is noteworthy that, in a public appeal, fourteen Assyrian civil and religious organizations in Turkey, while opposing the claims raised in the book, emphasize that Assyrians have "always been loyal and honest to the country".[16] The argument used in this appeal is precisely the response that the Turkish authorities wish to receive from the community. By expressing the loyalty of the Süryaniler, these organizations wrongly categorize minorities in terms of loyal and disloyal. The Turkish denialist approach makes persistent use of the argument of the disloyalty of Christians during the war as a way to justify the genocide of the First World War, using repeated claims such as "They stabbed us in the back!" Throughout the history of the Turkish Republic, whenever minorities faced oppression, they have always felt obliged to make statements regarding their 'loyalty' as a result of their deeply rooted fears.

In recent years, Assyrians as a group gained greater visibility due to Turkey's EU accession process. While some positive steps have been taken towards Assyrians in this period[17] (as will be discussed later in this article), they continue to

---

[13] BarAbrahem, 2011.
[14] Erol Dora was elected to the Turkish Parliament as a deputy of the pro-Kurdish Peace and Democracy Party (BDP) in the 2011 elections.
[15] Milliyet Daily Newspaper, 26 January 2012.
[16] BarAbrahem, 2011.
[17] There is an obvious growing interest in minorities (including Assyrians) from the side of Turkish government. The Turkish Ministry of Culture and Tourism, for example, has started the translation of a well-known poet by Mor Ephrem, "The Holy Noah Pipe" [*Sabah Daily Newspaper*, 19 December 2011]. Similarly, the Turkish government has also decided to support minority newspapers by allocating funds to help these newspapers to survive [Today's *Zaman*, 16 July 2011). For information on the publication of the first monthly Assyrian newspaper in Turkey,

face serious problems and challenges. Their sixteen centuries old monastery, Mor Gabriel, for example, is facing the risk of being confiscated. In history textbooks, Assyrians and other minorities continue to be portrayed as "traitors" and "collaborators with Western powers". The Supreme Court is still handing down verdicts against using surnames in languages other than Turkish (such as the case of Favlus Ay[18]). Overall, there is no formal recognition of Assyrians as an indigenous people of the country and the current Turkish policy towards Assyrians is far from consistent. All of these developments have rightly led Assyrians to become more careful and sceptical about the recent improvements in minority rights in Turkey. Those who support Turkey's EU membership do so as a way to find a remedy to their problems.

Syriac village in Tur Abdin. (M. Tozman)

Sabro, see also Cengiz, 2012. A Cabinet resolution established the Living Languages Institute at Mardin Artuklu University in 2009 [*Today's Zaman*, 2 December 2009]. Accordingly, the institute has started teaching Aramaic and other regional languages. The same institute recently organised the International Syriac Studies Symposium in Mardin.

[18] See Oran, 2011.

2. Unending amendments to the Law of Foundations

2.1. Resistance and unwillingness of Turkish authorities

One of the main problems regarding minority rights in Turkey relates to the problems and obstacles of minority foundations and their property rights. The Turkish Law of Foundations has received constant criticism at the international level for constituting a serious challenge to freedom of religion and religious tolerance in Turkey. Under this foundation system, non-Muslim minorities face restricted property rights and interference in the management of their foundations as well as a ban on training their own clergy.

The problems of minority foundations can be traced back to the Law of 1936 (the so-called '1936 Declarations'), which stripped all religious foundations of their autonomous status and placed them under the auspices of the General Directorate of Foundations (Vakiflar Genel Müdürlügü), which has long enjoyed formal and direct administration of foundations' properties and removed property from non-Muslim minority groups. In 1949 the Law of Foundations was amended and minority foundations regained their former status in relation to their administration. However, in the 1960s, the Turkish state developed additional bureaucratic obstacles for minority foundations. Following the verdict of the Turkish Appeal Court (Yargıtay) in 1974, acquisitions made after the 1936 declaration have been defined as 'illegally possessed' properties. As a result of this jurisprudence, minority foundations have lost innumerable amounts of real estate.

In the period 2002 to 2012, the Law of Foundations was amended six times as a result of the Europeanization process of Turkey. With the first amendment in 2002, within the context of EU harmonization laws, minority foundations were permitted to acquire real estate with the permission of the Committee of Ministers. However, with the bylaw of October 2002 and the circular of the Directorate of Foundations, the scope of the law was further restricted. In the face of criticism levelled against Law 4771 of 2002 (the amended version of the Law of Foundations), and the related bylaw and the circular, the ruling AKP government once again amended the Law of Foundations in 2003 within the context of the harmonization laws (Law 4778). Accordingly, the bureaucracy for acquiring new properties for minority foundations was reduced to seeking the permission of the Directorate of Foundations. In January 2004 the Secondary Committee for Minorities – which had been established by a secret decree in 1962 in order to carry out security surveillance of minorities – was abolished and replaced with the Minority Assessment Board which would be responsible for dealing with the problems of non-Muslim minorities. The Directorate General of Foundations is the most decisive body on the Minority Assessment Board.

In 2006, Turkish Parliament once again amended the Law of Foundations (Law No. 5555). However, the law was vetoed by former President Ahmet Necdet Sezer on nine articles, claiming that granting new rights and privileges to existing foundations would violate the Treaty of Lausanne, the fundamental principles of the Republic, the ban on discrimination, national interests and public interests.[19] In the reasons given by Sezer for his veto, it is plain to see that an improvement in minority rights is considered to be a threat against Turkish Republic's national interests and fundamental principles. This is a deeply rooted standpoint in the state bureaucracy, the Turkish army and in some political parties, such as the Republic People Party and the Nationalist Movement Party. The ruling AKP Government's policy in particular should be studied. Although AKP utilises a nationalist conservative approach, since 2002, it has been the most open and ambitious in driving the Europeanization project in Turkey. Nevertheless, there are many cases that also illustrate AKP's unwillingness to push the democratization reforms further and how the party has been avoiding working on solving chronic problems such as minority rights and the Law of Foundations radically and unconditionally.

With the 2008 Foundations Law (No. 5737), the law previously vetoed by the former president was amended, and religious communities have been permitted to apply for the return of confiscated properties. In August 2011, Turkish Prime Minister Recep Tayyip Erdogan passed a new omnibus decree that allows individuals or institutions to apply for the restitution of properties that were not specifically described during the registration in 1936. The new provision (Article 17 of the decree) is to be included as temporary Article 11 in the 2008 Law on Foundations. Unlike the 2008 decree, the new law also allows for applicants to receive monetary compensation for properties that were assigned to the Treasury or that were sold to third parties. According to Article 11, the immovable properties of minority foundations, along with the rights and obligations contained in the deed records, will be (re)assigned to them by the deed registry directorates after a positive decision is reached in their favour by the Assembly [Foundation Council], unless they submit an application within 12 months of the date of entry into effect of Article 11.[20] Since August 2011, 19 properties have been returned. Some 1,400 applications were submitted, of which 200 properties were returned as of

---

[19] Kurban and Hatemi, 2009.
[20] Zeldin, 2011.

The old church of Mor Afrem in Bote (Bardakci), now state property; it was used as refuge during the genocide. The majority of the Christian inhabitants were massacred nevertheless. (M. Tozman)

August 2011. Some 940 applications have been returned for not having sufficient documentation, of which only 500 were resubmitted.[21]

Despite the improvements in favour of minority foundations, Kurban and Hatemi, the authors of their 2009 report *A story of an alien(ation)*, criticize the 2008 Law of Foundations on five points: 1.) The last amendments to the Law of Foundations did not change the legal position of non-Muslim minority foundations. The foundations remain under the guardianship of the Directorate General Foundations. 2.) The law adopts the principle of reciprocity (Article 2), which opens up space for arbitrary praxis – conditional treatment of minorities in relation to other countries' praxis (for instance in relation to Greece or other countries). 3.) The requirement for the establishment of new foundations is linked to Article 5(2) of the Turkish Civil Code and Article 101(4) of the Civil Code, which stipulates that "no foundations may be established to support the members of a certain race or community". 4.) Although the new law permits foundations to engage in

---

[21] United States Commission on International Religious Freedom, 2012.

international activities and cooperation efforts in accordance with their purpose or activities, the condition is made that these activities must be mentioned in their statutes. These statutes, however, often date back to Ottoman times and therefore do not make mention of such activities. 5.) The final criticism relates to the return of properties belonging to non-Muslim foundations. The law dealing with the return of property was altered by Turkish Prime Minister's decree in 2011 (see above).

As Oehring concludes, although the new law has made life somewhat easier for community foundations, nothing has changed in their legal position.[22] Similar analyses were also reached in the 2012 Annual Report of the United States Commission on International Religious Freedom's (USCIRF), which states: "despite the 2008 amendments and the August 2011 decree, the Turkish government retains the right to expropriate land from religious communities, although it has not confiscated any religious foundations' properties since 2007".[23]

During the EU harmonization process, several significant and 'revolutionary'[24] improvements regarding the property rights of non-Muslim foundations were introduced, *albeit* limited and conditional in scope. Although the aim of this article is not to ignore Turkey's democratisation efforts, we must not close our eyes to the many cases that contradict the spirit of EU reforms in the field of minority policy. As Oehring rightly emphasizes, the Turkish governments demonstrated an unwillingness to solve the problem of minority foundations and their property rights promptly and adequately.[25] If the Turkish governments had worked more proactively, although changed six times over the past ten years, the property rights of non-Muslim minorities would not still be a problem. The persistent nature of the problems is an indication of the continuity of the traditional discourse towards non-Muslim minorities. Minority problems are still perceived to be national security and foreign policy issues rather than a human rights and citizenship issue.[26] In many circles this has raised the question of whether the current Turkish government has truly changed its traditional approach towards non-Muslim minorities. The following three sections offer a review of three cases in which the

---

[22] Oehring, 2008.
[23] The 2012 USCIRF annual report designated Turkey as a "country of particular concern (CPC)" due to its "systematic and egregious limitations on the freedom of religion". Turkey responded by calling the report 'partisan', saying that it turned a blind eye to the progress that had been made [*Today's Zaman*, 22 March 2012].
[24] Cengiz, 2012.
[25] Oehring, 2006.
[26] Kurban and Hatemi, 2009, p. 24.

Assyrian community and their respective religious foundations have encountered serious problems regarding the confiscation of their immovable properties.

Before discussing the examples, it should be noted that there is a clear dilemma in the treatment of Assyrians and their foundations. Although Article 3 of the Title Deeds Law mentions the names of twelve active non-Muslim foundations[27] belonging to the Assyrian community, no formal recognition of the group is made as a "non-Muslim minority", based on the provisions of the Treaty of Lausanne (1923).

2.2. The Case of Mor Gabriel Monastery

The attempts by Kurdish villagers with friendly relations with the Turkish authorities to confiscate the land of the Syriac Orthodox Monastery of Mor Gabriel (founded in 397 A.D.) has drawn worldwide criticism and has been discussed in almost all reports (such as the Annual progress reports of the EU commission and the annual reports of USCIRF) as a case that contradicts Turkey's democratization program and the reforms introduced in the country. Since 2008, the Monastery has struggled with five lawsuits which continue to this day. In addition, the monastery has also been the target of a smear campaign that aims to portray the monastery as a 'missionary centre' (an example of the old accusation of the 'gavur' as collaborators with Western powers) and is threatened in various ways.[28]

Two aspects of the case against the Mor Gabriel Monastery clearly demonstrate the fact that the main approach towards minorities has not changed. The first is the petition of the villagers. In the petition, the reason for the existence of "Christian clergy" is described as being "to agitate and provoke the public", and thus "to harm the spirit of national unity and solidarity". The petitioners go on to ask, "Where have these priests come from?"; as if the monastery did not have a history dating back more than sixteen centuries. The petitioners are the tribal leaders of the neighbouring Kurdish villagers, who have for many years exploited Assyrians in the region. The tribal chief of the two neighbouring villages is Sü-

---

[27] Foundation for the St. Mary's Syriac Apostolic Church in Diyarbakır; Foundation for the St. Mary's Syriac Apostolic Church in Beyoğlu; Foundation for the Syriac Catholic Church in Mardin, Foundation for the Syriac Apostolic Deyrulzafaran Monastery and Churches in Mardin; Foundation for the Mor Gabriel Monastery in Midyat; Foundation for the Syriac Apostolic Community Mar Barsaumo and Mart Shmuni Churches in Midyat; Foundation for the Mar Dodo Syriac Apostolic Church in İdil [Hazakh]; Foundation for the Chaldean Catholic Church in Diyarbakır; Foundation for the Chaldean Catholic Church; and Foundation for the Chaldean Catholic Church in Mardin.

[28] See also Aktas, 2008 and 2012.

leyman Çelebi, a former AKP deputy for Mardin (2007–2011). Moreover, these villages all enjoy very close relationships with the

View on Mor Gabriel's main church at night. (Mor Gabriel monastery)

Turkish State in their roles as 'village guards'[29]. Therefore, the message given in the petition should be taken seriously and analysed in its relationship with the state. The second sign is the involvement of the Turkish public authorities in the confiscation of lands belonging to the monastery – as described in the well-known 1936 Declaration by the monastery – on the basis of Cadastral Law no. 3402 and Forest Law no. 6831.[30] Five lawsuits are currently ongoing, including the lawsuit brought by the Treasury (the Turkish public authority, which is controlled by the government) and the lawsuit against the Forest Administration currently pending in the Court of Cassation. Oran rightly questioned the ruling party AKP's standpoint in 2011. Faced with international and domestic criticism regarding this case, the government has used the argument that "There is nothing we can do about it; it was the High Judiciary's decision". However, the ambitious involvement of the

---

[29] A paramilitary organization established in 1984 by the Turkish State during the war against the Kurdistan Worker Party (PKK); for more information on the PKK, see Makko's article in this book.

[30] For a comprehensive analysis, see also Oran's article in this book.

public authorities directly under the command of the government proves that the government is also part of this process.[31] Finally, we must wonder what role Kurdish tribal leader Süleyman Çelebi, who was a former deputy from the ruling AKP Party, had in this process. If the government were willing to solve the case it would not be a difficult task, considering that all of the individuals and public authorities that have filed lawsuits against the monastery are under the government's control. Therefore, with departure from the case of Mor Gabriel Monastery, it would be relevant to postulate that the 'Turkification' of non-Muslim properties is still continuing,[32] despite the reforms that have been introduced in this field and despite the 'positive' messages being sent by the Turkish government.[33]

2.3. The case of the Syriac Catholic Foundation in Istanbul

When the Syriac Catholic Community requested permission to use their church in Gümüssuyu, Istanbul, which was previously confiscated by the state, the local court decided in favour of the foundation and the church was registered in the name of the Syriac Catholic Community. The Directorate General of Foundations (DGF), however, filed a lawsuit claiming that, since the church is foundation property (and hence state property), the church should be re-registered to the Treasury. The DGF won the case and the church is once again registered to the Treasury. The DGF later filed a second lawsuit against the Syriac Catholic Foundation accusing them of not acting in good faith. The Syriac Catholic Foundation has brought the case to the ECtHR.[34] This example demonstrates how domestic judicial processes work in favour of protecting and favouring the interest of the state, rather than those of minority communities.

---

[31] A related discussion is ongoing regarding the Turkish governments' influence on the judiciary. The politicization of the judiciary or the judicialisation of politics is not a new phenomenon in Turkish politics. The AKP government and the so-called Gülen Community (the 'Cemaat') were recently accused of staffing the judicial mechanisms and forming a new 'power complex' covering all social, political and economic fields. For more on discussion, see Ertekin, 2012.

[32] Oran, 2011.

[33] For instance, during a visit in Germany the Turkish Minister of Foreign Affairs, A. Davutoglu declared that "the ancient Assyrian and Aramaic culture is part of Anatolian culture" and "the problems of the property rights of Mor Gabriel Church [monastery] in south-eastern province of Mardin will be solved" (Todays Zaman, 4 December 2011). Although with several occasions similar statements were made by the Turkish government, the problem still continues at the time of writing this article.

[34] See also Kurban & Hatemi, 2009, p. 23, for a general overview of this case.

2.4. The case of the Chaldean Catholic Church Foundation in Istanbul

In 1984, the Chaldean Catholic Church Foundation in Istanbul filed a lawsuit in Istanbul to get back its seized property. The court, however, rejected this request in 1989, citing the fact that the foundation did not legal exist because it had not submitted a declaration in 1936, and that the centre of the Chaldean Patriarchate was in Iraq. The foundation's lawsuit against the government and the DGF is still pending before the Council of State.[35] This example illustrates how the infamous 1936 Declarations are still taken as a point of reference to judge the legal existence of a foundation and its property rights.

Despite the reforms that have been introduced, the growing number of lawsuits and the public authorities' practices in this field show that much remains to be done. The issue of property rights of non-Muslim minorities is one of the core elements of minority rights in Turkey, because it touches upon a sensitive history of capital accumulation throughout the history of the Turkish Republic. Thus far the research conducted into the scope of capital accumulation from non-Muslim minorities to the state and Muslim third parties has been limited.[36] All that we know now is merely the tip of the iceberg. Many Assyrians struggle with the arbitrariness of the Deed and Cadastral rules in the Tur Abdin area. Many of them lost their properties and their lands were expropriated after their emigration to Western countries. Numerous lawsuits – approximately 300 court cases[37] – are awaiting a definitive solution.[38] Recent reforms have not provided sufficient and radical solutions in this field.[39]

3. The debate over a new constitution in Turkey and minorities

Since the 2011 elections, the Turkish Parliament has sped up the process of drawing up a new constitution. In this regard, the parliamentary Constitutional Reconciliation Commission, which has been assigned the task of drafting the text of a new Turkish Constitution, has invited various segments of Turkish society to offer their views for a new constitution. In February 2012, the Commission also heard presentations by representatives of religious groups, including representatives of the Syriac Orthodox and the Syriac Catholic Churches. A number of other civil

---

[35] Ibid.
[36] For information on studies into capital accumulation, see Onaran, 2010; Güngör and Polatel, 2011; and Cetinoglu, 2012.
[37] Oran, 2011.
[38] Journal of Turkish Weekly, 2 March 2012.
[39] For more information on this topic, see Tozman's article in this book.

Assyrian groups and individuals were also invited to the Turkish Parliament[40] – a move that was regarded as an historic gesture towards the country's minorities.

Lit candles in the Mor Gabriel monastery. (From the book by Y. Bilge)

These delegations addressed a number of problems they shared and submitted their proposals for a new constitution, in which they formulated the following demands: the legal recognition of Assyrians as a non-Muslim minority group; equal citizenship rights[41]; the removal of barriers on mother tongue education; an effective solution to the problems regarding their property rights; effective measures against discrimination (such as in school textbooks); the removal of obstacles from acquiring influential positions at top-level bureaucracy; funding from the Religious Affairs Directorate and so on.[42]

The current Constitution of the Turkish Republic, adopted in 1982, makes no reference to minorities. The preamble to the Constitution clearly warns against any

---

[40] The delegation consisted of representatives of the European Syriac Union (ESU), the Federation of Syriac Associations in Turkey, Mezo-Der and the Federation of Syriac People in Germany (HSA).

[41] The Syriac Catholic Chor Episcopus Yusuf Sağ, for example said "We hope the new constitution will highlight freedoms. We want a constitution that accepts and embraces everyone like a mother. We don't have expectations different from those of Muslim Turks. As Syriacs that have been living on this land for 4,500 years, we expect to receive the same rights as Muslim Turks." (*Today's Zaman*, 16 April 2012).

[42] See also *Today's Zaman*, 20 February 2012 and *Journal of Turkish Weekly*, 2 March 2012.

effort to promote cultures, languages or characteristics other than those defined as 'Turkish' and condemns any initiative or behaviour deemed to be anti-Turkish, secessionist or contrary to Turkish interests. In other words, under Turkish law, minority rights are criminalized. For example, the Turkish penal code (specifically the well-known Article 301 which deals with "denigration of Turkishness, the Republic and the foundation and institutions of the state"[43]); the 1991 Law on the Fight against Terrorism (amended in June 2006); the Law of Political Parties (Articles 81a and 82); and the Law of Associations (Article 101) are used against individuals who address the existence of minorities and their rights. Furthermore, legislation regarding religious communities represents a major problem for freedom of religion and religious tolerance.[44]

To develop a sustainable democracy and high standards in minority protection, the new constitution must include a clear ambition to recognize the 'others' and their collective rights, and should develop a new page in the history of Turkey by establishing peace and reconciliation in this region. The following sections focus briefly on each of these issues.

3.1. Definition of citizenship

During their visit to the Parliamentary Commission, representatives of various minority groups together underscored the need for a new definition of citizenship in the new constitution. In the current Turkish constitution, Turkish citizenship is defined strictly in ethnic terms and is equated with being a 'Turk'. Groups other than Turks do not fit into this definition, unless they deny their distinctive identities. The ethnic definition of citizenship has created the alienation of minorities in the history of the Turkish Republic. Members of minority groups have always had a problematic relationship with the definition of Turkish citizenship. Most of them grudgingly accepted the appellation of 'Turks' while others, as a result of the impact of assimilationist policies, began to identify themselves as Turks. The definition of citizenship in the new constitution is an important parameter for ending the Turkish nationalist and denialist approach and for opening up a new era for the recognition of the 'others'. For this reason, during the visit to the Parliamentary Committee, all of the minority groups voiced a common wish for the definition of citizenship to be modified. One good example that illustrates the dislike among minority groups for being called Turks was expressed in the objec-

---

[43] Amnesty International, 2006.
[44] For a comprehensive overview of Turkish Law regarding minority rights see MRG, 2007, and for a more specific overview of religious freedom, see Oehring, 2005.

tions made against the Ecumenical Greek Orthodox Patriarch Bartholomew, who noted during his visit to the parliamentary Constitutional Reconciliation Commission that, "Anybody who is tied to the Republic of Turkey through citizenship is a Turk".[45] Although the Greek Orthodox Patriarch demanded equal citizenship rights, his approach to definining citizenship is precisely the same definition as that of the current Turkish Constitution, which is strictly ethnic and excludes everyone other than 'Turks'.

There is a common tendency in the demands of minority groups to reformulate citizenship in more neutral terms (with no reference to ethnicity), specifically in favour of developing a geographical definition of citizenship. For instance, they would like to replace the terminology "Turkish Citizenship" with "Citizens of Turkey", without mention of a specific ethnic group. This represents a potential solution for considering the multiethnic structure of Turkey. This approach, however, should be combined with other protective measures for minorities – hence it is not merely the formulation of citizenship in the new Constitution, also the philosophy behind the process itself that is important. The driving logic behind the new constitution should be based on the recognition of the others that should be clearly emphasized, at least in the preamble of the new constitution. The new constitution, particularly the new definition of citizenship, should embrace everyone. Only then will those who are presently excluded be able to claim: "This constitution is ours".

3.2. *Collective or individual rights?*

The discussion around collective and individual rights is one of the prominent topics in the field of human rights. The positive and negative aspects of group rights have been widely discussed among scholars, focussing mainly on the theoretical discussion between liberal-individualist[46] and corporatist approaches.[47] In practice, while some countries favour individual rights in their constitutions, others have incorporated group rights in addition to individual rights. Rather than being mutually exclusive, collective and individual rights are mutually interactive and can be combined in legal texts.[48] The creative formulations for such combinations can only be understood in relation to a country's specific situation.

This discussion is also highly important for the debate over a new constitution in Turkey. Turkey's main standpoint during the EU membership negotiations

---

[45] *Today's Zaman*, 13 March 2012.
[46] See also Kymlicka, 1995, for the liberal-individualist approach.
[47] See also Taylor, 1989.
[48] See, for example, the Copenhagen Criteria for EU membership.

has been founded upon the rejection of group rights. In the views of the Turkish government, recognition of group rights is seen as a process which will lead to the creation of minorities other than Turks, and ultimately to the division of the country. This policy argumentation is no doubt based on the traditional denialist discourse and denies the existence of minorities in the country. At this moment, Turkish ruling elites aim to solve all problems related to minority rights within the general framework of democracy and individual rights. Within this context concepts such as democracy and individual rights are used to silence minorities' demands and to avoid a confrontation. In a demagogic way, it is also said that 'If we recognize group rights of minorities, then we will have a *Turkish problem*'.[49] By constructing an imaginary 'Turkish problem', Turkish elites are trying to press down or minimize the political demands of minorities.

When considering the intrinsic dominancy of Turkishness in the political and institutional culture, structural inequalities between groups, and the undeniable existence of resource-wise weak groups (such as Assyrians, Greeks and Armenians), group rights are necessary for a comprehensive protection of minorities. This is also in line with the international standards that promote *affirmative action* for minorities. Individual rights solely cannot solve the problems of discrimination and inequality between different ethnic groups in Turkey. Therefore, in the process of making a new constitution, it is very important to incorporate collective rights in the new constitution in order to develop a peaceful co-existence.

Turkey should legally acknowledge the minority status (and thus, group rights) of Assyrians based on their rights originating from the Treaty of Lausanne. The new constitution has the opportunity to incorporate international standards and norms for minority rights, and transcend the outdated provisions of the Treaty of Lausanne. A fruitful combination of group and individual rights has the potential to become a 'political model' for countries in the Middle East, most of which are multiethnic and multireligious in structure.

3.3. *The philosophy behind creating a new constitution*

One of the points being omitted in this debate is the moral dimension in creating a new constitution. Constitutions open a new phase in the history of a country. If it is hoped that the new constitution in Turkey will open a new era in the nation's

---

[49] The use of the term "Turkish problem" is related to the growing demands of minority groups in Turkey. It is another version of the so-called "Sévres syndrome", which refers to deeply rooted fear and mistrust of neighbouring countries, the Western world as well as its own citizens (non-Muslim minorities, Kurds, communists and others). To understand how the imaginary Turkish problem is constructed, see Özdag, 2012.

history, the driving philosophy of the new constitution should be based on three main elements. First, it should guarantee the recognition of the 'others'. Second, it should introduce a peaceful solution to the Kurdish problem. And third, it should develop a culture of reconciliation with the past (i.e. recognition of the 1915 genocide). Countries that avoid a confrontation with their past have never managed to turn a new page in their history. Therefore, it is essential to echo the spirit of the new constitution in the preamble. Without mentioning what happened in the past, without bringing justice to the forefront, without condemning the responsible policies and actors, without recognition of genocide of the First World War and without bringing peace to the country, the new constitution will not be a step forward.

References

Aktas, S., *Report on the Imminent Problems Facing the Syriac Monastery of St. Gabriel, in Midyat Turkey,* (2008). Retrieved from: www.aina.org/reports/rotiptsmomg.pdf.

Aktas, S., "Report on the Current Situation in Turabdin", presentation to the Turabdin/North Iraq on the occasion of the 20th anniversary of the group, 24 February 2012. Retrieved from: www.suryoyo.uni-goettingen.de/library/samuelaktas-turabdin2012-en.pdf.

Amnesty International, *Turkey: Article 301: How the law on 'denigrating Turkishness' is an insult to free expression,* 1 March 2006. Retrieved from: www.amnesty.org/en/library/info/EUR44/003/2006.

Atto, N., *Hostages in the Homeland, Orphans in the Diaspora: Identity Discourses of the Assyrian/Syriac Elite in the European Diaspora,* (2011), Leiden: Leiden University Press.

BarAbrahem, A., "Turkish High School History Book Portrays Assyrians as Traitors", 10 February 2011. Retrieved from: www.aina.org/releases/20111002110757.htm.

Cengiz, O.K., "Minority Foundations in Turkey: An Evaluation of Their Legal Problems", oral presentation for the working-level meeting of foreign Embassies, organised by the Dutch Embassy in Ankara on 4 April 2003. Retrieved from: www.rightsagenda.org/index.php?option=com_content&view=article&id=293:aliasminority-foundations-in-turkey-an-evaluation-of-their-legal-problems&catid=84:aliasminority-rights&Itemid=123.

Cengiz, O.K., "Welcome, Assyrian Sabro newspaper", in *Todays Zaman,* 20 March 2012.

Cetinoglu, S. "Ittihat terraki Komitesinin Etnik Temizlik Politikasi ve Mardin'de Mülkiyet Degisimi", paper presented at the Symposium Cok Kültürlü Yaşamda Süryaniler, Istanbul, 23 March 2012.

Deniz, F., *En minoritets odyssé : upprätthållande och transformation av etnisk identitet i förhållande till moderniseringsprocesser: det assyriska exemplet,* (1999), Uppsala: Uppsala University.

Ertekin, O.G., "The Cemaat' paranoya mi, tabu mu?", in *Radikal-2*, 19 February 2012.
Essed, P., *Understanding Everyday Racism: An Interdisciplinary Theory*, 1991, California: Sage Publications.
European Commission, *Turkey 2005 Progress Report*, November 2005.
Güngör, U., and Polatel, M., *Confiscation and Destruction. The Young Turk Seizure of Armenian Property,* (2011), London: Continuum.
Journal of Turkish Weekly, "Turkey's Syriacs Lay Out Vision for New Constitution", 2 March 2012. Retrieved from: www.turkishweekly.net/news/131897/turkey-39-s-syriacs-lay-out-vision-for-new-constitution-.html.
Kurban, D., and Hatemi, K., *The story of an alien(ation): Real Estate Ownership Problems of Non-Muslim Foundations and Communities in Turkey,* (2009), Istanbul: TESEV Publications.
Kymlicka, W., *Multicultural Citizenship: A Liberal Theory of Minority Rights,* (1995) Oxford: Oxford University Press.
Milliyet Daily Newspaper, "Bakan Dincer'den ders kitaplari ile ilgili aciklama", 26 January 2012.
Minority Rights Group International, *A Quest For Equality: Minorities in Turkey*, (2007).
Onaran, N., *Emval-i Metruke Olayı: Osmanlı'da ve Cumhuriyette Ermeni ve Rum Mallarının Türkleştirilmesi*, (2010), Istanbul: Belge.
Oehring, O., "Turkey: Is There Religious Freedom in Turkey?", in *FORUM 18*, 12 October 2005.
Oehring, O., "Turkey: Little progress on religious freedom", in *FORUM 18,* 26 July 2006.
Oehring, O., "What difference does the latest Foundations Law make?", in *FORUM 18*, 13 March 2008.
Oran, B., "The Minority Concept and Rights in Turkey: The Lausanne peace Treaty and Current Issues", in Z. F. Kabasakal Arat and R. Falk (eds.), *Human Rights in Turkey*, (2007), Philadelphia: University of Pennsylvania Press.
Oran, B., "AYM doğruladı: Gayrimüslim=yabancı", in *Radikal*, 26 July 2011.
Oran, B., "Reconciled by the St. Gabriel Assyrian Monastery in Turkey", in *Radikal* (in Turkish), 20 February 2011. Also available at: www.aina.org/news/20110220143506.htm.
Özmen, A., "Mülk-Adalaet-Din: Mülküne Yeniden Malik Olmaya dair Süryani Öyküleri", presentation at the Symposium Çok Kültürlü Yaşamda Süryaniler, Istanbul, 23 March 2012.
Today's Zaman, "Turkey establishes Living Languages Institute", 2 December 2009.
Today's Zaman, "Davutoglu meets with Turkey's Alevis and Christians in Germany", 4 December 2011.
Today's Zaman, "Turkey hopes to bring Syriacs back to Mardin", 13 April 2012.
Today's Zaman, "Turkey Slams US Report on Religious Freedoms", 22 March 2012.
Today's Zaman, "Turkish minorities: We want a constitution that embraces us all", 16 April 2012.
Today's Zaman, "Turkey's non-Muslim minorities seek equal citizenship rights in constitution", 20 February 2012.

Today's Zaman, "Atesyan wants neutral definition of citizenship in new constitution", 13 February 2012.
Sabah Daily Newspaper, "Ilk Süryani Eseri 2012'de basilacak", 19 December 2011.
Taylor, C., *Sources of the Self: The Making of the Modern Identity.* Cambridge, (1989), Massachusetts: Harvard University Press.
United States Commission on International Religious Freedom's (USCIRF), *2012 Annual Report*.
Zeldin, W., "Turkey: Minority Religious Congregation Property to Be Returned Under Historic Measure", 6 September 2011. Retrieved from: www.loc.gov/lawweb/servlet/lloc_news?disp3_l205402795_text.

Almost a Miracle – Syriacs are Returning to their Homelands[1]

By Horst Oberkampf

Horst Oberkampf is a retired pastor of the Evangelical Lutheran Church in Württemberg (Stuttgart). For many years he has stood up for the Christians in Tur Abdin and for the Christians in Iraq. He co-founded the Solidarity Group Tur Abdin and Northern Iraq. Today he is a member of the Solidarity Group's leadership. He has written several books and articles about his experiences in both regions and maintains the Solidarity Group's website www.nordirak-turabdin.de.

1. Kafro – a village in Tur Abdin

Today, Kafro [Tahtayto] (Turkish name: Elbegendi) is on everyone's lips. Were you to visit Tur Abdin, you too would have to stop in Kafro. This village has become well known for its inhabitants who have returned to Tur Abdin from the Diaspora. In the following chapter, using the example of Kafro, I would like to discuss certain aspects related to the topic of 'returning', including some general information, and then some of my personal experiences and thoughts.

I remember very well my last visit to 'old Kafro' in 1994. Many houses were abandoned and only a few families remained, the majority of the families having left their homelands. Sadness hung over the village like a shadow. Several other villages in Tur Abdin shared this same fate, as reflected in the numbers: although tens of thousands of Christians lived in Tur Abdin in the 1960s, today only some 2,400 Syriacs are left, most of whom live in the two dioceses of Tur Abdin and Mardin. In comparison, there are about 90,000 Christians from Tur Abdin currently living in Germany alone.

In a short historical article focussing on the years 1900 until 2002, the Kafro Development Organization wrote:

As the oral tradition goes, the village of Kafro was founded before the birth of Christ ... In 1900, about 30 families lived in Kafro. The Syriac Orthodox people were strongly affected by World War I (1914–1915). The ones who were able to flee hid themselves in

---

[1] The following text is based on the Book "Ohne Rechte Keine Zukunft – Die Syrischen Christen des Tur Abdin im Südosten der Türkei" (Oberkampf, 2011), pp. 88 to 101.This chapter will be based on it, even if it is not always explicitly mentioned.

caves and the village was abandoned. In 1916, the first eight families returned from the caves to their village.

In 1970, Kafro reached its highest population level with 46 families. Due to the emigration waves starting from the 1980s onwards mainly towards Europe, the number of inhabitants shrunk to five families in 1992. With the departure of the last three families in 1995, Kafro was abandoned completely. Within a few years the abandoned village was plundered and nearly completely destroyed: even the church and the graves were not spared. In the surrounding area, all trees were cut down. Today (2002), about 170 families originating from Kafro live in Europe, particularly in Germany, Sweden and Switzerland.[2]

If you were to visit Kafro today on your way to the Mor Malke Monastery and Arkah (Turkish name: Üçköy), coming from Midyat and Anhel (Turkish name: Yemişli), you would scarcely believe your eyes. From a distance you would see huge houses, some three stories tall. The traditional houses of Tur Abdin are much lower and smaller, most just one storey tall. Today, the village of Kafro is bristling with life. Indeed, a 'new Kafro' has come into existence. Life has returned to the abandoned village – families have resettled in the area and children, youngsters and adults fill the streets. Fifteen years ago if anyone had told me that this would happen, I would not have taken them seriously. It still seems like a miracle to me. I still find it difficult to comprehend what has happened there and in a number of other villages in Tur Abdin. The former inhabitants have returned and have rebuilt their village anew. Kafro is the embodiment of a pilot project: the 'return movement'.

2. Political changes in Turkey

At the beginning of the third millennium, Turkey underwent a 'climate change' that can still be felt in many places. The number of military posts in southeast Turkey has decreased, the state of emergency has been lifted and the military conflict between the Kurdish PKK and the Turkish Army has ceased with the imprisonment of Abdullah Öcalan, political head of the PKK, in the late 1990s.

Moreover, with its aspiration to become a member of the European Union, the political course of Turkey has changed. Of course, the path to full membership is long and a subject of much heated debate in Europe. It is a great challenge for Turkey that it is measured with European standards, for instance, when it comes to its minority rights regime, freedom of religion, human rights, adherence to the

---

[2] Kafro, 2002.

Almost a Miracle – Syriacs are Returning to their Homelands

Kafro (Tahtayto) with its new built houses in the background. (H. Oberkampf)

obligations of the Lausanne Treaty for non-Muslim minorities, dealing with the genocide and so on. In annual progress reports from the European Union, Turkey is judged based on its progress in several areas. The subjects mentioned here in particular still require a great deal of improvement.

Nevertheless, Turkey's concrete membership aspirations have led to an improvement of the 'political climate', which has also had an effect on Tur Abdin. For the first time, Syriacs who had left their homelands were encouraged to return by both politicians and the clergy of Tur Abdin. Archbishop Timotheus, who has his see in the Mor Gabriel Monastery, has also asked the Syriacs abroad to return to their homelands. In place of the term 'emigration', the term 'return' is increasingly being used.

Since then, this topic has been fiercely debated amongst the Syriacs in the Diaspora. Many questions and concerns have been raised, including: Will the Turkish authorities offer binding security guarantees? Will the provisions of the Lausanne Treaty finally be applied to the Syriacs, as well? Can the state offer the returnees any economic prospects? What will be done about the property and land that the Turkish state has often illegally seized from the Syriacs? And so on.

3. Personal motives for a return

Yacob Demir, who lived in Switzerland from 1977 until 2005, has to my mind been the driving force behind the return movement relating to former residents of the village of Kafro. As he told me:

In 2001 I visited the village together with my family. I was devastated when I saw how the graves of our relatives and ancestors had been defiled. Our old church, Mor Yaqub and Mor Barsaum, too, was badly damaged. Those who did it had no respect. Seeing this, I had to fight back my tears.

As a point of historical significance he added:

Looking at our history in Turkey, you will realize that any region of settlement which once belonged to the Syriacs and was lost, was never returned to our people again by any governments.

His decision was final:

What was done to the graves of our ancestors and to our church should never happen again. Therefore, I will return. Apart from that we should never give up our homelands and we have to do everything to save them. This is why we began to debate the advantages and disadvantages of a return from Switzerland and other European countries. An organization was founded consisting of the former inhabitants of Kafro and over the course of many meetings a return was gradually prepared. Eventually, 14 families have decided to return to their old village Kafro, to rebuild their houses anew and to resettle their village. Exile Syriacs returned to other villages as well.[3]

4. Invitation from the Turkish government

As mentioned earlier, in 2001 politicians began encouraging Syriacs living abroad to return to their former homelands in Turkey. This encouragement was justified *inter alia* by the fact that they were Turkish citizens and that their skills were urgently needed. Security and rights would be promised and guaranteed on behalf of the state.

The state voiced its encouragement in two documents. One is a circular letter from Turkey's then Prime Minister Bülent Ecevit dated 12 June 2001 (in which,

---

[3] Kafro, 2002.

the Christians are referred to as 'Assyriacs'). In addition to Ecevit, the then Turkish President Ahmet N. Sezer penned a similar message in the guest book of Deyrulzafaran Monastery in Mardin during a visit on 6 June 2001.

Both texts, written by high-profile politicians, opened up a surprising course for the Syriacs and both offer new opportunities. Whether these invitations will represent a new reality in Turkey will have to be judged in the years ahead. To my mind, the questions of security and rights for the Christians are pivotal. Unfortunately, not much has happened in this respect since the publication of these documents. The politicians must be asked how seriously they take their own vows. It is easy to make such promises, but keeping them appears to be much more difficult for them!

4.1. First document: Circular 2001/33 – 12 June 2001

There are allegations that Assyriac-origin Turkish citizens, who emigrated abroad for various reasons including PKK terrorism, were encountering certain problems when they want to return to their villages, including not being allowed to use their rights over their property in their villages, and that hurdles were raised for foreigners to visit villages where Assyriacs reside. It has been evaluated that international circles might bring these allegations in front of Turkey as a new human rights violation. In order not to let such allegations to turn into an anti-Turkey campaign, the Interior Ministry will conduct necessary works for allowing our Assyriac-origin citizens – who for various reasons moved to or settled in European countries from their villages in the state of emergency, region and in adjacent provinces – to return to their villages, if they make such a demand. I strongly request all public institutions and establishments show necessary care and sensitivity in letting our Assyriac citizens to freely use their Constitutional, legal and democratic rights that were under the guarantee of our state.

Bülent Ecevit, Prime Minister

The letter was distributed to all ministries and several other state institutions.

4.2. Second document: Message by the President of Turkey

I am very happy about the visit to the Monastery of Deyrulzafaran, the holiest place of the Syriac congregation, which is an inseparable part of our people.

The contribution of the self-sacrificing, intelligent and nationally loyal members of the Syriac congregation to the development and welfare of the Turkish Republic is great. These days when the problems of our southeastern Anatolian region are coming to an end and a new economic development programme is started this contribution becomes even more important.

It is my belief that the Monastery of Deyrulzafaran with its history of thousands of years will continue its tolerant and solidarian attitude – as it has done in the past. In this belief I extend my warmest congratulations to all the members of the Syriac congregation.

Ahmet N.Sezer, President of State

6 June 2001

5. Governor of Mardin approves the return to Kafro

On 28 February 2002, two representatives of the 19 families who were willing to return to Kafro came to Mardin accompanied by Archbishop Timotheus. The delegation filed an application to governor Kocaklar in Mardin and requested a permission to return. They also mentioned reasons for their return.

The governor approved their application and promised to support them if the Christians returned to their former village. He agreed to help with the construction of a new road, the installation of electricity, telephone and water lines and with the building of educational facilities.

As a result of these promises, the preconditions were created to gradually plan a return and the new houses could be built now as well as the infrastructure. The families, therefore, had to prepare themselves to bid farewell to their old places of residence, where some of them lived for 25 years or more.

6. Reasons for a return

There are numerous reasons for the Syriacs to return to their former homelands:
– A desire for their roots is highly apparent amongst the Syriacs, most have whom have never lost their ties to Tur Abdin. Many former inhabitants of Tur Abdin suffered from a sense of alienation in their countries of refuge and had difficulties adapting to the Western lifestyle. For many of them, the ties with Tur Abdin are part of their identity. In Tur Abdin, they were at home, while abroad they lived in their 'second home'.
– I can vividly remember what the Patriarch of the Syriac Orthodox Church, Ignatius Zakka I Iwas, said in the 1980s and 90s – those years in which waves of Syriacs fled Tur Abdin. "Do not forget where you come from", he said, "even in the Diaspora". Their roots lie within the soil of Tur Abdin, the Patriarch said, and "If anybody pulls his roots out they will wither away and the ties with Tur Abdin will vanish".
– All the richness of Tur Abdin – the impressive monasteries and churches, the traditions and cultural particularities, the fruits and the landscape, the scents and all those familiar things, the people and their property – can only be found there

and not in Germany, Switzerland or anywhere else. A statement Archbishop Timotheus once made, illustrates this feeling the majority of Syriacs have:

Syriac village of Chrabe Mishka (Dagici) within Tur Izlo; some of its former habitants have rebuild their old houses and are planning to return for good. (M. Tozman)

When I look down from my office, the Mor Gabriel Monastery, onto the wide lands of Tur Abdin, the *Mountain of the Servants of God*, then I feel and sense tranquillity in winter, colourfulness in spring, a cool breeze in summer that chills the hot air and the falling leaves in autumn. It is like paradise that has been given to us as gift from God.

However, he added that this was not the whole truth, alluding *inter alia* to the string of lawsuits the monastery has had to withstand relating to questions of property and ownership that the state and the monastery's neighbours claim for themselves. Yet, according to the Archbishop, there is even more at stake: the cases are about the very existence of Christianity in that region.

– Some Syriacs feel a huge sense of responsibility towards their homeland of Tur Abdin. The area is one of the oldest regions of Christianity. Churches and monasteries, which have been renovated in recent years to prevent them from falling into decay, are constant reminders of the long Christian tradition of that region. If nobody lived there any more to cherish this culture and its traditions, this heritage could no longer be passed on and preserved. This is one of the major concerns of the Syriacs and the clergy from Tur Abdin.

An article from one of Kafro's returning families reads:

> We [the parents and their three children] first came back in 2003 and it hurt to see what had happened to the village ... the houses had collapsed, the church was plundered, the graves became dilapidated and all the trees were cut down. Everything our ancestors had built up was reduced to ashes. Back then we realized: if nobody returns, everything Christians built up here in the course of the centuries will be lost for good.[4]

- With the families who have returned to Kafro and other villages, new experiences are brought to Tur Abdin, as well. Although the Syriacs were forced to flee Tur Abdin due to a lack of rule of law and a lack of security, it was an important time to many of those in which they were able to acquire a lot of new skills: a new language, ecumenical dialogue, education and work, many new contacts and so on. Experiences abroad and life in Tur Abdin melted together and something new emerged; a new chapter is being written. Tur Abdin will surely be renewed by the many experiences gained abroad. It will not be like it was before, like it has always been. It is changing – hopefully for a better future.

  The Syriacs who are returning want to give something back to their homelands and to those people who stayed in Tur Abdin when the great majority of their brethren decided to leave for greater security and liberty in the West.

- The decision about whether to or not to return is a very personal decision that every family must make for themselves. Every family must gauge whether they have the persistency to endure such a restart – whether they are mentally and physically strong enough to give up the ties and relationships they have built up while living in the Diaspora – and whether they want to face up to the challenges a return implies. It is a decision that must be made with complete freedom of will.

7. Return and Christian faith

I think that the decision to return also has a spiritual dimension connected to the Christian faith. Allow me to explain. Abraham, the father of faith in Judaism, Christianity and Islam, was called upon by God one day, as told in the Bible (Genesis 1:12). He was commanded to abandon his home, village, relatives and social network, not knowing what God had in mind for him. Abraham was faced

---

[4] Buck, 2008.

with great uncertainty, yet God made him a promise: "Abraham, go and set out, I will be with you". These words alone helped him to accept his new journey. The Christian faith, irrespective of the denomination, frequently resembles a journey; one does not know where it will lead. To believe means to be on a journey time and again.

At times, I am also reminded of the book of Joshua (1:5), where God says: "I will always be with you, I will never leave you alone". The Christian faith has an enormous power – a "dynamis", as Apostle Paul says – which encourages us and gives us strength at all times. Psalm 73:23 gives a vivid picture of God who accompanies us: "Nevertheless, I am continuously with you, you hold my right hand". God is a "God of life" and a "friend of life", as it says in Proverbs 3:32.

It was with this strength that the people from Tur Abdin set out on their journey from their homelands. And with the same strength and the promise made by God they return to their homeland again. The Christian faith bears up against good and bad times. The Syriacs who decided to return to Tur Abdin have set out with the faith in God's promise: I walk with you, I hold my hand above you without knowing where this 'adventure of a return' will lead. This is why the Christian faith always needs risk and courage, and above all faith in God.

8. Letter from Archbishop Timotheus, 2003

The question of whether or not to return is still widely discussed in Tur Abdin and the Diaspora, with heated debates and a wide range of opinions. Some of the former inhabitants of Kafro finally came to the conclusion that they would like to grab the opportunity presented by Turkey's 'climate change' and dare to return, despite several unresolved issues and questions. The Development Organization Kafro was founded and two booklets were published: one was a documentation of the village and the other was a concept for the return, in which an action plan and schedule were drafted for the entire process of return. Several talks followed with experts and friends in Turkey and abroad to prepare their undertaking effectively and thoroughly.

Part of this network were individuals in Tur Abdin, as well. The Mor Gabriel Monastery and Archbishop Timotheus in particular were crucial figures in this respect. He made his position clear in a letter he sent to Solidarity Group Tur Abdin. The topic of the Solidarity Group's annual meeting on February 2003 was "Return to Tur Abdin?" Naturally, the Solidarity Group dealt with this issue intensively and accompanied Kafro's inhabitants during the whole process. Back then, Archbishop Timotheus wrote:

Dear friends,

We send all of you greetings and blessings from your Christian brothers and sisters here in Tur Abdin.

The situation in Tur Abdin has been improving positively in the last several years. The immigration has stopped; instead there has been a growing interest among the Christians from Tur Abdin to return to their homeland. We have had families and individuals who have already returned and those who have planned to do so with those who consider the return. A concrete example for this is the village of Kafro Tahtayto from where two young men have already returned and 17 families have planned to return. We have people from other villages like Anhel, Miden, Midyat, Marbobo, Qelith, Hazakh who have people returned to them from Europe.

It is a very pleasing move to see our community coming back to the homeland. This will boost the morale of the Christians in Tur Abdin and encourage more of those living abroad to come back. The return process will not be without difficulties. The diocese works very hard to encourage the return activities and serve as a centre for those who want to return. It helps them with their bureaucratic and legal matters and with many other difficulties that might arise during the return process.

We need, however, your prayers for a more peaceful situation at this time and your solidarity to achieve this better. We must work hand in hand to morally and financially support the return activities. Peace has been dominant in the area for the last few years, let us pray so that all of us are protected by God's providence.

We appreciate your work of many years for your Christian brothers and sisters in Tur Abdin and we pray for you. May God's grace and love with you all and bless you.

Yours in Our Lord,

Timotheos Samuel Aktas
Archbishop of Tur Abdin

9. Kafro – a pilot project

Repeatedly it was said that the village of Kafro is a pilot project for the return of Syriacs to Tur Abdin and it is true: The inhabitants of Kafro had the most sophisticated planning and are far ahead of other families struggling with a decision. Fourteen families decided to return completely, albeit at different moments. They all originate from this village and return to it again as a community that knows each other for years. They shoulder this task together and they are aware that they must work extremely hard to make this project successful. They have already settled, though others are still at the beginning of their planning. The inhabitants of Kafro know about their responsibility: If their project does not succeed, they say,

Archbishop Samuel Aktas is reading in an old Syriac Bible. (From the book by Y. Bilge)

the whole return movement will be put back or will even perish. If they succeed, however, they will boost the whole movement and others will be encouraged to follow their example. All of those who think about returning to Tur Abdin, watch the village closely. So, this pilot project is a yardstick and role model at the same time. Kafro's inhabitants share their experiences with others and try to contribute to writing a 'new chapter' in Tur Abdin's history. It is not their aim to create a new Tur Abdin, but to develop Tur Abdin slowly and gently to fit into this century.

10. The consecration of the village Kafro

Finally, on 1 September 2006 the village of Kafro was consecrated. Several of those fourteen families mentioned had already moved into their new homes and Archbishop Timotheos came to celebrate the new beginning in a service with the community of Kafro. He expressed his gratitude to the villagers for returning to their homelands after so many years. They prayed together that their new journey would continue with God's blessings and that they would be able to live there safely and confidently. Refugees turned to returnees, who were welcomed by their fellow Christians and their people in Tur Abdin.

Yakub Demir said at that time:

Today we witness something that we could not imagine would ever become a reality. When we visited our village in the past, we always felt great concern. We felt called by the Lord to do something for the preservation of the spiritual values of our homelands. This prompted our return. We thank God that we are here now and that our dream has come true. We hope that with God's help we will be able to contribute to the good of this village and the region.

Archbishop Timotheos said:

Today a new chapter in the history of Tur Abdin has begun ... I congratulate you and your community on this village in our diocese. We pray for your everlasting love to the Lord and for your solidarity so that you become a role model for others in Tur Abdin. May God's grace always direct you.[5]

11. Return and daily routine

There are many variations and degrees of return. One option is a radical breach, as we see in Kafro. Families start completely afresh – the centre of their lives is no longer Germany, Switzerland or Sweden but Kafro. Another option many exile Syriacs use is to live for several months or even half a year in their newly renovated houses in Tur Abdin. The third option is that a family returns time and again during holidays to indulge in everything they miss in the Diaspora. During the summer months, Tur Abdin and its villages are populated by many visitors whose roots are in Tur Abdin. Consequently, the picture today is different: while

---

[5] ICO, 2006.

it was calm in the villages and there were very few visitors in monasteries some years ago, the joy of living has again returned to Tur Abdin.

Nevertheless, the children and teenagers of the returnees in Kafro and other villages in Tur Abdin have arguably had to make the biggest sacrifices: they have bid farewell to friends, teachers, educational opportunities, clubs, social networks and much more. Even when they visited their new homelands together with their parents previously, gained an impression of life there, and celebrated masses in the monasteries, the final and irreversible decision to return has changed their entire lives. Despite that, these young people must continue on their paths. When I consider what this must mean to a young person, I imagine that the challenge must be enormous.

Of course, the new Kafro also has its attractions. Many new experiences lie ahead, one of which is learning a new language: Turkish is the official language in Tur Abdin and is used at schools with various curricula. The youngsters will be required to learn a completely new language without forgetting the ones they grew up with. Their mother tongue, too, must be kept alive. They must be open to and accepting of these new challenges.

The children, parents and those responsible in the village have all had to make their contribution to this project. If they do not succeed in integrating and 'enrooting' future generations in Tur Abdin, the entire return project will have to be questioned. Yet, if they manage to give children and teenagers a perspective in their new homelands, then this new path will be a benefit for both young and old alike.

Meanwhile, the Development Organization Kafro has planned or even realized many new projects with a special focus on the youth: an internet café was opened in Kafro to offer them the opportunity to communicate with the rest of the world and to promote their education with the help of internet. Another project is the sports and leisure time facility in Kafro, which helps with the integration and interaction with others and is also beneficial to the young people's well-being. Several other projects were planned and realized for the community of Kafro, but they continue to dream up new projects. These projects require financial support and sponsors (such as a hotel in Tur Abdin, a travel agency, infirmaries, etc.), since Kafro cannot carry the financial burden alone.[6]

Though the families have finally arrived and settled well in Kafro, the adults still must find ways to earn their livelihood. Very little work is available in southeastern Turkey with a constant income. It will be up to the dexterity of the Syriacs

---

[6] Kafro, 2007.

to use the skills they have learnt abroad. I think that the Turkish government, too, has a responsibility to support the returnees and create employment opportunities. Though some individuals who have returned to Kafro have started their own construction firm with enough orders at the moment, there is still a dire need for further work opportunities. Not everybody can drive a taxi or a minibus to earn his living, become active in the agricultural or construction sector. This is a great challenge, but I am certain that they will solve this issue, as well.

12. Voices of the critics

Of course, there have also been critics of this pilot project. Criticism has been levelled that "Everything is too large scale, the houses are too pretentious and will only arouse the envy of the neighbourhood", and "the return movement will change Tur Abdin". This is severe criticism which cannot be simply brushed off. I myself also had doubts about this and was wondering if Tur Abdin would be able to cope with what the returnees brought with them from Europe. Would it fit into the landscape and the traditions of Tur Abdin? Or would a social imbalance occur?

In the meantime, however, after several visits and conversations with the new inhabitants of Kafro, I have changed my mind completely. I changed from an opponent to a proponent and my criticism gave way to praise for the positive aspects that do not receive their appropriate appreciation. I was impressed not only by the courage of the returnees and their willingness to take risks, but also by the reflection and the sophistication of the project Kafro, as well as the vision of the inhabitants.

I thought to myself, why should they not be allowed to build in whichever way they like? They have worked very hard abroad for several years to be able to set this up. It is not about the outside of the houses or the village. Instead it should be about the rationale and the concerns of the returnees who set out like Abraham to see their old homelands again and revitalize them. If we take a closer look at the other villages of Tur Abdin we will realize that they, too, rebuild and reconstruct their houses, churches and monasteries. This is a cause for rejoice, not for criticism!

13. Wait and see instead of returning today

Currently, the situation in south-eastern Turkey is not so positive that families would gladly and confidently return to Tur Abdin. New clashes with the PKK, which had ceased some years ago, have returned and bring back memories of those very hard times in the 1980s and 90s. The Mor Gabriel Monastery, which faces serious threats of expropriation by the state and its neighbours, has become the symbol for the current assaults on Christians. Yet, these cases are not only restricted to questions of property, they are about the very existence of Christians in that region. Unfortunately, there are still powers amongst Kurds and Muslims in south-eastern Turkey that would seek to 'drive off' the Christians. There are efforts to turn the Mor Gabriel Monastery into a museum, which according to Archbishop Timotheos, if successful, would spell the end for Christians in Tur Abdin.

Moreover, manifold conflicts with the land registry office, which regularly confiscates the lands of the Christian villages, pose an enormous problem. With much endurance, time, patience and unfortunately with much money, too, the Christians have to fight for their properties and possessions. All this surely does not motivate Syriacs abroad to return to their old homelands. Many prefer to wait and see if these dark clouds pass Tur Abdin again.

14. Conclusion: The Chapel of Our Lady

Many plans have been made and building has been done in Kafro in recent years. The desire for a village church naturally came up as well. In the Kafro of the olden days, there was a large church and a Chapel of our Lady, but both were destroyed. The villagers agreed upon rebuilding the Chapel. In an ecumenical project, both teenagers and adults from the Syriac Orthodox Church from Kafro and Germany, as well as Lutherans from Germany, have helped to rebuild the Chapel and make it a house of prayer for Kafro again. The initiator was Ernst Ludwig Vatter, a retired Canon, former staff member of the Evangelical Lutheran Church of Württemberg (Stuttgart), and for several years a member of the leadership of the Solidarity Group Tur Abdin and North Iraq.

As Ludwig wrote:

First new church in Tur Abdin in 400 years

On 15 August 2008, a new Chapel was able to be consecrated in Kafro with the financial support of the Evangelical Lutheran Church of Wurttemberg and the practical support of 12 teenagers and adults from Wurttemberg in 2007. Nearly 500 guests attended this ceremony from various parts of Tur Abdin. Archbishop Timotheos consecrated the Chapel in the presence of the mayor of Midyat, the chief of police, representatives of the army and the Evangelical Protestant Church of Wurttemberg.

Two Syrian Orthodox priests and a Malfono (Syriac and liturgical teacher) in Tur Abdin. (H. Oberkampf)

Unfortunately I was unable participate in the consecration of the Chapel. Instead, I sent them written salutations to demonstrate to the village and its inhabitants the bonds I share with them. The letter read:

Dear friends in Kafro!

I offer my congratulations to your new and renovated house of prayer! Today it will be consecrated and blessed. It will be handed over to you!

In future, you will be able to celebrate services in 'your church' once again. The prayers and hymns will resound again within these walls and will rise to God. The Eucharist will give you strength for your daily lives. You will find peace at this place. Joy and grief will have room in this house and will be brought before God.

This new church shall be 'in the midst of your faith' and 'locus of your community'. I send you from afar, but in mind connected to you, warm regards. I hope, you can walk confidently and courageously towards a common future in Kafro and Tur Abdin – God bless you on your ways!

Shlomo, your friend H.O.

To tell the truth, it still seems like a miracle to me that this happened in the midst of Tur Abdin in the first decade of this new century and at the dawn of the third millennium. Kafro has reawakened to new life. A miracle has become reality, and all because individuals believed in it!

References

Buck, K.D., Evangelisches Parish Paper for Württemberg, 27/2008 in *Neuanfang in der alten Heimat*, p. 10f.

Development Organisation Kafro, 'Geschichte von Kafro' in *Dokumentation über das Dorf Kafro tahtaito,* Entwicklungsverein Kafro (2002) p. 7f.

Development Organisation Kafro, Leaflet dated 24 February 2007. Retrieved from www.kafro.com.

Ecevit, Bülent, Circular Letter 2001/33, 12 June 2001.

'Kafro: a new chapter in the history of Tur Abdin', *Information Christlicher Orient (ICO),* November 2006, year 6, no. 24, p. 13.

Oberkampf, Horst,*Ohne Rechte Keine Zukunft – Die Syrischen Christen des Turabdin im Südosten der Türkei,* (2011) pp. 88–101.

Sezer, Ahmet N., Guest book inscription, 6 June 2001.

Solidarity Group Tur Abdin and Iraq. http://www.nordirak-turabdin.info/cms/index.php?option=com_content&task=view&id=403&Itemid=208

Timotheus, Archbishop Mor Gabriel Monastery, No. 21/03, 27 February 2003.

Cadastral Registration of Lands and Preservation Orders in Turkey's South-East: Subtle Forms of Discrimination?

By Markus Tozman

Markus Tozman is MA Student at Johns Hopkins University specializing in Middle East Studies; he dedicated his BA thesis to the Turkish minority rights regime and the topical situation of the Syriacs in south-eastern Turkey, after conducting field research in the region for five months; he worked for the Dutch MP Pieter Omtzigt on the portfolio "minorities in Turkey" from 2011 to 2012.

1. Introduction

The Turkish State does not know ethnical discrimination and does not accept any form of discrimination based on religion, ethnicity or language.... The Turkish State is ready to serve you.... Turkey is not your former home, it is still your home and it will always be your home.

Turkish Foreign Minister Ahmet Davutoglu
addressing a Syriac community in Germany in 2011

The expropriation of Mor Gabriel's lands as described in other chapters of this book might be seen as a crass act of arbitrariness and is known as a case in which the Turkish state, together with other individuals, is attempting to expropriate the most important spiritual centres of the Syriac community in Turkey. The trials of the monastery, however, are no exception to the rule in the Tur Abdin region. Rather, there are few if any villages that are not confronted with a similar situation. The majority of Syriac villages are faced with (state) measures which, taken together, I refer to as 'subtle discrimination'.

Turkey has thus far been unable to cope with its minorities and applies a nationalistic concept for its society which is based on exclusion of groups that are different from Sunni Turks. As the European Council correctly observed:

Sunni Islam has been functional in the nation-building process as a uniting common cultural factor of the majority of Turkey's inhabitants. A person who is not a Muslim is usually referred to as a minority person or a Turkish citizen but not as Turk. Turk designates an ethno-religious characteristic of a political community.[1]

---

[1] European Parliament, p. 10.

As a consequence, measures are implemented that aim at the expulsion, assimilation or marginalization of minorities in Turkey.[2] This state policy has been conducted throughout the whole history of the Turkish Republic[3] and is still apparent today, albeit in a more subtle form. Several authors and public reports by the European Union, the Council of Europe and national parliaments point to various forms of "systemic discrimination"[4] against minorities in Turkey.

Although much has been written regarding discrimination against minorities in Turkey with a plethora of examples, the following two occurrences have received barely any attention by scholars. Yet, in recent years, these measures have hit the Syriac minority in Tur Abdin particularly hard: the re-cadastration of lands and so-called preservation orders of holy sites. On the following pages I try to elaborate on these two measures.

2. Methods and limitations

2.1. Methods

When preparing to conduct my research, I decided to use the qualitative research method espoused by Gillham and Silverman, which utilises open-ended questions and helps in developing an understanding of how and why the situation of a particular group evolved. This research method offers the interviewee the opportunity to reply freely and in depth on questions and backgrounds in their own words. The open-ended questions helped to hone my interviews over time, deleting questions that proved to be superfluous or adding useful questions and inquiring into sub-topics wherever appropriate.

In total, I conducted 30 interviews in 27 different locations. I visited every possible location in which Aramaic was spoken by members of the community. The interviews were conducted in villages, towns and monasteries. I decided against visiting locations where Syriacs lived who no longer spoke the Aramaic language when it became apparent that these interviews were difficult to conduct with translators and were, therefore, inefficient.

My own roots are in the region: my parents fled the region, I speak Aramaic fluently and I am well acquainted with the culture. This enabled me to gain acceptance as part of their group – demonstrating the proper protocol (something which is of great importance within this ethnic group) and reading the nuances of the interviewees. As a result, I had good access to the group, which increases

---

[2] Tozman, 2011.
[3] See, for example, Icduygu & Soner, 2006 and Kurban, 2007.
[4] Kaya, p. 27.

the reliability of the results. Considering that I was born and raised in Germany, I myself do not have any direct ties to the region. This helped me to investigate the topic without emotional involvement and with the necessary distance to carry out scientific and unbiased research.

2.2. *Limitations*

Today, the Syriac community in Turkey is chiefly divided between Tur Abdin and Istanbul. While approximately 10,000–15,000 Syriacs live in Istanbul, only 2,400 Syriacs remain in Tur Abdin. The community in Istanbul emerged from the community in Tur Abdin through immigration from the 1950s onwards. Still, their situations are not comparable, since Istanbul is a metropolis, while Tur Abdin is a strongly rural area. I chose to conduct my research in the latter area, because of its remoteness. Moreover, a case study on the Syriac community in Istanbul was already carried out in 2007.[5]

Tur Abdin is situated within three Turkish districts that are still very fragile in security matters due to the Kurdish conflict. Hence, the Turkish state warns against travelling within that region and has declared certain parts of it to be restricted areas because of the skirmishes and bombings that still take place.[6] It is for that same fact that the Syriacs, having been caught for decades between those two hostile groups, are still highly intimidated. This situation also had repercussions for my interviews and resulted in several of my interviewees being very fearful of being interviewed. For this reason, I have rendered their names anonymous and, in cases in which the location would have been obvious, I have also changed the name of the village or town.

3. The situation of the Syriacs in the 1980s and 1990s

The conflict between the Kurds and the Turks, which started violently in 1984, had disastrous consequences for the Syriac minority. Living in exactly the same region as the Kurds, the Syriacs were caught in the crossfire between the two groups, suffering severe suppression, persecution, violation of basic human rights and daily terror.[7] Squeezed between the PKK, the military, the so-called 'village

---

[5] Thomsen, 2007.
[6] Auswärtiges Amt, 2012.
[7] Yonan, 2006. For more information on this topic, see also the chapter by Makko elsewhere in this book.

guards'[8], Turkish Hezbollah[9] and aghas[10] and with no relief in sight, thousands of Syriacs were forced to flee the region. In the words of one interviewee, "It simply was anarchy here back then".[11]

The situation only improved after the capture of PKK leader Öcalan in 1999. The Hezbollah was abolished, martial law was lifted in the area and as a result human rights violations decreased – or at least became less overt. But one of the most important changes in the region came as the results of a policy decision in Europe: the EU's decision to make Turkey a candidate for EU membership in 2005. The changes resulting from this application and from demands laid down by the EU were substantial and were felt throughout Turkey, including in the southeast. Today there is less overt violence and suppression than 20 years ago. However, state measures against the Syriac minority still make co-existence on an equal footing with their Muslim neighbours impossible.

4. Cadastral registration of lands

Although the cadastral registration of lands in Turkey officially commenced with the foundation of the Land Registry and Cadastre Directorates in 1936, a vast portion of the land in Turkey was not actually measured and registered until 1950. In the 1990s, however, it became clear that the measurements were insufficiently accurate, that different systems were used which were not all compatible and that not all parts of the country were actually registered. Because Turkish cadastral law could not meet international standards, the decision was made to change the law.

---

[8] Köy Korucu, Kurdish militia paid and armoured by the Turkish state to fight PKK rebels. According to Jung & Piccoli (2001), there were more than 80,000 Köy Korucu in the 1990s, and according to Smith (2005), approximately 60,000 remain.

[9] The Turkish Hezbollah was very active in Turkey from the late 1990s until the capture of PKK leader Abdullah Öcalan. Though they were against the Turkish laical state and wanted to create an Islamic state similar to Iran, the state used them during the conflict for executions of journalists, politicians and other 'undesirable' individuals. The Turkish Hezbollah also targeted Syriacs. For more information, see, Bruinessen, 1996, and Jacobi, 2004.

[10] Agas are Kurdish landlords, remnants of the feudal and archaic structures among the Kurdish people. The aghas are highly powerful in south east Turkey and, according to Smith (2007) 'own' entire regions. Inhabitants of agha-controlled villages are forced to pay regular tributes. With their cronies in the Government, police and politics, the aghas have a broad power base and maintain strict control over daily life there. The aghas even control most of the village guards, and hence they also have their own militia.

[11] Interview 30, 21 November 10.

Currently, Turkish cadastral law does not prescribe information related to the management of real estate – such as the form and aim of the use of real estate, the annual income generated or its production capacity.[12]

The monastery of Mor Gabriel with some of its lands; Mor Gabriel has severely been hit by consequences of the cadastral registration of its lands. (Mor Gabriel monastery)

For this reason, the lands, particularly in rural areas, have begun to be re-measured starting in the early 2000s. Starting in 2002, private companies have also been used in this process. Turkish law prohibits rivers, forests and so on from being held as private property; they are consequently state property. State documents (including some dating from the days of the Ottoman Empire) and ownership certificates but also eyewitness testimonies are used for the re-registration – the latter of which is a basis for random denunciation by average citizens.[13] Once parcels are registered, the state, the owner or any individual who feels disadvantaged has the right to submit an appeal within 10 years. Once that period has elapsed, ownership of the land can no longer be challenged. The administrative boundaries of

---
[12] Demir & Coruhlu, 2008, p. 112.
[13] Ibid.

a village must be taken into consideration, as well. If the boundaries shift, the parcels within them increase or decrease in size, as well.

For these reasons, there can be disagreements over the administrative boundaries of villages in connection with the determining of ownership in these areas. This results in many time-consuming lawsuits about the ownership of the parcels in these regions.[14]

Since 2008, this project has been financed by the World Bank.[15]

When the re-cadastration is carried out, the first step is the re-measurement of the village borders. Next, the boundaries of the individual parcels within the administrative borders of those villages are determined. Parcels of land can be awarded an ownership title, or they can be categorized as either a) forests, b) abandoned or c) unfarmed lands. The parcels declared to be forests immediately become the property of the state. Category b) and c) also become property of the state, but unlike category a) those lands can be resold to other individuals.[16]

The cadastral re-registration has led to huge expropriations amongst the Syriacs.[17] Few if any villages are unconcerned by these measures. Villages losing up to 4 million m² are no rarity.[18] The Kurds in the region began to claim Syriacs' lands in an attempt to co-opt fertile soils. Some interviewees indicated that false claims have been supported through ploys such as bogus witnesses and false testimonies in court.

Though the situation is clear and obvious – Christians have had tenancy agreements for several decades now – Muslims use bogus witnesses. Irrespective of this the judges are still in favour of the Muslims. So instead of deciding an obvious case for the Syriacs they declare the lands as forest and therefore, owned by the state. This was, the judge explained, due to the fact that "it could not be told anymore to whom the lands belong". In a couple of years the lands will probably be sold and then the Kurds can buy and own them legally. This happens regularly to us, even in the case where lands are already properly registered. I know about four cases from this village only that have already been negotiated in front of a judge.[19]

These issues have also been confirmed by several European parliaments and the

---

[14] Demir & Coruhlu, 2008, p. 118f.
[15] World Bank, 2010.
[16] Aktas & Özmen, 2006.
[17] Parliamentary Assembly of the Council of Europe, Resolution 1704.
[18] For example, Interview 14, Interview 19 and Interview 30.
[19] Interview 3, 4 September 2010.

European Union.[20] The Swiss Parliament mentions more than 10 million m² that have been consciously expropriated in more than 30 villages.[21] Some villages have lost more than 90 % of their land.[22] The town of Beth Zabday (Turkish name: Idil) is probably the most extreme example of this trend. The population of the town, until 30 years ago mainly Christian, owned some 10,000 hectares of land in the 1980s. Today, only 400 hectares remain.[23]

The case of Mor Gabriel Monastery has gained global notoriety. It is the perfect example of how the state, the agas and Kurds conspire to expropriate land owned by Christians. After the borders of the village of Kafarbe (Turkish name: Güngören) – the village to which the monastery administratively belongs – had been re-measured, the borders were changed to the monastery's disadvantage. Several parcels were awarded to the monastery's neighbours, despite uncontested title deeds and other evidence.[24] Other parcels within the monastery's walls were declared forest by the state, using as evidence the fact that "the lands look[ed] green in aerial photographs of the 1950s".[25] Since forests are state property, the monastery's walls and other parts lying within those claimed parcels will have to be demolished. The aga of the surrounding villages, Cellebio, who was an AKP deputy in the Turkish Parliament at the time the trials started, was chiefly responsible for initiating the trials against Mor Gabriel and had the full knowledge of his party.[26] Moreover, the state treasury issued an appeal against the positive verdicts of the regional courts, fighting the Monastery up to the highest courts in Turkey. It is inarguable, therefore, that the Turkish state and the governing AK Party are behind the expropriation of Mor Gabriel. As De Courtois noted, "Arabs, Turks and Kurds have all viewed the monasteries as their [favourite] targets".[27] Of the more than 80 original monasteries in Tur Abdin, only four remain inhabited and intact. Since this case is covered well by other chapters of this book, I will not elaborate on it further here. Nevertheless, I will say that it demonstrates very well how the re-cadastration is used in manifold ways against Mor Gabriel, just as it is used against the majority of Syriac villages.[28]

---

[20] See, for example, Tweede Kamer (2012), which is added as an appendix to this book and European Parliament (2008).
[21] Simoneschi-Cortesi, 2011.
[22] Syriac Universal Alliance, 2011.
[23] ABM, 2012.
[24] Bilge, 2011.
[25] Oran, 2012. For more information on this topic, see also Oran's chapter in this book.
[26] Deutscher Bundestag, 2012.
[27] Courtois, 2004, p. 282.
[28] Interview 26, 26 October 2010.

All of my interviewees believed that these new registrations have been used as means of subtle discrimination, seeing as how the state is behind the majority of the claims. Many of those Syriacs who were forced to flee from the Turkish-Kurdish conflict in the 1980s and 1990s have lost their land to the state. Their lands were categorized as abandoned or grew wild and were declared forests. Nor could many of them fight the expropriation, because many of the refugees had been required to surrender their Turkish nationality in their new home countries. As the European Council stated, "Syriacs who no longer have Turkish citizenship have not been able to register their properties in the Southeast".[29] Even if a refugee were a to win a case in court regarding expropriation by the state, without citizenship, they would no longer be able to register their lands in their own names.

The state seized land in nearly every village.[30] In other villages, even immovable properties were declared forest.[31] Villagers now fear that the government will sell the properties to Muslims from neighbouring areas in the years ahead to enable them to legally get closer to their villages and properties[32] – a fear that seems justified when looking, for example, at the villages of Bote and Ciwardo (Turkish names: Bardakci and Gülgöze), where the Turkish state has built mosques on land formerly owned by Syriacs.[33] Additionally, the firms involved in the cadastral registration frequently belong to agas. Kurdish villagers, too, would not take any actions against Christians belonging to an aga, if their agas would not tolerate this. With numerous exile Syriacs losing their lands to the state, the possibility of a return to Tur Abdin diminishes for them, too.[34]

However, there have also been cases in which villagers lost land because they were unmindful or were too afraid to go to court with their expropriations.[35] As Interviewee 17 explained:

They are very incautious and the state takes advantage of this.... In cases where the border of two villages and their lands are adjusted, you have a period of two weeks to hand in an appeal. Not very much time but still you have the possibility. What happens now? The civil servants give the mayor of a Christian village a totally wrong map where the properties are completely shifted to the Muslims, obviously wrong, and they make

---

[29] European Parliament, 2008, p. 8.
[30] See Interview 27.
[31] Aktas & Özmen, 2006.
[32] Interview 19 and Interview 30.
[33] Aktas & Özmen, 2006.
[34] For more information on this topic, see the chapter by Oberkampf elsewhere in this book.
[35] Dalen, 2011.

the mayor sign it. Why do the mayors do so? Because they are afraid and do not dare to contradict. Moreover, very frequently the mayors did not have any information about the lands and they just signed believing that they still had two weeks to hand in an appeal. The civil servants, however, wrote the wrong date on the form – for example, a date from two weeks ago – and the mayor signs his own defeat. People do not watch out for these things. There are several cases where we lost a tremendous amount of lands due to our insidious authorities and the fear or inattentiveness of our own people.[36]

Syriacs who work through the courts have difficulty in claiming their rights, because Kurdish agas are behind many of the suits and have strong levels of influence within the state institutions.[37] Their villages are flooded with trials by the state and their neighbours. In one Syriac village alone (I received copies of the official documents), more than 40 lawsuits are pending. The financial burdens of the lawsuits have left the villagers under a great deal of strain and psychological pressure. In the words of the

European Parliament: "Complaints regarding the seizure of their uninhabited property by both citizens in the region and the land registry authorities have recently reached a worrying level".[38]

5. Preservation orders

It appears as if measures against the Syriacs in Tur Abdin seeking to strip them of their financial and territorial basis for survival are insufficient. Instead, their spiritual foundation is now also under attack through the use of state measures. Faith is of particular importance to the Syriacs, because it has helped them to survive centuries of oppression and persecution.[39] Since the beginning of the last decade, the state started placing preservation orders (Turkish: 'sit alani') on churches and monasteries. If applied, the state must approve any changes, new building constructions or renovations – approval which it never grants. The Council of Europe confirmed this trend in 2011 in its *ECRI Report on Turkey*:

This has meant that even minor maintenance work on buildings owned by non-Muslim foundations could not be carried out without a decision of the Directorate General for Foundations to the effect that they were necessary; the latter reportedly rarely found this to be the case, meaning numerous properties fell into a state of disrepair.[40]

---

[36] Interview 17, 22 September 2010.
[37] See, for example, Interview 30, 21 November 2010, and ABM, 2012.
[38] European Parliament, 2008, p. 8.
[39] Courtois, 2004.
[40] Council of Europe (2011), p. 32

One of the Christian villages in Tur Abdin severely hit by state expropriations of land. (M. Tozman)

In other words, the state wants those ancient witnesses of Christianity to fall into decay – silently and inconspicuously.

The United Nations has been aware of this situation since as early as 2000. A special Rapporteur on freedom of religion and belief, Abdelfattah Amor, presented a report on 25 October 2000:

With respect to places of worship, the authorities have imposed restrictions on the renovation of churches and monasteries in south eastern Turkey (Tur Abdin region), the Rapporteur writes: Yet in many cases this stance in fact seems to represent interference by the authorities, inspired by a nationalism that rejects all minorities, particularly Christians. The report also presents the problem of the confiscation of places of worship declared 'unused' by the General Director of Foundations, which sometimes will convert them into mosques.[41]

In 2012, this judgment was repeated by the current UN Rapporteur Heiner Bielefeldt, who also noted that a structural and systemic impediment of minorities' religious life in Turkey.[42]

In my interviews, I heard from people in at least nine villages with an intact Syriac community who reported that their places of worship had been placed under preservation order.[43] In villages such as Kerburan and Bote (Turkish names: Dargecit and Bardakci) which no longer have any Syriac residents, churches without a functioning legal foundation to administer them have been confiscated by the state treasury.[44] As a result, some of the oldest churches in the Tur Abdin region have already been lost to the state.[45]

When I asked Interviewee 26 (26 October 2010) if the measures might not represent an honest effort to preserve the buildings, he replied:

You've got to be kidding! The state does not care about preservation, it wants our buildings to fall into decay and to crumble. The state thinks that the churches and monasteries are part of Christianity and that after Islam came to take over this allegedly outdated faith, the Christians' places of worship, consequently, have to be destroyed, too.

---

[41] Yacoub, 2006, p. 44.
[42] Bielefeldt, 2012.
[43] See, for example, Interview 3, Interview 9, Interview 12, Interview 13, Interview 21, Interview 23 and Interview 27
[44] Toktas and Özmen, 2006. For an incomplete list of the preservation orders placed on Christian places of worship in Tur Abdin (in this case under the administration of the Mardin Culture and Tourism Directorate), see: www.mardinkulturturizm.gov.tr/belge/1-60907/kiliseler---manastirlar.html.
[45] See Interview 9, Interview 26 and Interview 17.

Monastery of Mor Augin from below; received a preservation order by the state, too. (M. Tozman)

It would be our money we would be spending, so what does the state want? If they got experts to help us, send them, they are welcome! Or send us an official to observe what we are doing but give us the permission to do something!

Along with the Mor Gabriel monastery, another one of the monasteries was also running the risk of being partly destroyed by the state authorities, ostensibly because new buildings had been built without permission.

Just recently we received an order that we have to tear down the last rooms we have built and the water depot. The case is with the judge now but we will most likely lose it anyway. Our advocates know what is possible in this respect but if necessary we will go to Europe with this case. It is not that we have any other choice. Turkey is everything here. The judges, the advocates, the laws; they are all made by Turks and for Turks and thus not for, but against us Christians.

We only want to build our monastery in a way that fits our needs. Nothing more, nothing less. What does the state want from us? Do we ask for money? No! Do we bother them with anything in general? No! What is all this about? Do they want to chase us away from

Cadastral Registration of Lands and Preservation Orders in Turkey's South-East

our indigenous lands? What is the message behind all this? "You build up what you like and we destroy not just your work but also your hope" – is this their message?

The state has not changed a bit. We had a bit of hope for a short period of time but they killed the last bit of that until now, too.[46]

The church of the Holy Virgin Mary in Beth Zabday (Idil) has faced similar issues to those dogging the Mon Gabriel monastery. Following the renovation of the main church and the parish hall, the state threatened to demolish both. As a member of the community said:

If we want to renovate or re-build a church or a building, the authorities work against us and the churches are threatened to be expropriated or demolished. Instead of thanking us for paying for the renovation of our ancient buildings ourselves, the state threatens to expropriate or demolish them[47]

The preservation orders, too, appear to be only directed against Christians. When I asked interviewee 17 (22 September 2010) if mosques faced the same problems, he responded:

No, why should they? This is simply subtle discrimination and suppression. 100 years ago there were barely any Muslims here [i.e. Tur Abdin], let alone mosques. As a result there is not a mosque anywhere in the region older than 100 years, and hence they use all of these preservation orders only against our churches. The older mosques in Tur Abdin were all churches several decades ago; they simply took them from us and converted them into mosques.

Yet, the worst case I heard of was from interviewee 27. After placing a preservation order on their church, the government declared their *entire village* an archaeological site, which means that they are no longer permitted to make even the most mundane renovations to even their own backyards without approval from the government. Nor can they work through the courts, because archaeological sites appear to be a special case. "They just completely sacked us", he concluded correctly.[48]

This type of discrimination seems to be the general trend in the Tur Abdin region.[49] Although several churches have been renovated in recent years, those villages appear to have simply renovated their churches without informing the state in advance. In many instances preservation orders were placed on the churches

---

[46] Interview 22, 7 October 2010.
[47] ABM, 2012.
[48] Interview 27, 2 November 2010.
[49] See Öhring, 2008–2011, and Yacoub, 2006.

Apse of the church of the Holy Virgin of Hah; the church has been put under preservation order. (M. Tozman)

only after renovation was completed.[50] Again, the Mor Gabriel monastery is also suffering as a result of these measures. The entire monastery and its surrounding buildings have also been placed under such a preservation order. Although parts of the monastery require urgent repair, they have not yet been granted permission to do so, and the state has thus far not demonstrated a willingness to help.

6. Conclusion

In this chapter, I have attempted to shed light on two of the main problems facing the Syriacs in southeast Anatolia today. One could argue that discrimination has decreased in the region in recent years as compared to the 1980s and 1990s. But when looking more closely at their situation, it becomes apparent that only the manner in which the state and the environment discriminates against them has changed, and thus not the fact that severe discrimination *still persists.*

Ironically the cadastral registration demanded by the European Union and financed by the World Bank has become a useful tool to take Syriac land silently and inconspicuously. As many of my interviewees reported, even when they successfully defend their right in court, others will claim their lands again; a ploy that can be repeated until the 10 year deadline to raise objections has expired. The consequences have been disastrous. With the state or Kurdish neighbours backed by their powerful agas, the Syriac minority feels vulnerable and exposed to these attacks that are intended to send the clear message that there is no room left for them in their indigenous lands.

If the cadastral registration disposes of the territorial and financial basis for the survival of the Syriacs in Tur Abdin, the preservation orders hit another, even more sensitive foundation of this people: their faith. As we have seen, their faith and their holy places have traditionally been a haven for Syriacs for surviving discrimination and suppression. To steal them from their Syriac owners, and consequently to allow them to fall into decay, is likely the worst measure the state could take against this minority and has a huge psychological impact on both those Syriacs still living in Tur Abdin and those living in the Diaspora.

Though several national parliaments and the EU are aware of these developments, these bodies have not placed these issues high enough on their agendas. Mor Gabriel has become their focus of attention and at times it seems to be an excuse not to show more commitment to the other daily hardships of the Syriacs in Turkey. Yet, if these problems are not solved soon, the Syriacs of Tur Abdin will lose both their lands and their places of worship. This would not only be a slap in

---

[50] Interview 8 and Interview 11.

the face to anyone who believes in the progress of Turkey's minority rights regime under the AKP government, it would likely also put an end to the millennia-old existence of the Syriacs in Tur Abdin.

References

Aktas, S., & Özmen, S., Open letter to the chair of the human rights commission of the Turkish Great National Assembly Mehmet Elkatmis: *Ersuchen um Schutz für die syrischen Christen und für ihr kulturelles Erbe in der Türkei*, (2006). Retrieved on 21 May 12 from: http://huyodo.com/index.php?p=cheats&action=displaycheat&system=56&area=1&cheatid=466.

Aramese Beweging voor Mensenrechten (ABM), (2012). *Discriminatie en onteigening van het Aramese erfgoed ten gevolge van de nieuwe Kadasterregistratie.*

Auswärtiges Amt, *Türkei: Reise- und Sicherheitshinweise*, (2011). Retrieved 10 May 2012 from: http://www.auswaertiges-amt.de/DE/Laenderinformationen/00-SiHi/TuerkeiSicherheit.html?nn=338384#doc336356bodyText1.

Baskin, O. "Reconciled by Mor Gabriel", (2012).

Bielefeldt, H., *Festvortrag: Gleichberechtigung von Minderheiten als Forderung der Religionsfreiheit – Überlegungen und Beobachtungen mit Blick im Blick auf Türkei und Nordirak* (2012). Retrieved on 21 May 2012 from: http://nordirak-turabdin.de/2012/03/01/festvortrag-von-prof-dr-heiner-bielefeldt-erlangen/.

Bilge, Y., *1600 Yillik Gelenek Mor Gabriel Manastiri*, (2011) Istanbul: Gerceğe Dogru Katiplari.

Brown, J., "The Turkish Imbroglio: Its Kurds", in *Annals of the American Academy of Political and Social Sciences 541*, (1995) pp. 116–129.

Bruinessen, M. van, "Turkey's Death Squads", in *Middle East Report, 199* (2), (1996) pp. 20–23.

Council of Europe, *European Commission against Racism and Intolerance* [ECRI]*Report on Turkey*, (2011) Strasbourg: Directorate General of Human Rights and Legal Affairs.

Council of Europe, Resolution 1704, (2011). Retrieved from: www.assembly.coe.int/Mainf.asp?link=/Documents/AdoptedText/ta10/ERES1704.htm.

Courtois, S. de, *The forgotten Genocide: Eastern Christians, The Last Arameans*, (2004) New Jersey: Gorgias Press LLC.

Dalen, P. Van, "Reisverslag Turkije, deel 2", (2011). Retrieved on 21 May 2012 from www.petervandalen.eu/k/n23997/news/view/499072/359195/Reisverslag-Turkije-deel-2-Kernwaarden-van-het-christelijk-geloof-zijn-liefde-en-respect.html.

Davutoglu, A. *Die Türkei wird immer eure Heimat bleiben*, 2011. Retrieved on 21 May 2012 from: www.deutsch-tuerkische-nachrichten.de/2011/12/11391/%E2%80%9Edie-tuerkei-wird-immer-eure-heimat-bleiben%E2%80%9C/.

Demir, O., & Coruhlu, Y.E., "Determining the property ownership on cadastral works in Turkey", in *Land Use Policy, 26*, (2008), pp. 112–120.

Deutscher Bundestag, *Antrag: Fortbestand des Klosters Mor Gabriel sicherstellen,* (2012) Berlin: 17/9185.
European Parliament, *Religious Freedom in Turkey: Situation of Religious Minorities* (2008), Brussels.
Frankfurter Allgemeine Zeitung (FAZ), *Verbrecherische Assimilation?,* (2008). Retrieved 30 January 2010 from: www.faz.net/s/Rub594835B672714A1DB1A121534F010EE1/Doc~ED8E3047E719842E19BF98F7584EEA8D5~ATpl~Ecommon~Scontent.html.
Gillham, B., *Research Interviewing: The Range of Techniques,* (2005) Maidenhead: Open University Press.
Icduygu, A., & Soner, A., "Turkish Minority Rights Regime: Between Difference and Equality" in *Middle Eastern Studies, 42* (3) (2006), pp. 447–468.
Jacobi, T., *Political Violence, the 'War on Terror' and the Turkish State*, (2004) University of Manchester: Institute for Development Policy and Management.
Jung, D. & Piccoli, W., *Turkey at the Crossroads. Ottoman Legacies and a greater Middle East,* (2001) London: Palgrave.
Kaya, N., *Forgotten or Assimilated? Minorities in the Education System of Turkey*, (2009) Minority Rights Group International.
Kurban, D., *A Quest for Equality. Minorities in Turkey*, (2007) Minority Rights Group International.
Öhring, O., "Turkey: Turkish nationalism, Ergenekon and denial of religious freedom", (2008) Oslo: Forum 18.
Öhring, O., "Turkey: No progress on religious property in 2009", (2009) Oslo: Forum 18.
Öhring, O., "Turkey: Hopes for 2009 disappointed", (2009) Oslo: Forum 18.
Öhring, O., "Turkey: Syrian Orthodox land – All people are equal, but some are less equal than others?", (2010) Oslo: Forum 18.
Öhring, O., & Ceyhan, G. "Turkey: Religious freedom survey, November 2009", (2009) Oslo: Forum 18.
Silverman, D. (Ed.), *Qualitative Research. Theory, Method and Practice*, (2002) London: SAGE Publications.
Simoneschi-Cortesi, C., Parliamentary Question to the Swiss Parliament. Heavy Discrimination against the Aramean (Syriac) Minority, (2011) Bern: 11.5410.
Smith, T.W., "Civic Nationalism and Ethnocultural justice in Turkey" in *Human Rights Quarterly, 27,* (2005), pp. 436–470.
Syriac Universal Alliance, 2010 Tur-Abdin Report: The Aramean Question in South East Turkey. Report to the United Nations, Committee on Economic, Social and Cultural Rights. 46th Session, 2011.
Thomsen, J., *The Assyrians/Syriacs of Turkey. A forgotten people*, (2007) Malmö University: School of International Migration and Ethnic Relations.
Tozman, M., *Turkiye Türklerendir. Syrian Orthodox Arameans in southeast Anatolia*, (2011) Maastricht: Maastricht University.
Tweede Kamer der Staten-Generaal, *Initiatiefnota van het lid Omtzigt over de zorg-*

wekkende situatie van het Mor Gabriel klooster en de Aramees Sprekende Christenen in Turkije – De Süryoye, (2012) The Hague: 33 195.

World Bank, "Turkey Land Registration and Cadastre Modernization", (2010). Retrieved 29 April 2012 from: web.worldbank.org/external/projects/main?Projectid= P106284&theSitePK=40941&piPK=73230&pagePK=64283627&menuPK=228424.

Yacoub, J., "Minorities and Religions in Europe. Case Study: The Assyro-Chaldeans of Turkey", in *European Yearbook of Minority Issues, 4* (5), (2006) pp. 29–49.

Yonan, G., *Ein Vergessener Holocaust. Die Vernichtung der christlichen Assyrer in der Türkei*, (2006) Göttingen: Pogrom.

The Role of Religious Freedom in the Context of the Accession Negotiations between the European Union and Turkey – The Example of the Arameans

By Renate Sommer

Dr. Renate Sommer is Member of the European Parliament for the Christian Democrats and Member of the Delegation to the EU-Turkey Joint Parliamentary Committee. In this context she focuses inter alia on civil and human rights and the fight against discrimination in Turkey.

1. Introduction

Religious freedom is the emblem of a democratic society; it should be seen as a source of social strength and stability.

Madeleine Albright,
Former United States Deputy of State[1]

The intrinsic link between democracy and the endorsement of religious freedom is not only important in American politics, but constitutes the cornerstone of European values and policies. Looking back at a violent history of religious wars, the principle of protection of ethnic and religious minorities has become a key aspect in European internal and external policies. Among the most important elements in the attempt to promote freedom and democracy are the accession negotiations with potential candidate countries within the context of the EU neighbourhood policy. By granting Turkey candidate status, the EU has made clear that Europe does not consider itself to be a 'Christian Club' and is willing to promote these values even beyond European borders. However, economic and political assistance is linked to strict criteria, one of which is the respect for religious freedom. Unfortunately, despite of lengthy discussions, the European Commission's annual reports on the progress made on the Copenhagen Criteria reveals only limited progress on the situation of religious minorities in Turkey. The remaining discriminations religious minorities suffer from become particularly evident when analysing the situation of the indigenous Aramean people who live mainly in the South East of Turkey. Given the lack of progress, the EU must ask itself whether the instruments provided for in the negotiation framework are sufficient and how we can continue

---

[1] Albright, 2011.

to influence the Republic of Turkey to enable the country to become the envisaged role model as a democratic, pluralistic and yet Muslim democracy.

2. Role of religious freedom in EU and EU politics

Although the EU has no spoken 'common policy approach' on religious freedom, and EU member states maintain sovereignty to enact legislation regarding churches and religious associations, religious freedom is one of the basic values in the European Union.[2] The claim that "the fundamental values that hold Europe together were essentially achieved in the face of what used to be the lack of religious freedom and its devastating consequences"[3] reflects how long and difficult the path was to achieve this basic freedom. Today, religious freedom is enshrined both in primary and secondary law of the European Union. The Lisbon Treaty made the Charter on Fundamental Rights – which stipulates the freedom of thought, conscience and religion in Article 10 – legally binding. Furthermore, religious freedom is enshrined in Article 9 of the European Convention on Human Rights (ECHR), Article 18 of the International Covenant on Civil and Political Rights (ICCPR) and in Article 18 of the Universal Declaration of Human Rights (UDHR)[4], all of which have been ratified by the EU member states. In secondary law, the European Union has strengthened the concept of religious freedom by means of directives aiming at the elimination of discrimination. The Employment Equality Directive, for example, prohibits discrimination, harassment, instructions to discriminate and victimization on grounds of religion and belief[5]. While the implementation of these directives remains in the hands of national governments, the decisions are always being scrutinized by the European Court of Human Rights. In an important decision, the Court clarified that "freedom of thought, conscience and religion is one of the foundations of a democratic society",[6] and has repeatedly protected this concept by overruling national decisions.[7]

Of course, the concept of religious freedom is a dynamic one, and one that requires continuous reassessment. The differences in interpretation of the relationship between the individual, religious communities and the state result from our national history and it is not the objective of the EU to overcome this. Moreover, the increasing migration from Arab and African countries into the European

---

[2] Carrera & Parkin, 2010, p. 2.
[3] Schirmacher, 2010, p. 1.
[4] CDU, 2011, p. 1.
[5] Carrera & Parkin, 2010, p. 9.
[6] Schirmacher, 2010, p. 1.
[7] De Wall, 2004, p. 11.

Union has raised questions with regard to the conflict between religious freedom and other basic rights. While the practice of female circumcision in some religious communities is widely rejected as inhuman by EU citizens, the debates on the burqa ban in some countries and the responses to religious cartoons have drawn attention to the differing approaches to interpreting religious freedom. Nevertheless, the principle of religious freedom itself is uncontested and the EU has even managed to advance this principle in areas in which the treaties do not expressly recognise a commission to enact legislation. This soft power approach utilising support and incentives to guide national policies plays a prominent role in EU policy towards candidate countries.[8] As William Hale has described, "As the European Union's program for enlargement into Eastern Europe got off the ground, respect for human rights was made a sine qua non for candidate countries".[9] The Copenhagen Criteria adopted in June 1993 name the respect for and protection of minorities, such as religious communities, as prerequisites for EU membership. This moral norm imposes strict rules that are difficult to comply with. However, the need for "a total transformation of the domestic landscape"[10] in candidate countries has made it abundantly clear that accession to the EU is not merely a gateway to an Economic Union that grants financial support. Rather, joining the EU is a long-term mission in which each and every citizen must commit himself or herself to the fundamental common values – a concept that has yet to be grasped by the Turkish government and Turkish society.

3. Situation of religious minorities in Turkey

The situation of religious minorities in Turkey is dire, and has only worsened rather than improved within the recent century. Following the horrific genocide during the First World War, in which approximately 1.5 million Armenians were murdered, hopes were high when Ataturk came to power. Having founded the modern Turkish nation on the principle of laicism, many religious groups hoped for a clear separation between religion and the private sphere. Unfortunately, the opposite was the case. Although the Treaty of Lausanne grants special legal minority status to 'non-Muslim minorities' and even the Turkish Constitution enshrines freedom of belief, these principles were invalidated by discriminatory laws and practices, such as an extra wealth tax for religious minorities imposed in 1942. The reasons were twofold. On the one hand, the definition of the 'Turkish' nation

---

[8] Carrera & Parkin, 2010, p. 1.
[9] Hale, 2003, p. 108.
[10] Toktas & Bülent, 2010, p. 717.

that served as the foundation for the modern state was always equated with a 'Muslim' nation, denying rights to non-Muslim communities. At the same time, the deep fear that greater religious freedom could result in Islamic fundamentalism led to a situation in which no religious authority could exist independent of the state.[11] Because the state-led religious authority accepted only the Sunni interpretation of Islam, even Muslim minorities in Turkey face major impediments with regard to the exercise of their belief.

Singing in a hymn book (Fenqitho) during church service. (S. de Courtois)

Due to the discriminatory regime that resulted from this "conspiracy mentality",[12] the number of religious minorities of Christian and Jewish decent has diminished significantly. Today, less than 1 % of the Turkish population is Christian or Jewish, constituting only 92,000 citizens of Armenian Orthodox, Greek Orthodox or Jewish belief. The number of Syriacs – who are not even granted religious minority status under the Treaty of Lausanne – has decreased from 250,000 to approximately 25,000 people.[13]

---

[11] Ibid, p. 715.
[12] Karaosmanoglu, 2010, p. 198.
[13] Updegraff, 2009.

In spite of demands by the United Nations, the United States and the European Union, the steps taken by the Turkish government have been nothing more than "a glossing of minority rights on paper".[14] A number of recent reports point out how Turkey continues to intervene in the internal governance and education of religious communities. The prohibition of the training of priests by non-Turkish citizens accompanied by the closing of several seminaries makes it practically impossible to train young priests. Many congregations continue to struggle with unlawful expropriations and delays in court cases regarding these expropriations.[15] While citizens now have the option to leave the religious affiliation blank on the official Turkish identification card, those who choose this option face the same harassment by state officials and policemen as individuals who clearly indicate their minority status. Non-Muslim communities continue to face problems in establishing places of worship.[16] In most regions, religious instruction on Islam remains compulsory and, even those students who are granted exemptions often still face discrimination in the form of lower marks.[17] To date, Turkey has failed to sign, ratify and comply with relevant international conventions.[18] The list of legal hurdles is nearly endless. The major issue, however, is the fact that neither the 26 constitutional amendments brought forward by the current Turkish government[19] nor the multiple amendments to the law on foundations have managed to get to the core issue: the lack of a legal status for religions minorities in Turkey.

To date, religious minorities and churches are considered foundations, whose rights are strictly regulated by the General Directorate for Foundations. Although some improvements have been permitted, such as the latest adoption in August 2011 broadening the scope of the restoration of property rights[20], a study by TESEV nevertheless describes the legislation regarding non-Muslim foundations as "complete chaos".[21] The bureaucratic obstacles imposed on non Muslim foundations when trying to register their property are cumbersome. Consequently, only 29 % of the requests filed with the DGF have been accepted.[22] In its 2010 legal evaluation of the law on foundations, the Venice Commission also reached the same conclusion: that denial to grant religious communities legal personality con-

---

[14] Toktas & Bülent, 2010, p. 711.
[15] US Department of State, 2011, p. 10.
[16] For more information on this topic, see Pastoor's article in this book.
[17] European Commission, 2011, p. 29–31.
[18] Syriac Universal Alliance, 2011, p. 14.
[19] Ibid, p. 15.
[20] European Commission, "Progress Report on Turkey 2011", (12 October 2011), p. 29–31.
[21] Kurban & Hatemi, 2009, p. 34.
[22] Kurban & Hatemi, 2009, p. 26.

siderably affects their access to court and property rights. Therefore, the Turkish system "amounts to an interference with the rights of these communities under Article 9 in conjunction with Article 11 ECHR".[23] It remains to be seen whether the new Constitution drafting process[24] following recent elections will replace the restricting manifestations with these Articles.[25]

Unfortunately, even the correction on paper will not bring about immediate freedom of religion. "The discriminatory legal regime for non-Muslims encouraged and legitimized existing prejudice in the collective subconscious".[26] This fact is reflected in the growing amount of misinformative and contemptuous media coverage that stirs social harassment and violence. No government programmes are in place that address the prejudice towards religious minorities in Turkish society. On the contrary: the Turkish government further ignites these prejudices through its actions and discriminatory language. The growing Anti-Semitism in Turkish society and the Turkish media is, to a large extent, the result of the bellicose rhetoric of Prime Minister Erdogan following the unfortunate raid by the Israeli military on a Turkish-based flotilla attempting to breach the Gaza blockade. At the same time, the Turkish government is being criticised for its halfhearted investigation of the killing of Hrant Dink and the three Protestant Christians in Malatya in April 2007. European Parliament rapporteur on Turkey Ria Oomen-Ruijten voiced sharp criticism of the negligence on the part of the competent authorities to address the alleged complicity of state officials.[27]

Overall, the steps undertaken by the ruling AK Party in recent years indicate a trend towards subtle Islamisation. Proposals such as the criminalisation of adultery, an increase in the age limit for children in Quran schools, bans on alcohol and the establishment of separate beaches and parks for women and men are just some examples of this trend. For Prime Minister Erdogan, the desire for an Islamic Turkey might mean that, in the short run, he will be forced to allow for a slight opening towards religious freedom. Ironically, when lifting the headscarf ban in public buildings, he availed himself of the rather liberal argument of wanting to preserve individual basic rights, only to penetrate the secularist concrete of the Ataturk regime.

The trend has left religious minorities caught between a rock and a hard place – misinterpreted secularism on the one hand, and Islamisation on the other.

---

[23] European Commission for Democracy through Law (Venice Commission), 2010, p. 16.
[24] For more information on this topic, see Onder's article in this book.
[25] Yildrim, 2011.
[26] Kurban, 2009, p. 19.
[27] Oomen-Ruijten, 2012.

Should Islamisation prevail, many fear that this will result in even greater discrimination against non-Muslim communities both in the private and public spheres.

4. The situation of Syriacs in Turkey

The historical significance of the Syriac population both for Turkey and 'the West' has been remarkable. The Arameans are the indigenous people of Mesopotamia, which is widely considered to be the cradle of civilization where the first advancements were made in astronomy and mathematics. It is also the Aramean history that proves that Christianity belongs to Turkey. It was in the Turkish city of Antakya that Jesus' devotees for the first time referred to themselves as Christians. Anatolia was the heart of the Christian Byzantine Empire and millions of Christians and other religious minorities lived in the Ottoman Empire. In the opinion of numerous experts, Arameans are "one of the points of departure for us in the West".[28]

Considering this importance, the oppression and discrimination that Syriacs in Turkey have suffered is a disgrace. Following the violence that unfolded after World War I, thousands of Syriacs living in Turkey emigrated to other countries. Their respite was evanescent. The majority of Syriacs have always lived in the south eastern area of Turkey and, as the level of violence between the Turkish military and the Kurdish minority increased, the Syriacs found themselves in the firing line.[29] As a result of the dire security situation, another 45,000 Syriacs migrated from Turkey between 1960 and 2000.[30] In total, the number of Syriacs living in Turkish territory dwindled from 250,000 under Ataturk to just 25,000 today. Most of the migrants forfeited their Turkish citizenship, thus making a return difficult.

In addition to the concrete threats to their security, the Arameans have always faced discrimination that had its roots in the Treaty of Lausanne. Although the Treaty grants special legal minority status to "non-Muslim minorities", the Turkish government only extended the definition of minority to Armenians, Greeks and Jews. As a consequence, Arameans were not permitted to establish schools to train their own clergy. The clergy from other countries had difficulties obtaining residence or work permits, thus jeopardizing the survival of the entire community. Communities who did not have enough clergy and personal to maintain activities were confiscated and declared unused by the General Directory of Foundations

---

[28] Syriac Universal Alliance, 2011, p. 5.
[29] For more information on this topic, see Makko's article in this book.
[30] Samur, 2009, p. 329.

(GDF). Returning Syriacs who lost or gave up their nationality are also unable to re-register their properties.[31] Today, the remaining 25,000 Syriacs have only 19 foundations, all of which face further expropriations.[32] The case of the Mor Gabriel monastery, considered by Syriacs to be the second Jerusalem,[33] is the most well-known example of the struggle with unlawful expropriations. With the five trials based on "ludicrous complaints"[34] currently ongoing, the monastery faces losing up to 1,000,000 square metres of its property.[35] Although the Turkish government makes constant reference to judicial independence, it is inarguable that the lawsuits could only have been filed with the help of the Turkish government. The latest delay to the ongoing lawsuit against the chairman of the foundation of Mor Gabriel for his alleged illegal seizure of land is yet another evidence of the delaying tactics being employed by the Turkish government.

Any positive signal, such as the authorisation of church services or the first appointment of a Syriac member to the Turkish Parliament[36] are soon overshadowed by discriminatory actions. The accusation of treason, as quoted in Turkish school books used last year, is not only an unacceptable offence, but also perverts historic facts. In the entire history of Turkey, "Aramean Christians did not ask for secession, did not ally themselves with any Anti-Ottoman (and later Anti-Turkish) force, and did not harm in any sense either the Empire or the Republic".[37]

The only thing that can reverse this trend of discrimination targeting Syriacs in Turkey is a change of perception among Turkish citizens. A major study has shown that return migration will be very important to achieve this goal, as returning Syriacs will not only restore buildings and entire villages, but will also "contribute to the Europeanisation process in terms of normative change and citizenship education".[38] However, the Syriac Community requires the strong support of the European Union to spark this return migration. The ups and downs in the return statistics are a good indicator of Turkish policies. Considering the fact that Syriacs point to infrastructural problems and denial of religious freedom as major obstacles to their return,[39] it is up to the European Commission to make the fight for religious freedom the priority.

---

[31] US Department of State, 2011, p. 8.
[32] Vingas, 2011, p. 3.
[33] Updegraff, 2009, p. 2.
[34] Megalommatis, 2011, p. 3.
[35] Syriac Universal Alliance, 2011, p. 8.
[36] Dora, 2011.
[37] Megalommatis, 2011, p. 1.
[38] Samur, 2009, p. 337.
[39] Samur, 2009, p. 335.

The Patriarch of the Syrian Orthodox church Ignatius Afrem I in the centre (1933–1957) and bishop Iavanis Afrem Bilgic of Tur Abdin (1952–1982) who had his Sea in the Mor Gabriel monastery (front row, first right) together with other bishops, monks and priests. (From the book by Y. Bilge)

5. EU policy towards Turkey and the role of religious freedom in the accession negotiations

Although Turkey applied for membership in the European Union in 1987, it took 12 years until the country became a candidate. EU member states were divided in their opinion on accession negotiations. While supporters hoped that Turkey's military strength and geopolitical role could also increase the power and profile of the EU in the world, opponents envisaging a political union raised concerns early on about the EU's absorption capacity. What united both camps and eventually led to the acceptance of Turkey as a candidate country was the belief that the negotiation process as such would enhance alignment with European democratic standards. With regard to the fundamental value of religious freedom, hopes were high that Turkey could become a role model for modern Islam.

Due to the remaining scepticism, the candidate status was granted under very strict conditions. In the negotiating framework of 2005, the member states emphasized that "the pace will depend on Turkey's progress" and that the negotiations are an "open-ended process". It further stipulates the "zero tolerance policy" in the fight against ill-treatment relating to freedom of religion.[40] As with other countries before, the EU Commission announced that it would apply very strict standards on Turkey and would closely monitor and comment upon the progress made, particularly on the Copenhagen Criteria. This control mechanism is complemented by annual reports and statements from the European Parliament and the Council commenting on the findings. In addition, the Joint Parliamentary Committee (JPC), which brings together parliamentarians from the Grand National Assembly of Turkey and of the European Parliament, discussed the problems raised in multiple meetings.

Due to the lack of progress with regard to the rights of religious minorities in Turkey, the EU changed its strategy when the new AK Party came into power in 2002. Rather than insisting specifically on solving the Kurdish problem, the EU addressed the need for a wide-range of improvements for all minorities.[41] Turkey, however, failed to fulfil the demands. As a result the reports increase in length every year until finally "the assessment of minorities, cultural rights, and religious freedom occupies more space in the reports".[42] Seeing the lack of progress, the Council renewed the priorities and conditions in its decision of 2008,[43] making the freedom of religion a top priority among the short-term objectives.

The mere number of amendments to the annual reports in European Parliament and heated debates during JPC meetings show the level of emotion that accompanies the topic of religious freedom and that underscores its pivotal role in the negotiations. We as parliamentarians are in personal contact with numerous representatives of the Diasporas of displaced religious minorities and have heard heartbreaking stories. Given their importance for Christianity in Europe, the destiny of the indigenous Syriac community was always of importance to us. In the latest resolutions on the Commission progress reports, we specifically criticise the problems of the property ownership encountered by Syriacs and the arbitrary court cases against the monastery of Mor Gabriel. Numerous MEPs have tabled written questions asking the Commission to clarify what actions are being undertaken to protect the rights of Arameans in Turkey. My Christian Democratic Group of the European Peoples Party has even established a Working Group on Interreligious Dialogue that has delved into the situation of religious minorities in

---

[40] European Council, 2005.
[41] Yilmaz, 2011, p. 9.
[42] Toktas & Bülent, 2010, p. 707.
[43] Council Decision of 18 February 2008.

Turkey on several occasions. Even the rather 'sober' Commission representatives have grown disillusioned by the lack of progress. Over the past three years, the reports have made specific reference to the problems facing Turkish Arameans. The latest progress report points out that "Syriacs can provide only informal training (of clergy), outside any officials established schools", and that the Syriac community "continued to face difficulties with property and land registration". The Commission has repeatedly dedicated several paragraphs criticising the proceedings targeting monastery Mor Gabriel.[44] Among EU member states, the lack of progress on religious freedom has prompted even original advocates of Turkish accession to the EU to revoke their support. German and France have even voiced their preference for a "privileged partnership".

6. Conclusions – Support for religious freedom in Turkey in light of the "Arab Spring"

Having outlined the fierce criticism voiced by all European institutions and member states on the limitations of the rights of religious minorities in Turkey, the question must be raised as to whether the current approach by the EU can be maintained. The annual progress report repeatedly reads like the same old story. Consequently, it does not come as a surprise that organisations such as the Open Doors Institute or the Pew Forum, which monitor religious freedom in the world, have signalled a deterioration in the situation and have assigned Turkey ranks lower than those of just a few years ago.[45] In allowing this to happen, the European Commission and the EU member states betray the principle of "Unity in Diversity" and contradict their own contractual basis. The negotiation framework from 2005 clearly states that:

[I]n the case of a serious and persistent breach in Turkey of the principles of liberty, democracy, respect for human rights and fundamental freedoms … the Commission will … recommend the suspension of negotiations and propose the conditions for eventual resumption.[46]

If the EU blocks negotiations on eight chapters due to Turkey's reluctance to sign the Ankara Protocol, but nevertheless treats the violation of the fundamental freedom of religion as a trivial offence, the threat implied in this framework becomes void and the Turkish government will continue to mock the EU.

---

[44] European Commission, 2011, pp. 29–31.
[45] Open Doors Institute, 2011; for more information, see Pastoor's article in this book.
[46] European Council, 2005.

Tomb of Mor Yaqub from Nisibis. (S. de Courtois)

Aside from the people in Turkey suffering from the ongoing discrimination, this approach could also have other dangerous consequences. It could send the wrong message to other candidate countries. Recent riots at the border between Kosovo and Serbia have shown how fragile the peace in that former ethnic and religious melting pot is. Only the perspective on serious sanctions in response to the breach of social and political rights has kept the countries in this region on track.

Even more important is the role of a future democratic Turkey that respects the rights of minorities for the developments in the Middle East after the Arab Spring. Arameans in particular are not only indigenous to Turkey, but also to Lebanon, Iraq, Jordan and Syria. As a result of the war in Iraq, Arameans in the country came under attack. If the revolutionary developments in countries such as Syria result not in greater democracy but in Islamisation, even more Arameans will be displaced. Despite the democratic deficiencies in Turkey described in this article, the Turkish model of political Islam in a secular and democratic setting is still considered to be a role model that "can have significant impact in the Arab world".[47] And despite the remaining deficiencies, experts claim that "EU membership has

---

[47] Ülgen, 2001, pp. 1 and 5.

been a great incentive for structural reforms in Turkey" and that "there would be no Turkish model to emulate without this external anchor".[48] If we do not want to lose this anchor by permitting Turkey to turn into an Islamist society, greater weight must be given to the respect of religious freedom in the negotiations – even if this means that we must block additional negotiation chapters or cut financial assistance. We owe this credibility not only to the Arameans and other religious minorities in Turkey, but to our own cultural heritage.

References

Albright, M., Forum Religionsfreiheit Europa. Retrieved on 16 December 2012 from: www.foref.info/zitate/.
Carrera, S., & Parkin, J., "The Place of Religion in European Union Law and Policy: Competing Approaches and Actors inside the European Commission", in *RELIGARE Working Document No.1*, (September 2010).
Christian Democratic Union (CDU), "Implementing Religious Freedom Worldwide", Resolution by the CDU Federal Committee on Development Cooperation and Human Rights of 19 April 2011.
Council Decision of 18 February 2008 on the principles, priorities and conditions contained in the Accession Partnership with the Republic of Turkey and repealing Decision 2006/35/EC (26 February 2008).
De Wall, H., "Die Religionen in der Verfassung der Europäischen Union".
Dora, E., "Syriacs send their first deputy to Parliament", in *Journal of Turkish Weekly*, 13 June 2011.
European Commission, Progress Report on Turkey 2011, (12 October 2011).
European Commission for Democracy through Law (Venice Commission), "Opinion on the legal status of religious communities in Turkey and the right of the orthodox patriarchate of Istanbul to use the adjective Ècumenical", adopted by the Venice Commission at its 82nd Plenary Session in Venice, (13 March 2010).
European Council, Negotiating Framework EU-Turkey, European Council, (3 October 2005). Retrieved from: www.ec.europa.eu/enlargement/pdf/st20002_05_tr_framedoc_en.pdf.
Hale, W., "Human Rights, the European Union and the Turkish Accession Process", in *Turkish Studies*, Volume 4, Issue 1, (March 2003).
Karaosmanoglu, K., "Reimagining Minorities in Turkey: Before and After the AKP", in *Insight Turkey*, Volume 12, No. 2, (2010).
Kurban, D., & Hatemi, K., "The Story of Alien(ation): Real Estate Ownership Problems of Non-Muslim Foundations and Communities in Turkey", *TESEV*, (14 March 2009).

---

[48] Tocci & Taspinar et. al, 2011, p. 13.

Megalommatis, M.S., "Turkey's Ongoing Colonization, the Arameans, the Kurds, the Armenians, Pan-Arabism and Islamism", in *American Chronicle*, (15 December 2011). Retrieved from: www.armericanchronicle.com/article/.

Tocci, N., Taspinar, Ö. et al, "Turkey and the Arab Spring: Implications for Turkish Foreign Policy from a Transatlantic Perspective", in *Mediterranean Paper Series 2011*, (October 2011), published by the German Marshall Fund of the United States.

Oomen-Ruijten, R. (MEP), "Verdict in Hrant Dink murder case is disappointing", Group of the European People's Part (Christian Democrats). Retrieved on 18 January 2012 from: www.eppgroup.eu/press/showpr.asp?prcontroldoctypeid=1&prcontrolid=10903&prcontentid=18303&prcontentlg=en.

Open Doors Institute, "Weltverfolgungsindex 2011", (19 April 2011).

Samur, H., "Turkey's Europeanization Process and the return of the Syriacs", in *Turkish Studies*, Volume 10, Issue 3, (September 2009).

Schirrmacher, T., "Collective list of questions for the public hearing by the German Parliaments Commission for Human Rights and Humanitarian Aid on October 27, 2010 on the topic of 'Freedom of Religion and European Identity'", International Institute for Religious Freedom. Retrieved on 15 January 2012 from: www.thomasschirrmacher.net/wp-content/uploads/2011/08/Schirrmacher-Fragenkatalog-Menschenrechtsausschuss-27102010-zweite-Fassung_English.pdf.

Syriac Universal Alliance, *2011 Turkey Report: Recommendations for promoting and protecting the human rights of Syriac (Aramean Christians)*, (9 March 2011). Retrieved from: www.anca.org/return/pdfs/sua_2011_report.pdf.

Toktas, S. & Bülent, A., "The EU and Minority Rights in Turkey", in *Political Science Quarterly*, Volume 124, Number 4, (October 2010).

Ülgen, S., "From Inspiration to Aspiration, Turkey in the New Middle East", in *The Carnegie Papers*, published by Carnegie Endowment for International Peace, (December 2001).

Updegraff, R., "Mor Gabriel case raises questions about Syriac Minority". Retrieved on 20 January 2012 from: www.turkishpoliticsinaction.com/2009/07/mor-gabriel-case-raises-questions-about.html.

U.S. Department of State, *International Religious Freedom Report: Turkey, July-December 2010*, (13 September 2011).

Vingas, L., "Turkish Minority Foundations Entering a New Stage", in *Journal of Turkish Weekly*, (2 July 2011).

Yildrim, M., "Turkey: The new Constitution drafting process and freedom of religion and belief", in *Forum 18 News Service*, (30 November 2011).

Yilmaz, G., "Is there a puzzle? Compliance with minority rights in Turkey", in *KFG Working Paper Series*, No. 23, (January 2011).

Persecution of Christians in Turkey

A state caught between secular aspiration and Islamic tradition

By Ingrid Fischbach

Ingrid Fischbach is a German MP for the Christian Democrats and vice chair of the parliamentary group CDU/CSU in the German Parliament. On of her core tasks is the position of the Church within the state. She is especially interested in and committed to the Mor Gabriel law cases.[1]

In his speech in Düsseldorf on 27 February 2011 to his compatriots living in Germany, Turkish Prime Minister Recep Tayyip Erdogan stated that everyone has the right to practise his or her faith. Inevitably attention focuses on Turkey. Do Erdogan's words also apply to Turkey itself? What is the position regarding religious freedom in this country that sits astride East and West? How do Christians fare in Turkey? Despite all the question marks, this German perspective on Turkey derives from ties of friendship.

Turkey is based on the secular principle – the strict separation of state and religion. This is its theoretical basis, and officially it is not an Islamic state. Islam as the state religion was abolished in 1928. But the reality is rather different: state and religion are closely linked in Islam, seen by many political and social organisations in Turkey as the force that binds the Turkish nation together.

Article 24 of the Turkish Constitution guarantees freedom of religion. Article 18 of the Universal Declaration of Human Rights, recognised by Turkey when it became a member of the United Nations in 1945, declares freedom of thought, conscience and religion to be an individual right, as does Article 9 of the European Convention on Human Rights, which Turkey ratified in 1954. Article 18 of the UN's International Covenant on Civil and Political Rights, in force in Turkey since 2003, guarantees a statutory right to freedom of thought, conscience and religion. In reality, however, there is no religious freedom in Turkey. And whilst those chiefly affected are non-Muslim minorities – Christians in particular – Muslims too are affected, because Islam is not free in the way we understand religious freedom to be. The conclusions of the EU Commission's 2010 Progress Report on religious freedom in Turkey are sobering: religious instruction in the Islamic

---

[1] Translated by Alison Gaunt in cooperation with the Language Service of the German Bundestag.

faith continues to be mandatory, and training for the Orthodox priesthood, banned in 1971, is still banned.

According to official statistics, more than 95 per cent of the population are Muslim, and roughly 0.2 per cent (about 120 000 people) are Christian. The Christian churches are not recognised in law; they are not allowed to train their priests, own property or operate bank accounts; the building of centres of prayer and worship is subject to strict constraints. Christians encounter daily harassment, bureaucratic obstruction and discrimination. They are unlawfully arrested, and hindered in the practice of their religion – with intimidation and the disruption of religious services. In the south-east of Turkey, the Syriac Orthodox Christians are increasingly oppressed. Media reporting about Christians is flippant in tone, opinion polls reflect a growing hostility towards Christians, and attacks on churches and church workers are on the rise. Physical assaults and killings of Christians in recent years point to increasing violence against this group. In this climate of fear, Christians in Turkey wonder if they will be properly protected by the forces of law and order against frequently threatened attacks on buildings and people's lives.[2]

1. Aramaic Christians and Mor Gabriel

Typical of the acute difficulties facing Christians in Turkey is the situation of the 22,000 or so Aramaic Christians, or Arameans. The Treaty of Lausanne, concluded on 24 July 1923 between Turkey, the UK, France, Italy, Japan, Greece, Romania and the Serb-Croat-Slovene state following the Greco-Turkish war, which Turkey had won, makes provision in Articles 37 to 45 for the protection of minorities, safeguarding the rights of the non-Muslim minorities remaining in Turkey. Articles 40 and 41 expressly state that Turkey will give minorities the right to establish, manage and control their own schools and religious institutions, provide public funds for these institutions and allow cultural freedom and the free practice of their religion. But the Turkish view is that the Aramean minority are not covered by these safeguards – unlike the Armenians, Greeks and Jews. This conflicts with the text, meaning and purpose of the international Treaty of Lausanne, which applies the concept of "non-Muslim minority" without distinction.[3]

The latest events concerning the Syriac Orthodox monastery of Mor Gabriel in the south-eastern Tur Abdin region of Turkey are a particularly blatant example of the reprisals suffered by the Aramaic Christians: In expropriation proceedings against the Mor Gabriel monastery, the Supreme Court in Ankara, in January

---

[2] For more information on this topic, see Pastoor's article in this book.
[3] For more information on the Lausanne Treaty, see Hurst's article in this book.

2011, awarded some 27.6 hectares of land which the monastery had owned for centuries to the state forestry department. In June 2012, the Supreme Court had ruled against the Mor Gabriel monastery and given 24.4 hectares of land to the Treasury. So to date a total of some 52 hectares of land have been seized – a development which is extremely worrying.

Mor Gabriel monastery; main church from the outside. (M. Tozman)

The monastery, founded in A.D. 397, is one of the oldest Christian monasteries in the world. So these expropriations threaten not just the monastery's property rights, but its very existence and the future of the Arameans in Turkey. The monastery of Mor Gabriel with its 1,600-year-long tradition is the spiritual home of the international Aramean Diaspora and symbolic of the difficulties that face Christians in Turkey. This example shows very clearly that the fear of systematic oppression by the state cannot be discounted and that Turkey is very far from allowing true freedom of religion.

2. Geographically and socially divided

What is the cause of this conflict between a secular state, guarantees concerning religious freedom, and the actual reality? One reason might be the various tensions to which Turkey, to the outside observer, appears vulnerable.

Geographically, Turkey is literally divided: straddling the two continents of Asia and Europe as it does, Turkey looks westwards to the modern world, embracing the idea of European integration, but is at the same time mindful of her traditions and the conservative values of Islam, dreaming dreams of latter-day Ottoman imperial power in her foreign policy. The social groups that reflect these two tendencies engender tension within the country: Turkey has to reconcile the influences and ideologies of the educationally sophisticated and pro-European urban elite, where women enjoy considerable decision-making freedom and freedom of movement, with the influences and ideologies of those who support traditional Islam, in which the roles of men and women are conservatively segregated.

Further divisions are caused by tension between the Islamic Justice and Development Party (AKP) and the nationalists. The nationalists seek to discredit Christians, in order to cause difficulties for the ruling AKP *vis à vis* the rest of the world. A mixture of radical nationalism and religious extremism is brought to bear here, seeking to resist any Western 'Christian' influence in Turkey. Christianity is seen as a direct threat and something that divides the nation. Because Islam is undergoing a renaissance in the life of Turkey and its influence is increasing, these tendencies are becoming more pronounced and the link between state and religion is becoming stronger.

3. Role in the EU and for the Arab world

Turkey's aspiration to join the EU also creates tensions: The nationalists oppose it, seeing it as a threat to Turkey's unity and national sovereignty.

All these difficulties are a kind of "tensile test" for the country and may account for the conflict between this secular state, guarantees concerning freedom of religion, and the actual reality.

With a view to possible accession to the EU, Turkey has definitely made a start. The EU's accession talks with Turkey, which after forty years of trying finally started on 3 October 2005, have clearly brought positive developments. But no real improvement is apparent in the legally indefensible position of her Christian communities. Indeed, it is to be feared that Turkey is systematically dragging her feet over the changes demanded by the EU. So much more remains to be done if EU accession on the basis of common values is to be a realistic prospect any time soon. And a fundamental requirement of the EU is that religious freedom should exist not just *de jure* but *de facto*.

Precisely now, in view of current developments in the Arab world, it is hugely important that Turkey should guarantee full religious freedom – to secure peaceful coexistence in mutual respect and tolerance. Turkey's role is an important one, because with a foot in two continents she can be a trailblazer and a model for the countries of the Arab world, placed as she is on the road to becoming a democratic country in which fundamental rights – including the right to freedom of religion – are safeguarded by the state.

What role can Germany play if it wants to take effective action against the persecution of Christians and work to secure religious freedom in Turkey?

4. What Germany should do

Germany must continue its dialogue with Turkey, even though they know that mutual understanding will continue to be difficult, because the two countries apply totally different parameters to their understanding of the relationship between state and religion. This basic premise is a *sine qua non* of any constructive relationship. The necessary dialogue will require an awareness of the other party's sensitivities: Western arrogance, hauteur and an attitude of always knowing what is best would understandably create distaste for the 'Christian club' and make the prospect of joining it undesirable rather than attractive. The way in which dialogue is conducted will decide whether Turkey is willing to keep pursuing her goal of joining the EU and make the efforts needed to achieve it.

On the other hand, however, the dialogue must insist loud and clear on freedom of religion – we must not get used to seeing religious minorities routinely stripped of their rights. Dialogue thus demands commitment, and work to persuade Turkey to espouse the core values of the European Union: unconditional recognition of a democratic constitution based on the rule of law, and legislation that reflects this, respect for human dignity, recognition of the freedoms guaranteed in western societies – particularly freedom of thought and religion – respect for other faiths and the repudiation of force, violence or threats against their adherents.

These ideas were echoed by Pope Benedict XVI during his visit to Turkey in November 2006, when he urged the civil authorities to meet their obligation to guarantee the members of all faiths true freedom and allow them to organise themselves freely. The Pope was anxious to encourage the "small pockets" of Christianity in Turkey, he said, because they faced difficulties and challenges.

Mosaic above the monastery's main church apse from the 6th century. (Mor Gabriel monastery)

Germany's Federal President Christian Wulff, addressing the Turkish parliament in October 2010, did some straight talking of his own: in Germany, he said, Muslims were able to practise their religion with dignity. At the same time we expected 'that Christians in Muslim countries be given the same rights to practise their beliefs in public, to educate new religious leaders and to build churches'. Christianity, he said, unquestionably belonged to Turkey.

In the light of the difficulties being experienced by the Arameans, the Chairman of the German Bishops' Conference, Archbishop Robert Zollitsch, and the Chairman of the Council of the Evangelical Church in Germany, Provost Nikolaus Schneider, voiced serious concern in February 2011 about the increasing oppression against the Syriac Orthodox church in Turkey and made their position clear.

The CDU/CSU parliamentary group also stands squarely behind the Aramean community and will tirelessly pursue its calls on the Turkish state to guarantee all religious minorities the right to freedom of religion. The CDU/CSU parliamentary group is very much in favour of a value-based foreign policy which works nationally and internationally to secure the basic human right of religious freedom. Working with our EU partners as part of the common foreign and security policy, we must devise a coordinated strategy to safeguard religious freedom. This objective was voiced by the Christian-Liberal coalition in the motion for a resolution on the protection of freedom of religion worldwide, which received final consideration in the German Bundestag on 17 December 2010.

Efforts to secure peaceful coexistence across national borders, cultures or faiths are now more important than ever. Safeguarding the right to religious freedom demands not only legislation but also input from the whole of society. People in Germany and in Turkey can play their part here. Turks living in Germany are important ambassadors in this respect – as are the many Germans who happily spend their holidays in Turkey year after year.

Part 2:

The Mor Gabriel Monastery

The Monastery of Mor Gabriel: A Historical Overview and its Wider Significance Today

By Sebastian Brock

Dr. Sebastian Brock is internationally acknowledged as one of the most influential academics in the field of Syriac studies today. He is an Emiritus Reader in Syriac Studies at the University of Oxford's Oriental Institute and an Emiritus Fellow at Wolfson College. He is a Fellow of the British Academy.

The Syrian Orthodox Monastery of Mor Gabriel in Tur Abdin can rightfully claim to be among the world's oldest Christian monasteries still in use. While it is true that the monastery has, at times, been forced to close for a period of several years owing to invasions and raids that brought about wholesale destruction, the religious life was nevertheless always taken up again once it became possible to return to the monastery with its church and buildings. The date of its foundation, which is traditionally given as A.D. 397, but in fact was probably earlier, makes the Monastery of Mor Gabriel older by a century and a half than the better-known Monastery of St. Catherine on Mount Sinai, and a great deal older than any monastic foundation in Western Europe.

Since no narrative histories have been preserved, our knowledge of the history of the monastery has had to be pieced together from a variety of different sources. For the early period, biographies survive of the three main saints connected with the monastery: the founder St. Samuel (Shmu'il) of the village of Eshtin; his disciple St. Simeon (Shem'un) of Qartmin (the neighbouring village of the monastery), who died in A.D. 433; and St. Gabriel of Beth Qustan, abbot of the monastery in the first half of the seventh century, who died in A.D. 645. Although these biographies were written down quite some time after the deaths of their subjects, which has led the narratives have accumulated elements that are legendary in nature, they nevertheless offer a considerable amount of valuable historical information.

Another important source is an anonymous chronicle which was almost certainly composed in the monastery. Its brief entries cover the period up to the year A.D. 819. The most informative source for most of the duration of the second millennium A.D. is a work known as "The Book of Life", produced in the village of Beth Sbirino which had close connections with the monastery, providing many of its monks and abbots. This "Book of Life" consists of a commemorative record of benefactors, incorporating a considerable number of historical notices, several of which involve the monastery.

In additions to these sources, valuable information has at times been preserved in inscriptions (several of which have precise dates) and at the end of manuscripts where the scribe has added some incidental information about himself and the location and circumstances in which he had been copying the manuscript.

1. The beginnings and early history

No information survives concerning just how Christianity first reached Tur Abdin. The first local Christian known to us by name is Karpos, a Martyr bishop who was killed by the Persians. This may well have taken place during a raid carried out while the Persians were besieging the city of Nisibis in A.D. 350 – this dramatic event, in which the Persian Shah, Shahpur II, diverted the local river to create a flood around the town, was described by the great poet St. Ephrem, who compared the city with Noah's Ark. Karpos was buried in the village church of Qartmin, his relics having been brought there by Samuel of Eshtin when he fled from the Persian incursion. Samuel subsequently acquired a young disciple from Qartmin named Simeon, and it was Simeon's dream of an angel commanding him to build an open-air 'prayer house' (*Beth Slutho*) which led to their initial building activity on the site of the future monastery. A flourishing monastic community was soon established, and it was perhaps partly thanks to tales of miracles performed by some of the monks that resulted in reports of the monastery reaching the ears of the emperors Honorius and Arcadius, which in turn resulted in the first of several imperial benefactions in A.D. 397. This benefaction led to major building activities being commenced, which has led to A.D. 397 being commemorated today as the year of the monastery's foundation. A further imperial benefaction occurred some ten years later, under Theodosius II, but it is to the time of the third benefaction, by Anastasius in the early sixth century, that several still-existing structures and decorations (including the mosaics) date back. Details of all these benefactions are given in the "Biography of Gabriel". Among the intriguing items described are two bronze trees, placed in the church either side of the sanctuary entrance and decorated with all sorts of different hanging metal objects and thus anticipating modern Christmas trees!

Over the course of the centuries the monastery would provide the church with a significant number of its bishops. The first of these for whom there is a record was the monk John So'uro who, in A.D. 484, was made metropolitan bishop of Amid (present-day Diyarbakir), where he undertook some notable building activities, including having a bridge built over the river Tigris. It must have been while John So'uro was still a monk at the monastery that a young student from across the border with the Persian Empire studied there, before going to the famous Persian School in Edessa. That student was Philoxenus (d. A.D. 523), who would later become bishop of Mabbug, and who was one of the main Syrian Orthodox theologians who defended the "one nature" (Miaphysite) Christology, in opposition to the dyophysite formula of faith set down at the Council of Chalcedon in A.D. 451.

Acolytes in Mor Gabriel celebrating a Mass following the ancient rites of the Syrian Orthodox church. (From the book by Y. Bilge)

A damaged inscription dated A.D. 534 would once have told us the name of the abbot at that time, but unfortunately all but one letter of his name is lost. By that time the imperial ecclesiastical policy had changed, with the emperor Justinian's imposition of written acceptance of the doctrinal formula of the Council of Chalcedon as the condition for holding episcopal office. Because this 'two nature' formula was unacceptable to many people in the eastern provinces of the Roman Empire, separate hierarchies from those of the state began to emerge – lines which continue today in the Syrian Orthodox and other Oriental Orthodox Churches.

2. Under Arab rule: The seventh century to the mid-thirteenth century

Some 45 years after the dated inscription of A.D. 534, the monastery suffered considerably as a result of a Persian raid into Roman territory in A.D. 580. Sixty years later, the Arab conquests in the region brought a permanent change of rule. This transition occurred while during the abbothood of Gabriel of Beth Qustan, the person after whom the monastery is generally named today. It may well have been during his time as abbot that a zealous monk of the Church of the East, curiously nicknamed 'Gabriel the Cow', held a theological debate with the monks of the monastery. This Gabriel was a monk of the monastery of Mor Abraham, today a recently revived Syrian Orthodox monastery, but in the seventh century still an East Syriac foundation.

The biography of 'Simeon of the Olives' tells of an enterprising monk, educated in the monastery, who in due course became bishop of Harran in A.D. 700. Simeon was able to put his entrepreneurial skills to good use thanks to a chance find, by his nephew David, of some buried treasure. This treasure financed Simeon, not only for numerous charitable works and for the renovation of the monastery – which was still not fully repaired following the damage done by the Persians in A.D. 580 – but also enabled him to purchase extensive agricultural lands where he planted 12.000 olive trees. Once the trees began producing fruit, he was soon able to supply oil to all of the churches and monasteries of Tur Abdin. It is interesting to note in passing that Simeon also undertook several church building activities in Nisibis where, being on excellent terms with the Arab authorities, he also had a mosque and madrasa built for them.

After Simeon's death in A.D. 734, the monastery appears to have continued to flourish during the eighth century. Two monks from the monastery were selected by the reigning caliph to be imposed as patriarchs, only to be excluded subsequently from the Church's official list of patriarchs. Many years later the monastery would produce two additional patriarchs: Theodosius (887–896), who is commemorated in a building inscription in the monastery, and Dionysius III (958–961).

Building activities during the eighth century are recorded in some dated inscriptions: in A.D. 758 the abbot Gabriel, briefly recorded his building activity, and in A.D. 785 the abbot Denho and a number of other office-holders in the monastery commemorated the construction of a winepress. Another, much longer, inscription dating to A.D. 777 tells of the difficult transport of a large slab of cut stone from the site where it had been carved out eight years earlier to the monastery, evidently to be used as a kneading trough for the monastery's bakery. In the course of this interval of time there comes the oldest surviving manuscript to have been copied in the monastery – this is a beautifully calligraphed manuscript, dating to A.D. 770 and now in the British Library, containing the biblical books of Ezra and Nehemiah written on parchment. In the following decades parchment must have become scarce, because the scribe of another manuscript written in the monastery in around A.D. 800 has reused some old parchment leaves after sponging off their original text. Traces of the under-writing reveal a surprise: the original manuscript was written not in Syriac, but in Greek. Even more surprising is the fact that the two Greek texts involved are both secular, one being from Homer's Iliad, and the other a mathematical work by Euclid. Were these Greek texts rejections from the monastery's library, or had they been bought elsewhere as parchment to be recycled? If the former, then they serve as evidence of an excellent knowledge of Greek among at least some monks in the monastery at an earlier period, no doubt during the sixth and seventh centuries when Greek was still widely known.

That the number of monks in the monastery towards the end of the eighth century was quite large is evidenced by the information in a chronicle indicating that 94 monks had died in a period of pestilence.

Little information is available on the monastery's fortunes in the ninth and tenth centuries. A single manuscript written there, probably from the ninth century, survives. The manuscript contains a work by the former alumnus of the monastery's school, Philoxenus. An indication that the monastery continued to play an important role within the Syrian Orthodox Church during these centuries is offered by the lists of episcopal consecrations in the Chronicle of Patriarch Michael the Great (d. 1199): no less than 34 monks from the monastery were consecrated as bishops by successive patriarchs during these two centuries. These include one appointed to distant Sigistan and another to the important see of Tikrit.

In his Church history, the Syrian Orthodox polymath Barhebraeus (Bar 'Ebroyo; d. 1286) includes some important information about a revival of the old Estrangelo script in the monastery around A.D. 1000 by one of the monastery's bishops, John, Bishop of Tur Abdin:

Patriarch Athanasius consecrated John bishop of the monastery of Qartmin in 1299 of the Greeks (= A.D. 988), and he renewed the writing of Estrangelo in Tur Abdin that had been out of use for a hundred years. He learnt it from examples in books, and he taught it to his (three) nephews. Perfect grace was granted to Emmanuel in writing, and in illumination to his brother Nihe. The bishop sent Petros their brother to Melitene [modern region of Malatya], and he purchased parchment. Rabban Emmanuel wrote 70 bound volumes of the Peshitta, Syrohexapla and Harklean [all Biblical versions], and a volume of poems in three columns. He donated the books, which have no comparison in the world, to the monastery of Qartmin.

Fortunately at least two of these illustrated manuscripts have survived and can be identified today, one dated 1041 in the Patriarchal Library, Damascus, and the other, undated, in the British Library. Barhebraeus goes on to tell us that already in 1169 only 17 of these 70 manuscripts were still in the monastery's possession, the rest presumably having been victims of plunder and fire. One such occasion may well have been the sack of the monastery by the Seljuks in 1100; an event recorded some five years later in a long inscription which also usefully lists the names of the bishops of the monastery, some together with their places of origin, during the previous two and a half centuries:

The names of the bishops of this monastery from the year 1160 of the Greeks (= A.D. 849): Nonnus of Harran, Ezekiel of Hah, Samuel of Beth Man'em, Ezekiel, John, Iwannis, Ignatius, Severus, Habbib of Beth Man'em, Yeshu' of Qartmin, Joseph of Beth Sbirino, John of Beth Sbirino, Zakay – he acceded amidst a dispute –, Lazarus of Beth Sbirino, Shamli, a sinner, of Beth Man'em, who acceded in the year 1400 (= A.D. 1089) and who wrote this record. In his difficult and disaster-filled time this monastery suffered a terrible raid by the Persians [in fact, Seljuks]; it was laid waste and in ruins for five years, along with the whole of Tur Abdin. The raiders camped in the main church for fourteen days.

This traumatic event was also recorded in the "Book of Life", where mention is also specifically made of the destruction of, and the damage to, books – among which the precious 'Book of Life' itself is a victim, having been torn apart and its pages being scattered as far as Nisibis. At the first possible opportunity, an intensive search for these torn-out pages was carried out. In the end all but one of the pages were recovered and the manuscript was restored, with the record added concerning its dire adventures.

As both the inscription and the note in the 'Book of Life' indicate, monastic life resumed once the interlopers had departed. From later in the twelfth century we learn that some cells were built in 1167 by the Headman of Beth Sbirino – perhaps an indication that the number of monks was increasing. Scribal activity also continued, as is witnessed by a manuscript containing Anaphoras, dated 1182, now in the British Library. The high quality of the scribal art practiced at the monastery around this time is evidenced in the illuminated Gospel Lectionary of Ainwardo, which had been copied in the monastery in 1201. As is the case in several of the magnificent Gospel Lectionaries from this period, several of the

View on Mor Gabriel and parts of its outer wall. (H. Oberkampf)

lectionary headings are written in gold ink. The date is notable, since it comes only two years after the outbreak of a pestilence in which 35 monks of the monastery had died.

3. Late thirteenth to early sixteenth century: Under the Mongols and others

It is the nature of historical records that disasters are more often recorded than are periods of peace. This is certainly true for the history of the monastery during most of the remainder of the second millennium A.D. Thus we learn that in 1296 the monastery was once again sacked, this time by the Mongols, and remained deserted for four months before the monks were finally able to return.

In the case of one episode towards the end of the fourteenth century, we have several small pieces of information in various sources, and out of these a vivid picture for once emerges. It is quite rare that two manuscripts written by the same scribe survive, particularly for the fourteenth century, from which very few Syriac manuscripts survive today. Having two manuscripts written by the monk

Barsaumo, both dated 1364 and both written in Mor Gabriel monastery, is quite exceptional. Both the texts that Barsaumo copied are learned works: one an extensive Syriac-Arabic lexicon, the other a collection of writings by the polymath Syrian Orthodox scholar of the thirteenth century, Barhebraeus. This in itself is an indication of the relatively high intellectual level of the monastery in this otherwise dark period for all the Christian Churches in the Middle East. What is of particular interest, however, is a note in the second manuscript (preserved today in the British Library) which was added by a later reader named Aziz, from the nearby village of Fofyat. The note reads:

Aziz of Fofyat took a look at this book when he was 75 years old, of weak sight and having shaking hands, since I read the name of the scribe, Rabban Barsaumo, whose family was from Fofyat. He copied many books in our region of Tur Abdin, so that teachers from distant parts came to examine his manuscripts and his wonderful handwriting ... He died by suffocation from smoke, along with the bishop of the monastery and forty monks with them.

Unfortunately the end of the note is too damaged to make much sense, but fortunately we can learn of the circumstances of his death from two different sources: the "Book of Life" of Beth Sbirino and the continuation of the Chronicle of Barhebraeus. Both sources record the ravages of the Mongol Timur Leng in the region of Tur Abdin. Evidently many people took refuge by hiding in caves, but when they were discovered, the Mongols lit fires at the cave entrances, creating smoke and suffocating the refugees inside. One of these sources specifically mentions one cave where everyone was suffocated by smoke, indicating that there were "forty monks along with their bishop, John Thomas of Beth Sbirino, and some 500 people from the vicinity". The date given from this terrible event is 1395.

The late thirteenth and early fourteenth century was a time of numerous raids, either by the Mongols themselves or by Kurds. From a note in another manuscript in the British Library, we learn that in 1413 only one monk was left after the monastery had yet again been sacked. The continuation of Barhebraeus' chronicle informs us that, just three years later, the Kurds burnt down the monastery's gate and stole not only the sacred vessels, but also the precious relic of Mor Gabriel's hand.

Some respite came towards the end of the fourteenth century with the rule of the Aq Quyunlu. A small number of dated manuscripts written in the monastery in the early 1480s survive, the most important of which (now in Paris) contains an anonymous theological work entitled "The Cause of Causes", which is remarkable for its ecumenical outlook.

It is interesting to find that, around this time, a number of monks from Mor Gabriel Monastery found their way to the famous 'Syrian monastery' (Dayr al-Surian) in Egypt, situated between Cairo and Alexandria. This monastery had had a mixed Syriac and Coptic presence ever since the ninth century, and this continued up to the mid-seventeenth century, since when it has continued to this day as solely Coptic Orthodox. A number of manuscripts dated to the early 1490s record the activity of two monks from Mor Gabriel, Rabban Gabriel and his nephew Rabban Abraham, both from Beth Sbirino. In two of these manuscripts, both dated 1492, we find them helping in the library of the Syrian monastery. Another manuscript mentions that, on his way back, Rabban Gabriel rebound a lectionary in the Syrian Orthodox Monastery of St. Mark in Jerusalem. A connection between Mor Gabriel monastery and Jerusalem is also known from the continuation to Barhebraeus' Chronicle, which informs us that in 1490 the bishop of the monastery went to Jerusalem and bought a house there for use by Syrian Orthodox pilgrims. One wonders whether the names "Gabriel and Abraham, monks from Beth Sbirino", carved on the column at the entrance of the Church of the Holy Sepulchre in Jerusalem might not actually have been Rabban Gabriel and his nephew Rabban Abraham!

A rare piece of incidental information from the sixteenth century concerns the re-tiling of the roof of the monastery's church, carried out as a community effort by the inhabitants of Beth Sbirino. This comes from the 'Book of Life', where we read:

In the year 1813 of the Greeks (= A.D. 1502) the people from Beth Sbirino, the priests, headmen and the faithful, took counsel together and at the beginning of June they set off for the monastery of Mor Gabriel, along with their wives and children, and they re-tiled the large broad church of Mor Gabriel in the midst of the monastery complex. This was because in the winter a lot of water had got in. Over the course of a week they re-tiled the east and west sides of the roof, completing the work with God's help. This was the cause of great joy to the bishop Stephan and to the monks, since they had sought for help in their great need but had not been able to achieve anything. (The people brought) food and drink with them from their homes.

4. The sixteenth to nineteenth centuries: The Ottoman period

The Ottomans, who captured Constantinople in 1453 thus bringing an end to the Byzantine Empire, had gained control of most of the Middle East by the end of the second decade of the sixteenth century. Owing to a total lack of relevant sources, the course of the monastery's history in the sixteenth and seventeenth centuries remains completely obscure. It is not until 1710 that we find another manuscript copied in the monastery that still survives. This manuscript, now in Berlin, appropriately contains the biography of Bishop Simeon 'of the Olives', the great benefactor of the monastery in the early eighth century. A later note informs us that the manuscript was rebound in 1789. This, however, was almost certainly not done in the monastery, since we learn from an important liturgical manuscript copied at the monastery in 1838 that the monastery had only recently been re-inhabited after being depopulated as a result of a number of devastating raids in the second and third decades of the eighteenth century. The manuscript in question is a 'Fenqitho', or hymnary for Sundays and feasts throughout the liturgical year. At the end of the manuscript, the scribe, who identifies himself as the deacon Zaytun, a monk of 'the monastery of Mor Shmu'il, Mor Shem 'un and Mor Gabriel', gives the names of the patriarch and bishops of his time, after which he provides us with the following important information:

In the year 2145 of the Greeks (= A.D. 1834), after the holy monastery, known as the monastery of Qartmin, had been left desolate for a period of 120 years as a result of the various pillages that had taken place, God in his grace chose Mor Baselios Hadbeshabba and performed through him a deliverance. Since he had access to kings and judges, they gave him permission to remove the pagans and Muslims who were occupying the monastery. He dispersed them all over the place and recovered from them everything that they had stolen and appropriated from the monastery. He also gained possession of the large valley below the monastery to the north, from the ruined village of Arzon to the high rock where there is a cavern which serves as a place of reclusion for monks; from the village Fofyat and northwards: this rock is the boundary mark of the valley. In connection with this he paid 1000 *zuze* as gift money, until he succeeded in recovering the valley from the hands of the pagan 'sayyids' who were living in the caves in the valley. He also received a document of authorization from the Sultan in witness to the return of the valley, so that no one might have the audacity to make difficulties and contest the matter, in order that it might indisputably belong to the holy monastery.

The scribe Zaytun then goes on to list the names of the members of the newly restored monastic community, which comprises ten monks, one priest, seven deacons (including Zaytun himself) and three nuns. To conclude his labours Zaytun cites a tag that is found not only in many Syriac manuscripts, but also in Greek and Latin ones:

As a sailor rejoices when his ship has arrived in harbour, so too does the scribe rejoice on reaching the final line.

The manuscript's subsequent history appears to have been an eventful one. It must have been stolen, probably in the course of the massacres of 1915, because a later note tells us that it had been bought (at a great price) from a Muslim in 1929, and that the purchaser had later donated it to the village church in Kfarze. This was probably after 1936 when, as the same note tells us, it had at last been possible to rebuild the ruined church there and have it re-consecrated by the Bishop of Tur Abdin. There the manuscript remained until the mid 1970s, when Rabban Samuel Aktash, the abbot of Mor Gabriel monastery (now the Metropolitan of Tur Abdin, Mor Timotheos) and the head teacher, Malfono Isa Gülten (Garis), learnt of it and arranged for a new Fenqitho to be copied for the church in Kfarze so that the historic one of 1838 might return to its proper home.

Scattered glimpses of the monastery's history during the subsequent years of the nineteenth century can be gleaned from notes in manuscripts and from the rare Western visitor; one reported that brigands infested the road between Midyat and the monastery. Several other manuscripts which were written in 1838 and 1839 in the monastery survive, one of which contains the book of weekday prayers for monks called the "Shebitho", while the other has a collection of verse homilies by the famous poet, Jacob of Serugh (d. 521). Among other surviving manuscripts copied in the monastery during the nineteenth century are several provided with exact dates: 1859, 1865, 1877 and 1879. The 1879 manuscript appropriately includes a biography of Simeon of the Olives, as well as of Samuel, Simeon and Gabriel. Moreover, at the end of the manuscript the copyist tells us that there were thirteen monks living in the monastery at the time, six of whom were novices. In several cases the copyist also mentions the village from which these monks originated. Nine years earlier, the German Orientalist Albert Socin reported that he had counted fourteen monks in the monastery church during a service. Somewhat later, however, in 1892, during his six-month stay in Deyrulzafaran outside Mardin (at that time the seat of the patriarch) the Englishman Oswald Parry was able to pay a short visit to Mor Gabriel monastery, where he found only four monks in addition to the bishop.

5. The twentieth century onwards

An inscription in the monastery dated 1900, records that some restoration work was undertaken in that year. A few years later, in 1909, when Gertrude Bell visited the monastery, there was apparently only one monk and one nun (whose name, Besne, is still remembered and whose photograph is preserved in the Gertrude Bell Archive in Newcastle University).

At the time of Seyfo, '(the year of) the sword' (1915), when the widespread massacres commenced in earnest, there were six monks living in the monastery

The main church of Mor Gabriel monastery. (Mor Gabriel monastery)

(the bishop at the time happened to be in the large village of Ainwardo, where he died shortly after). The monks were soon joined by refugees from the nearby village of Kfarbe, who had been warned by their Kurdish neighbours in the village to escape before hostile Kurds from elsewhere came to massacre them. In the autumn of 1917 the monastery itself was attacked and all its inhabitants, with the exception of two children who escaped, were killed, the monks having first been subjected to appalling forms of torture. The monastery remained under Kurdish occupation for the next four years, and it was only after the end of World War I that the government gave orders for the properties to be restored to the Syrian Orthodox Church. Once this had been done, monastic life in the monastery was once again restored.

It was not, however, until the second half of the twentieth century, after the Turkish Government had started to establish state schools in the region, that the monastery truly began to flourish again, albeit in often difficult circumstances. In 1956 Patriarch Aphrem Barsaum appointed Father Shabo Gunesh from Syria as abbot of the monastery, with instructions to set up a school, with the support of the Bishop of Tur Abdin, Mor Iwannis Ephrem. Amongst the teachers was the monk Yeshu' Çiçek, who himself became abbot in 1962 following the death of Father Shabo. Subsequently he was to become the first Bishop of Central Europe, with the episcopal name Mor Julius. This came after a period spent studying in the United States. After the departure of Rabban Yeshu' for America, Rabban Samuel Aktash, the present abbot, was appointed to the office in 1973. Later, in 1985, he was consecrated Bishop of Tur Abdin, with the episcopal title Mor Timotheos.

From the 1960s onwards various restoration and refurbishment works in the monastery have been undertaken, such as the installation of a new kitchen in 1965. Several of these activities are recorded in Syriac inscriptions. One of the longest of these inscriptions is dated 2006 and sums up the achievements over the previous decades:

To the glory of God and in honour of the Bearer of God (Mary), and of the saints and Martyrs, this monastery has been restored, renovated and embellished, with monks and nuns, with teachers and students, with buildings and gardens, through the great care of Mor Timotheos Samuel Aktash, bishop of Tur Abdin and abbot of Mor Gabriel, at the expense of the Syrian Orthodox faithful and of Christians in general. This was inscribed as a record in the year 2006. Let everyone who reads this pray for all who have been, and continue to be, involved.

A number of inscriptions specify that the financial support for specific building activities came from Mor Athanasius Samuel Yeshu', the first Syrian Orthodox archbishop in North America (d. 1995). In one of these inscriptions his mother is also included:

Built at the expense of Mor Athanasius Yeshu', Metropolitan of Canada and America, and of his mother, Hatun, in the year A.D. 1968.

In a number of cases the support came from other churches, as in the following:

To meet the needs of those living in the monastery this well was dug, to the depth of 350 metres; above it and to the north of it this cistern was constructed, above the old one that had been excavated. And piped water and electricity has been brought into the monastery. All this at the expense of the associations of the friends of Tur Abdin: [in English script] Solidarity Group & Friends of Tur Abdin. May the Lord reward them well. In the year A.D. 2004.

Syriac inscriptions also record a number of visits by the Syrian Orthodox Patriarch of the time. Thus, in 1965, Patriarch Ignatius Yakub III undertook the elaborate consecration of the Holy Myron in the monastery, while the present Patriarch,

Ignatius Zakka I Iwas, has made two visits: first in 1982 and then again in 2004, as commemorated in the following inscription:

His Holiness Mor Ignatius Zakka I Iwas has made two apostolic visits to the holy Monastery of Mor Gabriel. The first one was in May 1982, in the time of Bishop Ephrem Bilgiç and the abbot, Rabban Samuel Aktash, when His Holiness was accompanied by four bishops and thousands of the Syrian Orthodox people. The second time was on the 14th May 2004, in the days of Mor Timotheos Samuel Aktash, bishop of Tur Abdin and abbot of the monastery. Accompanying the Patriarch were four bishops, monks from the Monastery of Mor Ephrem at Maʿarrat Saidnaya, near Damascus, and nuns of the Convent of Mor Jacob Burdʿono, in Atshane, Lebanon, together with thousands of the Syrian Orthodox faithful.

6. Monastic life

In the late 1960s the number of monks in the Syrian Orthodox Church was at a low ebb, which had become a serious problem since bishops are appointed only from among the ranks of monks. However, as happened with monastic life on Mount Athos in the Greek Church, and a bit earlier in Egypt in the Coptic Church, just when there appeared to be a threat that the monastic life might fade out, there has been a revival, and in recent decades the number of monastic vocations in the Syrian Orthodox Church has increased. One source of inspiration behind this revival has been the monastic school in the monastery, set up in 1956 and developed very considerably under the leadership of one of the early teachers, Isa Gülten, (now Archdeacon). The monastery school functions alongside the state educational system and provides excellent training in Syriac language, liturgy and church music outside of state school hours. While most of the students of course end up in secular careers, the monastic life of the school has inspired several to become priests or monks. In his recent book on the history and life of the monastery, Yakup Bilge lists eight former students who have become bishops, nine more who have become monks and 31 who have become priests.

It is important to note that, along with the monks who helped revived the religious life in the monastery in 1834, there were also three nuns. As evidenced by the photograph taken by Gertrude Bell in 1909 mentioned previously, at least one nun was living in the monastery in the years immediately preceding Seyfo. For several decades following World War I, life in the region of Tur Abdin remained too dangerous to allow the re-establishment of the monastic life for women. This, however, was to change with the revival of the monastery's fortunes from the 1960s onwards, and the story of how the revival of the monastic life for women came about has been told in an article by Elishbah Gülten, the wife of Malfono ('teacher') Isa Gülten. Young girls of a marriageable age in the surrounding villages were (and sometimes still are) in danger of being forcibly abducted, and this looming threat has been the cause of many families emigrating. In one case the parents of three daughters decided to send their children to relatives in Western Europe for safety. During their wait for passports, the father stayed with his daughters with the venerable Bishop of Mardin, Mor Filoksinos Dolabani. So captivated were they by the stories of the saints with which Mor Filoksinos regaled them that the girls announced that they wished to become nuns. The bishop sent them to Mor Gabriel Monastery to test their vocation and there they have remained. Today there are fourteen nuns living in the monastery.

7. Importance of the monastery

Like all monasteries that have continued to exist over centuries, the Monastery of Mor Gabriel has experienced periods of splendour and periods of decline. As the outline of the history of the monastery indicates, the monastery has had its ups and downs over the years, but even after the worst periods when it was sacked and the monks were driven out, the monastery has always managed to revive and to continue to play a significant role within the wider Syrian Orthodox Church. In recent decades this role has become all the more important, paradoxically at precisely the same time that the surrounding villages have become largely emptied of their Syrian Orthodox inhabitants as a result of emigration.

These two phenomena are of course not unconnected, since the Suryoye (Syrian Orthodox) who have emigrated and resettled in various Western European countries (mainly Sweden and Germany) have a need for priests and teachers, of which the monastery is the chief source of supply.

The first priest to serve in the European Diaspora was a former teacher from Tur Abdin, Father Butrus (Peter) Öguç, who settled in Augsburg where he still lives. As the number of Suryoye coming to Western Europe increased, Patriarch Yakub III established dioceses (patriarchal vicariates) in both Sweden and Central Europe. As mentioned earlier, the first Syrian Orthodox Bishop of Middle Europe was Mor Julius Çiçek, who had earlier been a monk and abbot of the monastery. While the majority of his flock were in Germany, he himself was based in the Netherlands in the Monastery of St. Ephrem (consecrated in 1984), which he had founded as soon as a suitable building became available. A man of great vision and energy, he quickly established and organised churches throughout his diocese, providing them with priests, many of whom had started out as students at the monastery's school. Other former students were appointed teachers of Syriac for local Suryoyo communities, and in due course in Germany these teachers became officially recognized by the German government. Most of those who had emigrated from Tur Abdin, whether for work or as refugees, have retained an emotional attachment to their former homes and, probably thanks to the specific association which many of the priests and teachers had with the Monastery of Mor Gabriel, the monastery itself became the symbolic focus of people's attachment. As a result, among the many visitors that the monastery receives, particularly during the summer, the majority are Suryoye from Europe who have come back on visits. The strength of this attachment to the monastery was made evident in Berlin on 25 January 2009 when, on a bitterly cold January day, some 19,000 Suryoye held a demonstration to show their support for the monastery in connection with the ongoing court cases over boundary disputes.

A picture of Archbishop Samuel Aktas, the monks, teachers and pupils of Mor Gabriel monastery. (From the book by Y. Bilge)

As a result of this type of effort and others, the Suryoyo Diaspora in Western European countries has succeeded in drawing the attention of official bodies of the European Union and other organisations to these court cases involving the monastery. This new European awareness has, for example, led to the fact-finding visit by representatives of nineteen different member states of the European Union to the monastery made in March 2011.

Within the Syrian Orthodox worldwide, the Monastery of Mor Gabriel is highly regarded, and it is to this monastery that monks are often sent from the large Syrian Orthodox community in Kerala, South India, to learn Syriac and to deepen their knowledge of the liturgical tradition of the Church. Moreover, the fact that quite a large proportion of the younger bishops of the Syrian Orthodox Church today were once monks at the monastery is a clear indication of the great contemporary significance of the monastery within the Church.

8. The wider significance of the monastery

That concern for the welfare of the monastery is by no means confined to members of the Syrian Orthodox Church is demonstrated not only by the financial help given to the monastery by bodies such as Missio (commemorated in an inscription of 1994), but also by the establishment in some Western European countries of support groups, such as The Friends of Tur Abdin in Austria (Linz) and the Tur Abdin Solidarity Group in England. The Friends of Tur Abdin in Austria was founded by Fr. Hans Hollerweger, whose beautifully illustrated book, *Tur Abdin: Living Cultural Heritage* (1999), with text in English, German and Turkish, has done a great deal to make this remote part of Turkey and its Syrian Orthodox background more widely known. The Friends of Tur Abdin also publish a quarterly newsletter, incorporated into *Information Christlicher Orient*. Exhibitions of photographs of the monastery and of Tur Abdin in general have been held in a number of different European cities, notably Milan and London, thus bringing awareness of the monastery and its situation to a much wider public.

From various different cultural points of view, the monastery, along with Tur Abdin in general, has received the attention of architectural and art historians, archaeologists, linguists, ethnomusicologists, sociologists and historians, resulting in various specialist publications in recent times. The architectural interest of Mor Gabriel monastery and other churches in the area was pointed out early in the twentieth century by the famous traveller Gertrude Bell in various publications, two of the most important of which have been brought together by M.M. Mango and republished with a valuable supplement under the title *The Churches and Monasteries of the Tur Abdin* (1982). The preservation of sixth-century mosaics in the apse of the main church of the monastery, all the more remarkable in view of the various sacks and pillages that the monastery has endured, is of particular interest for art historians, given the rarity of all but floor mosaics that survive from the pre-Islamic period.

For anyone interested in the riches of Classical Syriac literature, the use of Classical Syriac as an everyday spoken language in the monastery and its school is a notable testimony to the longevity of Classical Syriac, now attested in writing for just over two thousand years. Mention might also be made here of the local Aramaic (Modern Syriac) dialects spoken in the area. In the past these dialects, collectively known by scholars as 'Turoyo' (the 'mountain' dialect) have only very rarely been used in a written form (Classical Syriac being used instead). However, this is now changing in the Diaspora, where Turoyo is not only maintained as a widely spoken language within the community, but is also used for literary purposes, using either Syriac or European script (for which a standard transliteration has been developed in Sweden under the auspices of the Swedish educational authorities). Introductory and descriptive grammars of Turoyo have been produced in recent years by German scholars, with the result that the place of Turoyo among the other Modern Aramaic dialects is now better appreciated. Its particular interest lies in the fact that it is situated geographically between the small group of towns in Syria where Modern Western Aramaic still survives and the much larger group of Modern Eastern Aramaic dialects which are spoken in northern Iraq, northwest Iran and elsewhere.

A wider interest in the monastery has also been developed in academic circles. Thus, for example, in the late 1970s a course of lectures on historical aspects of the monastery and Tur Abdin was held in Oxford University, and in the last few decades a number of academic links between universities and Suryoye communities have been developed all over the world, such as Beth Mardutho in New Jersey, USA; the Society for Syriac Studies based at the University of Toronto; the Société des Études syriaques in Paris; the annual Deutsches Syrologen-Symposium in Germany; and the Syriac section of the Accademia Ambrosiana in Milan, at one of whose conferences, in 2003, Mor Julius Çiçek gave an important lecture, on the growth of the Suryoyo Diaspora in Western Europe.

Finally, it should be mentioned that, partly as a result of its numerous visitors, the monastery has acquired many ecumenical contacts with other Churches, while others have grown up through its former students, now teachers, monks and bishops living in the Diaspora, today spread all over the world. It has only been in the last half century that ecumenical dialogue between the Syrian Orthodox Church and the other Churches – Eastern Orthodox, Catholic, and Reformed – has taken place, and this has led to a growing realisation among the other Churches that the Syrian Orthodox Church, and the Syriac tradition in general, represents a hitherto largely forgotten strand of Christian tradition that has much to offer to the other Churches, all of which have an essentially European background. Seeing that the monastery of Mor Gabriel preserves this specifically Syriac aspect of Christian tradition in a pre-eminent way, its welfare is obviously a matter of very wide concern.

References

Aydin, Hanna, *Das Mönchtum im Tur-Abdin* (1988).
Barsaum, Ephrem, *History of Tur Abdin* (*Maktbonuto d-'al atro d-Tur Abdin*) (1985), with a supplement by Mor Julius Çiçek.
Bilge, Y., *1600 Yillik Gelenek Mor Gabriel Manastırı* (2011), in Turkish (English translation is in preparation).
Brock, S.P. (ed.), *The Hidden Pearl: The Syrian Orthodox Church and its Ancient Aramaic Heritage,* Vol. 3. *At the Turn of the Third Millennium: the Syrian Orthodox Witness* (2001).
Dolabani, Filoksinos Yuhanon, *Chronicles of the holy monastery of Qartmin* (*Maktabzabne d-'umro qadisho d-Qartmin),* (1959), in Syriac.
Gülcan [Gülten], Elishbah, 'The Renewal of monastic life for women in a monastery in Tür Abdin', *Sobornost* 7:4 (1977), pp. 288–98.
O'Mahony, A. (ed.), 'The Syrian Orthodox Church in modern history', in *Christianity in the Middle East. Studies in Modern History, Theology and Politics* (2008), pp. 17–38
Atto, N., *Hostages in the Homeland, Orphans in the Diaspora* (2011)
Palmer, A.N., *Monk and Mason on the Tigris Frontier* (1990)
Palmer, A.N. (ed.), *The Lives of Samuel, Simeon and Gabriel* (1983)
Palmer, A.N. 'Mor Gabriel Monastery", in *The Gorgias Encyclopedic Dictionary of the Syriac Heritage* (2011).

Reconciled by Mor Gabriel[1]

By Baskin Oran[2]

Baskin Oran is professor emeritus of International Relations at Ankara University with a special focus on nationalism, minorities, religion-state relations and Turkish foreign affairs; he is a well known Turkish human rights activist and advocate with various publications on human rights in Turkey and the legal position of minorities in Turkey, amongst which one of his best known is the master piece "Turkish Foreign Policy 1919–2006, facts and analyses with documents" (Translated by Mustafa Aksin, University of Utah Press, 2010, 968 p.).

The struggle between the Government and the High Judiciary has frightened everyone. This will no longer be the case, because the two sides have now reached an agreement. Established in A.D. 397 in the district of Midyat is the Mor Gabriel Monastery (Deyrulumur) of the Syriacs (Turkish: Süryani, also known as Assyrians) – the most peaceful and the most oppressed people of the Middle East. The Government and the High Judiciary have decided to join together to "Turkify" the lands that have belonged to Mor Gabriel for centuries.

However, the whole thing ended up with me getting into trouble. I had written an article entitled "the Syriacs have had enough" in the 21 November 2008 issue of Radikal-2.[3] I had mocked the petitions of the Kurdish villagers of Midyat, who at that time had undertaken the mission of occupying Syriac lands. I made these remarks in response to the odd things that were written in the petition, including: "We don't claim that you should cut off the head of this bishop, but you should prevent his illegal occupation and looting", and "The Christian clergy is here to agitate and provoke the public. They are engaging in all kinds of activity to harm the spirit of national unity and solidarity". Those are some claims! So these Syriacs have not only apparently saved themselves from getting their heads cut off,

---

[1] This article appeared in the Turkish daily *Radikal*'s Sunday supplement *Radikal-2* on 6 February 2011. Retrieved from:
 http://www.radikal.com.tr/Radikal.aspx?aType=RadikalEklerDetayV3&ArticleID=1039217.
 See also B. Oran, *Türkiyeli Gayrimüslimler Üzerine Yazilar* (Writings on Non-Muslims of Turkey), Istanbul, Iletisim Publishers (2011), pp. 744–748.
 Abdulmesih BarAbraham and Andrew Palmer helped to get the permission to reprint this article.
[2] Reyhan Durmaz translated this article from Turkish to English.
[3] Sunday supplement of an important Turkish daily newspaper.

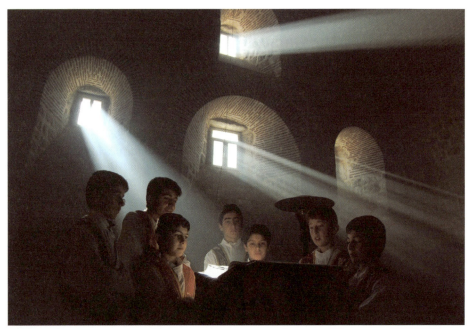

Acolytes in Mor Gabriel singing hymns in Aramaic, the language Jesus Christ and his disciples used. (From the book by Y. Bilge)

they are also agitating the public. Elsewhere in the petition is written, "Where have these priests come from? What kind of education are they getting there and for what purpose?" In fact, this monastery has been in existence for nearly seventeen centuries. Now I come to understand that the petition was not in vain: the petitioners apparently knew very well what they were doing. In fact, now, with all its grandeur, the all mighty Turkish State has made its entry onto the scene.

1. How the State confiscates

The number of court cases brought against the Syriacs – a people (comparable to the endangered bird species of the same region called "bald ibis") on the verge of disappearing from their ancient homeland in the Mardin-Midyat/Tur Abdin region (now numbering no more then 3,000) – is now approaching 300. The AKP government blames the EU, stating on the one hand, "We will not pull the plug. You do it!", while on the other hand it is encouraging various government institutions to go to court against the 1,614-year old Mor Gabriel Monastery in order to destroy it. This despite the fact that the entire world is watching the case closely. Do you know when this process began to gain momentum? It was when the Syriac [speaking] people started to return from abroad and wanted to resettle in their villages.

The State is using two methods to achieve its goals: 1) According to the Court of Cassation's interpretation of Cadastral Law no. 3402 and Forest Law no. 6831, arid land that goes unused for agricultural purposes for more than 20 years becomes "State property." 2) According to the Forest Law, land which looks green in aerial photography is registered by the State as forest.[4] How many people have you ever heard of being charged based on these "Laws of the Turkish Republic"? As a result of these methods Mor Gabriel is now struggling with five lawsuits:

1. The two neighbouring Kurdish villages of Yayvantepe and Eğlence litigated against the Monastery in 2008. The reason: "Our lands, when the Cadastre was here, were officially left within the territory of the village of Güngören, and thus of the monastery." The tribal chief of these two villages is Süleyman Çelebi, an AKP deputy for Mardin. This case ended with the Midyat Cadastral Court approving the decision of the Cadastre, that is, in favour of the monastery.
2. Upon hearing this decision the villagers began occupying the monastery's land. The villagers of Güngören, the village within the administrative boundaries of which the monastery stands, having had good relations with the monastery for centuries, litigated to determine the administrative boundaries. While the villagers were successful at the Midyat Court of the First Instance, the decision was later overturned in the Court of Cassation, who ruled that: "This lawsuit is within the jurisdiction of the Administrative Court. The court should have decided that the case is not its subject-matter jurisdiction". The case is now to be sent to the Administrative Court. Good luck!

If it's deserted, confiscate it. If it's green, confiscate it any way

3. There are some 260,000m^2 of land within the monastery's walls and some 60.000m^2 of land immediately outside the outer walls. All of the land has been in the monastery's possession for centuries. During the cadastral survey, these lands were registered as Treasury lands. The reasoning cited was, "The land constitutes forest land." The monastery had once planted trees there and, as you know, forests belong to the State. In response, in October 2009, the Monastery Foundation sued the Forest Administration in the Midyat Cadastral Court, only to have the Court overrule its claim, stating that: "In aerial photographs from

---

[4] For an example of this application see the case the Court of Cassation, 20th Civil Chamber, E. 2009/15971; K. 2009/18101; T. 07.12.2009

the 1950s, the land looks green." The foundation later brought an appeal against this decision. The file is now at the Court of Cassation. Good luck!

4. In response to complaints from the village chiefs of Eğlence, Yayvantepe and Çandarl, the Chief Prosecutor of Midyat brought a criminal lawsuit against Kuryakos Ergün, chairman of the Mor Gabriel Foundation, claiming "Illegal occupation of forest land." The lawsuit rests on the claim that "The monastery's outer wall is partially within this 276,000m^2 area of forest land". The old wall was reinforced when clashes in the region and attacks against the Monastery multiplied in the 1990s. The case is ongoing, pending the result of the lawsuit brought by the Foundation against the Forest Administration. If the Court of Cassation approves the decision of the Midyat Cadastral Court against the Foundation, K. Ergün will be fined and the wall will be demolished.

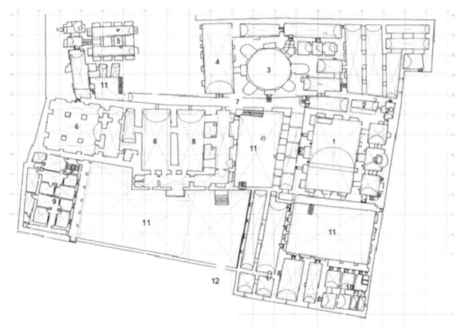

1 Main Church
2 Mor Gabriel's hermitage
3 Dome of Theodora
4 Old Kitchen
5 Tombs of the Saints
6 Church of the Holy Mother of God
7 Hallways
8 Old stable (today used as dining & common room)
9 Accommodation facilities / deacon's house
10 Guest rooms
11 Court
12 Entrance

Footprint of the Mor Gabriel monastery, ground floor (without the outer wall and its surrounding lands). (From the book by Y. Bilge)

And most importantly:

5. On 29 January 2009 the Treasury brought a lawsuit against the Foundation in Midyat Cadastral Court, looking to gain possession of the 12 plots (244,000m^2) that were registered as monastery land during the cadastral survey. The Court denied the Treasury's case, only to be overruled by the Court of Cassation on appeal, which quashes the decision and orders the land to be registered as being the property of the Treasury. Their reasoning was very interesting, stating that "According to Section 14 of the Cadastral Law, when a plot of non-registered land is claimed by someone who can prove that he has been its *de facto* possessor for at least 20 years, this land cannot exceed 100,000m^2 in dry areas, whereas the land registered here is 244,000m^2".[5]

2. Does the Court of Cassation recognize legal documents?

I say that this decision was "very interesting" because Section 14 continues as follows: "In case one of the following documents is submitted, more than 100.000^2 can be registered". The first document in the list is "Tax records prior to 31 December 1981". In accordance with the Land Registry Law, the monastery has paid taxes on this land since 1 September 1937. Based on this fact, the Midyat Cadastral Court decided in favour of the monastery. The Court of Cassation, however, refused to accept the validity of the document. Moreover, let me add this: The monastery had mentioned this land in the well-known 1936 Declaration.[6] As it stands now, the monastery will apply to the same chamber of the Court of Cassation. Good Luck!

Our State does not even allow the Syriacs to benefit from the minority protection clauses of the Lausanne Treaty of 1923, simply because these people are located in a distant corner of Anatolia. The European Court of Human Rights, however, does not differentiate between villagers and urban dwellers. Whatever the Treaty requires for the compensation of real estate in Beyoğlu [central Istanbul], it will require the same for the monastery lands. This, of course, is of no concern either to the Government or the Court of Cassation, because the public

---

[5] Since this article was written before the first judgements on the trials, it should be noted that the 3rd and 5th trial described here have been lost by the monastery. In January 2011 and in June 2012 the monastery has lost approx. 24,4 and 27,6 hectares respectively. The monastery has filed a complaint against the courts first decision (January 2011) at the European Court of Human Rights in Strasbourg. The second case (June 2012) will also be brought to the Court in Strasbourg. The other cases are still pending; since the Turkish courts have regularly postponed the cases.

[6] For more on this concept, see the box at the end of this article.

Snow in Mor Gabriel monastery. (From the book by Y. Bilge)

will pay for it with their taxes. Which is all well and fine, but what about the honour of our State?

To the AKP I would like to say: it will be difficult to save yourselves this time by saying "There is nothing we can do about it. That's what the High Judiciary has decided". After all, who is in command of the Treasury?

To the State I would like to say: Since 1915 capital accumulation in Turkey has been accomplished by "Turkifying" non-Muslim property. Are we still continuing this practice? Haven't we exhausted all of it yet?

> **The 1936 Declaration**
> The Law on Foundations came into force in 1936 as a Republican reform law. The state called on each foundation to declare all real property in its possession. The purpose of the declaration (in fact a circular order) was to make arrangements that would deprive the Islamists of their financial means. But Atatürk died shortly thereafter, and the declaration fell into oblivion.
> After 1972 the Directorate General of Foundations, as a means of pressuring Greece in the Cyprus affair, wanted to put pressure on Greek (Rum) Orthodox foundations and started calling on non-Muslim foundations to submit their founding charters. These foundations had no such charter, however, because they had been set up through imperial decrees during the Ottoman era. The Directorate General informed these foundations that the 1936 declaration would be accepted in lieu of a charter and started appropriating all real estate acquired after 1936. The legal justification for this was that the 1936 declaration did not indicate that these foundations could acquire new properties.
> The argument that the 1936 declaration was merely a listing of all real property and therefore could not contain such a clause was to no avail, and all property acquired through purchase, donation, legacy, or other means and not listed in the declaration was expropriated. The property thus expropriated was returned, free of charge, to the sellers or their legal heirs or, in the event of their absence, to the Treasury. This violation of the Lausanne Treaty as well as of the right to property came to an end in 2003 with the promulgation of an EU Harmonization Package. Seizures were stopped, real estate buys were permitted, and confiscated real estate was planned to be returned to the owner foundations. But no solution had yet been found (by the end of 2010) for real estate sold to third parties, nor for properties already confiscated.
> *(Excerpt from: Baskin Oran (ed.),* Turkish Foreign Policy 1919–2006, facts and analyses with documents, *Utah, University of Utah Press (2010).*

The Saint Gabriel Monastery Trust[1]

By Yakup Bilge

Yakup Bilge was born in Bote, Tur Abdin, Turkey and received his M.A. at the Institute of Social Science at Istanbul University's Department of Political Science and International Relations. He has worked as a journalist in both Ankara and Istanbul for such diverse national Turkish newspapers as Hürriyet, Cumhuriyet and Yeni Yüzyıl, and has published several works on the Syriac community. One of his most recent books is 1600 Yıllık Gelenek: Mor Gabriel Manastırı (A 1,600 Year Old Tradition: The Monastery of St. Gabriel), published in 2012. He currently lives in Sweden where he works as a teacher of social studies at a secondary school.

The St. Gabriel Monastery Trust is a parallel organisation which developed in tandem with the Monastery of St. Gabriel for the sake of serving its physical needs. As such it has played an important role in enabling the monastery to develop into the region's most famous religious institution whose residents, at times, numbered more than a thousand.

As told in the *Qartmin Trilogy*, the life stories of the monastery's founders, St. Samuel and St. Simeon, and that of its 7th century abbot St. Gabriel describe the monastery of St. Gabriel as a holy centre that regularly received imperial grants.[2] In order to complete construction of the monastery's Great Church, the Eastern Roman Emperor Anastasius[3] (491–518 A.D.) provided financial support as well as architects, stone masons and marble workers. It is also said that Anastasius donated seven villages, the names of each of which started with the letter "K" (?). The names of the villages given to the Monastery Trust were: Kfarşoma (Budaklı), Kfarallap (Yollbaşı), Kfararap, Kfarhıvvar (Gelinkaya), Kfarninağ (Alıçlı), Kafro (Tahtayto?) and Kivah (Mağara köyü).[4]

In addition to the grounds surrounding its immediate vicinity, written sources attest to the fact that the monastery had real estate holdings as far away as Mount Şigur (Sinjar) in a region known as Roğulo d'Gihano ('Hell's Creek'), a valley to

---

[1] This article is a précis of a chapter by the same name from Yakup Bilge's book *1600 Yıllık Gelenek: Mor Gabriel Manastırı* ("A 1600 Year Tradition: The Monastery of St. Gabriel"). The book's author reviewed this article prior to publication. The text has been translated into English from the original Turkish by Peter Pikkert.
[2] *Qartmin Trilogy*, XXVII:10–19, XXVII:1–4; XXXI:13:19, XXXII:1–4, LIX:7–10.
[3] *Qartmin Trilogy*, LIX:7–13.
[4] Dolapönü, 1971, pp. 22–23; Mor Gabriel Öğretim Kadrosu, 1988, p. 17.

Dome of Theodora, part of the Mor Gabriel monastery; built in the 6th century by Theodora the wife of Byzantine Emperor Justinian I, the Great. (From the book by Y. Bilge)

the north of Idil running from south to west in the province of Şırnak; in Nisibin (Nusaybin); in Servan, an old settlement approximately halfway between Nusaybin and Idil; Harmoşo, a region near Beyaz Su ("White Water") between Midyat and Nusaybin; Hazzo, the district of Kozluk in Batman; as well as in Kanik, the village of Bakacik, affiliated with Nusaybin.[5]

Monasteries established in the Roman Empire during the early Christian Era commonly received land grants from emperors and governors.[6] In fact, granting land endowments to famous monasteries became a common tradition, something which emperors did upon their coronation. From the *Qartmin Trilogy* we learn that the Roman emperors Honorius (395–423), Arcadius (395–408), Theodosius II (408–450) and later Anastasius (491–518) made great contributions towards the construction of new buildings as well as with respect to the granting of regular gifts meant to meet the monastery's annual expenditures.[7]

From this generous imperial response it is clear that St. Gabriel was, from its earliest days, a monastery known throughout the Christian world. It is also known

---

[5] Dolapönü, 1971, pp. 22–23; Mor Gabriel Öğretim Kadrosu, 1988, p. 17.
[6] Rasmussen & Thomassen, 2007, p. 203; Palmer, 1990, p. 58; and Alkan 2009, pp. 95–96.
[7] *Qartmin Trilogy,* XXVII:10–13, XXXI:13:19, XXXII:1–4, LIX:7–10.

that believers living in the region of Tur Abdin, where the monastery is located, also donated land to the Monastery. To this day, believers with close ties to the church and the monastery regularly donate land grants to the monastery. In some cases, the land belonging to the monastery or to village churches is partially owned by one of the church faithful; the church or the monastery takes full ownership of these properties upon the death of the church member.

An important source testifying to the monastery's wealth is the life-story of St. Simeon of the Olives: one of St. Gabriel's monks who lived in the 7th and 8th century and was appointed Bishop of Harran in the year 700 and who died at the monastery of St. Gabriel in the year 734 A.D. According to his biographer, the costs incurred in building the Church of St. Theodorus in Nisibin, widely known for the marble used in its construction, its ornamentation, as well as for the fact that it was the largest, most important church in the region, were met by the St. Gabriel Monastery Foundation. The same account states that St. Simeon of the Olives purchased land near a monastery related to St. Gabriel located in Servan (a settlement halfway between Nusaybin and Idil) in the region of Beth Araboya (a region south and west of Mount Sinjar which included Nisibin), where he had 12,000 olive shoots planted, the produce of which was taken to the monastery of St. Gabriel where the monks processed it into olive oil.[8]

St. Simeon of the Olives was one of the people who contributed greatly to the expansion of the St. Gabriel Monastery Foundation. From his biography we learn that he bought several villages, orchards, mills, stores, farmland, inns and baths for the church and the monastery.[9] Some of the churches and buildings that were founded, as well as the monasteries that were restored by the Monastery Foundation, are remarkable:[10]

– He had a large inn built for travellers and traders near Nisibin's eastern gate, towards the south of a monastery. He also bought five mills, a garden full of fruit trees and a large piece of ground towards the east of that city.
– He had the Church of the Virgin Mary built on the ruins of the Monastery of the Martyr Fabruniye. He also had the large St. Theodorus Church built in the same area. Known for its great beauty, this church was consecrated in the year 707 A.D. by the Patriarch Yulyanos (d. 708 A.D.). In order to provide a regular income for the St. Theodorus Church, he had a large mill built outside the city walls which he then enclosed with its own protective wall. He also had a gate punched through the city wall to reach this enclosed mill. The costs

---

[8] Palmer, 1990, p. 12; Brock, 2001b, p. 62.
[9] Brock, 1999, p. 24.
[10] Dolapönü, 1971, pp. 79–81.

of the construction of the church were covered by the St. Gabriel Monastery Foundation.
- He had three monasteries built, one of which was called St. Dimet. He then purchased such properties as houses, stores and a mill to support them.
- He bought baths for the support of the Monastery of St. Elisha which he had built.

The growing profits from all the foundations which St. Simeon of the Olives established in Nisibin were tied to the St. Gabriel Foundation by a title deed signed by the Patriarch Yulyanos (d. 708 A.D.).[11] In that way all of the remaining profits from the churches and monasteries in the city of Nisibin went to the monastery of St. Gabriel.

Thanks to the foundations St. Simeon of the Olives established in Nisibin, and in particular to the olive oil harvested from the twelve thousand trees he had planted in the olive groves in Servan in the district of Beth Araboye, the monastery entered one of its most glorious periods. The income from the foundations he had founded went towards the restoration of many churches and monasteries in the area. For more than a century this income ensured the survival of the churches and monasteries of the Tur Abdin region.[12]

The wars and disorders which plagued the region throughout the course of history, as well as the fact that nearby villages and other groups occupied land belonging to the monastery, led to the loss of most of the monastery's holdings. Various documents testify how land belonging to the monastery was occupied by local villagers.

One example is found in a colophon (notes on empty pages of manuscripts) in a manuscript going back the first half of the 19th century. A monk called Zeytun writes in the colophon of a prayer book he was copying how a valley belonging to the monastery which had been occupied for some time by local villagers had been restored thanks to the efforts of the Mafriyan of Tur Abdin, Ablahad (d. 1844).[13]

A decision by the Ottoman Ecclesiastical Court endorses the event referred to in this colophon. A decision by the Ecclesiastical Court held in the governor's office of Amed (Omid; Diyarbakir) in the year 1841 ordered local villagers to restore to the monastery land they had occupied. It is interesting to see from this decision by the Ecclesiastical Court that local villagers had occupied the monastery's land for an extended period of time.

---

[11] Dolapönü, 1971, p. 81.
[12] Dolapönü, 1971, pp. 76–89; Brock, 1999, p. 24.
[13] Brock, 1979, p. 169.; see also, Brock's article in this book.

From the court's decision it is understood that a certain "Ali Bin Temur and Seyyid Emin and Seyyid Ömer" were called to the court because they had unlawfully usurped land belonging to the monastery "from a cave known as Zinevle on the one side to Govare Kine and the border of Kferbe on the other side, to tenbushel fields on the border of Qartmin, a total of six pieces of land belonging to the monastery". After looking into the matter the Ecclesiatical Court decided to return the said properties to the monastery:

[T]he said fields and vineyards belonging to the church's foundation were to be relinquished by the said individuals [Ali Bin Temur, Seyyid Emin and Seyyid Ömer] who themselves admitted to occupying and using the fields and vineyards, to be restored upon request to the said Mafiryan responsible for the properties as ordered by this Ecclesiastical Command.

In addition to this decision taken by the Ecclesiastical Court, two other documents in the Ottoman archives dating back to 1910 testify to communication between various departments of the Ottoman state pertaining to the "occupation" of land belonging to the monastery, most likely by local villagers. These two documents are located in the Ottoman archives,[14] and indicate that new information sent from the Midyat district governor's office to the Diyarbakir provincial census bureau (the Diyarbakir Governor's Clerk's Office), which in turn forwarded the documents to the Ministry of the Interior and the Ministry of Justice and Religion. It is evident from the documents sent to the Diyarbakir Governor's Office that a part of the land belonging to the monastery was occupied by a number of people or groups of people and that the monastery's abbot, Athanasios Afrem (d. 1915), requested help with respect to their restoration from the administrative authorities. It is unclear at the time of writing whether all of the documents from that era pertaining to the monastery's assets are complete, and if any of these documents exist that have not yet been released to the public.

After the establishment of the Republic of Turkey, manifests listing the properties belonging to foundations were requested, as stipulated within the framework of the laws and regulations governing foundations.[15] The foundations were given one year to declare their assets, hence these reports came to be known as the 1936 Manifest. Within this framework the properties belonging to the "Midyat Syriac

---

[14] Ministry of Interior, File Number 43/-1, Cover Number: 6; 12 / L (Şevval)/1328, 16 October 1910.
[15] Ruling number 2762, 13 June 1935.

Deyrulumur Mor Gabriel Monastery Foundation"[16] were declared and given to the General Directory of Foundation Affairs. According to the manifest presented and signed by Tuma Araz, the Bishop of Tur Abdin at that time, the monastery was in possession of "22 fields without water access, two vineyards, 10 wells, the monastery building and the surrounding lands for which there were no title deeds". The phrase "lands for which there were no title deeds" indicate that the monastery owned the land surrounding it but did not hold a title deed. This sentence played an important role in the legal proceedings which have been ongoing since 2008 between the monastery, local villagers and the internal revenue department with respect to the issues pertaining to its cadastral surveys.[17]

The Syrian Orthodox Church Patriach, Mor Ignatius Zakka I (second from right), and accompanying delegation visited Prime Minister Recep Tayyip Erdoğan (first from right) on 30 March 2011, at which time they communicated the problems they were experiencing with the Treasury. The Patriarch informed the Prime Minister that the entire Syriac community was carefully following the progress of the property dispute. (From the book by Y. Bilge)

Seeing how other articles published in this book deal with the court cases between the St. Gabriel Monastery Trust and the surrounding villages, the Treasury

---
[16] Kurban & Hatemi, 2009, p. 25; Alkan, 2009, p. 110; Website of the General Directorate of Foundations: www.vgm.gov.tr/02_VakiflarHakkinda/004_CemaatVakiflar/cemaat.cfm.
[17] For more information on the monastery's trials, see Oran's article in this book.

and the Department of Forestry, I will not go into the details of these matters here. Other chapters in this book provide detailed information on the particulars concerning these matters.

However, the difference between the court cases of the Ottoman era and the post 2008 era is that, today, the state, working through the Treasury department, is bringing court cases against the monastery foundation, and thus is seeking to register property belonging to the monastery in its own name. According to the documents from the Ottoman era, the state and courts insisted that property belonging to the monastery which had been "occupied" by local villagers was to be restored, while in the cases brought after 2008 the state itself sought to register land belonging to the monastery in its own name.

The various court cases which the Monastery of St. Gabriel has faced as of late 2008 have received a great deal of attention from both the Turkish media[18] and from major international news agencies such as Reuters.[19] The lawsuits have also been brought to the attention of parliamentarians in various European nations and have been placed on the agenda of the European Parliament. Inasmuch as the monastery of St. Gabriel is both a holy place and an important religious centre, the Syriac Diaspora and their institutions have brought this subject before both Turkish ambassadors and the political establishment of their countries of residence. The Monastery of St. Gabriel has often been on the agenda of those European countries such as Sweden, Germany and the Netherlands, which have a sizeable Syriac community. Thanks to the efforts of Yılmaz Kerimo, Robert Halef and other politicians of Syriac extraction, along with those of their Swedish, German and Dutch colleagues, the Monastery of St. Gabriel is, from time to time, on the agenda of the Swedish, German and Dutch Parliament.[20]

Suroyo TV and Suryoyo Sat satellite television stations broadcasting in Syriac from Sweden to Europe, North America and the Middle East have followed

---

[18] Many Turkish newspapers, including *Hürriyet*, *Milliyet*, *Cumhuriyet*, *Vatan*, *Sabah* and *Taraf*, reported on the court cases brought against the Monastery of St. Gabriel, while the newspaper *Radikal* made it headline news on 12 December 2008. Various columnists also discussed the subject of the monastery: Cengiz Çandar on 13 December 2008 in *Radikal*; Baskın Oran on 21 December 2008 and 6 February 2011 also in *Radikal*; and Orhan Miroğlu on 10 October 2008 in *Taraf*.

[19] On 22 May 2009, Reuters reported on the decision of the Midyat Regional Court, along with its reasoning and further developments.

[20] On 8 June 2009, the Swedish Minister of Foreign Affairs, Carl Bildt, suggested to the Swedish parliament that they were aware of the issues pertaining to the Monastery of St. Gabriel and were monitoring the situation closely and implied that the issue might be placed on the Swedish Government's agenda.

the St. Gabriel's property controversies closely, and have kept the global Syriac community up to date on the latest developments. Furthermore, an Internet site run by the Izmir Peace Assembly called "Mor Gabriel'e Dokunma" (Don't Touch St. Gabriel) and collecting signatures for petitions has attracted considerable interest.

The Syrian Orthodox Church Patriach, Mor Ignatius Zakka I, and accompanying delegation had the opportunity to visit Prime Minister Recep Tayyip Erdoğan on 30 March 2011, and met with the President of the Republic of Turkey, Abdullah Gül, on 31 March 2011, at which time they communicated the problems they were experiencing with the Treasury and requested a resolution of the issue. During these discussions Mor Ignatius Zakka I explained that the Monastery of St. Gabriel was an important religious centre – a "Second Jerusalem" – for the Syriac community, noted that it was important to the entire community that the problems be resolved, and expressed his hope that the state would exercise due diligence in resolving the problems between the Treasury and the monastery. The representatives of the ministers pertinent to the subjects under discussion were also present at these discussions.

In order to inform state officials of the disagreements between the Monastery of St. Gabriel and the Treasury with respect to the surrounding land claims, the Patriarch of the Syriac Church, Mor Ignatius Zakka Iwas I (fourth from the left), together with accompanying delegation, visited the President of Turkey Abdullah Gül (center) on 31 March 2011. (From the book by Y. Bilge)

Today, the monastery of St. Gabriel is the residence and main office of the Bishop of Tur Abdin, Timotheos Samuel Aktaş and as such, is an important religious centre for both the Syriac people as well as being one of the most important religious centres in Turkey. The expenses incurred by the monastery and the bishopric of Tur Abdin are met by the gifts of the community living in Mardin, Diyarbakır, Adıyaman, Elazığ and Istanbul, as well as from the Syriac Diaspora in Europe, North America and Australia.

The first director of the St. Gabriel Foundation upon its foundation in 1935 under the new Law Pertaining to Foundations, was the bishop of Tur Abdin, Tuma Araz. He was succeeded in the administration of the monastery foundation by the priests Sefer Gabriel Kittino (Akyön) of Arbolu and Şabo Güneş, who was in turn succeeded as head of the foundation by priest Samuel Aktaş (1973–1986), Yakup Türker (1986–1987), priest Avcin [Augin] Kaplan (1987–1990) and Isa Gülten (1990–2007). Since 2007, Kuryakos Ergün has served as the head of the foundation and Isa Doğdu has served as the deputy head.

The Monastery of St. Gabriel is not just a holy place for Syriacs living in Tur Abdin, but for Syriacs worldwide; indeed, especially for those living in the Diaspora. Additionally, as one of the world's oldest active monasteries, the Monastery of St. Gabriel is a place of importance for all of Christendom. Hence, the legal battles which the Monastery of St. Gabriel faces are being followed closely by both the Syriac community and Christians around the world. In fact, the court cases in which the Monastery of St. Gabriel is embroiled are followed closely not just by the Syriacs and global Christian communities, but also by those who believe in the democratic process and the rule of law.

People around the globe are following with amazement a series of events in which certain local authorities, along with the State Treasury, are seeking to expropriate property that has been in the possession of one of the oldest and most unique monasteries in the world since it was established some 1,600 years ago – an institution the likes of which can be counted on one hand.

Unfortunately, when cases pertaining to minorities reach the Supreme Court in Ankara the decision generally goes against the minorities. The lawsuit with respect to the Monastery of St. Gabriel was no different. Although the Midyat Cadastral Court (Land Registration) awarded the properties in question to the monastery two times, the Supreme Court, in its review of the Treasury's objection, followed its customary trend with respect to cases involving minorities and has taken away property which has belonged to the monastery for some 1600 years. The Supreme Court's negative disposition regarding cases concerning minority groups is a great misfortune in Turkey's judicial system.

References

Alkan, M., "Azınlık Vakıfları: Tarihi Arkaplanı, Hukuki Yapısı ve İç Analizi" (Foundations of Minorities: Historical Background, Legal Structure and Interal Analysis), in *Akademik Bakış*, Number 4, (2009) pp. 93–111.

Brock, S., "The Fenqitho of the Monastery of Mor Gabriel in Tur Abdin", in*Ostkirchliche Studien* 2 (1979), pp. 168–182.

Brock, S., "Tur 'Abdin – a Homeland of Ancient Syro-Aramaean Culture", in H. Hollerweger (ed.), *The Living Cultural Heritage*, (1999), Linz: Friends of Tur Abdin, pp. 24–25.

Dolapönü [Dolabani], H., *[Mar Gabriel] Deyr-el-umur Tarihi* (The History of [Mor Gabriel] Deyr-el-umur), Translated into English by Cebrail Aydın, (1971) İstanbul: Baha Matbaası.

Kurban, D., & Kezban, H., *Bir 'Yabancılaştırma' Hikayesi: Türkiye'de Gayrimüslim Cemaatlerin Vakıf ve Taşınmaz Mülkiyet Sorunu.* (A Story of Alienation: Real Estate Problems of the Non-Muslim Communities' Foundations of Turkey), (2009) İstanbul: TESEV Yayınları.

Mor Gabriel Öğretim Kadrosu, "Mor Gabriel Manastırı'nın Kuruluş Hikayesi (The Story of the Founding of the Monastery of St. Gabriel)", in *The Voice of Tur Abdin*, (1997) Linz: June 1997, p. 12.

Palmer, A. *Monk and Mason on the Tigris Frontier*, (1990) Cambridge: University of Cambridge.

Rasmussen, T., & Thomassen, E. *Kristendomen*, (2007) Skellefteå: Artos&Norma.

Qartmin Trilogy [*Taş'itho d'Mor Şmuel u Mor Şemun u Mor Gabriel dab'Umro Kohnoyo d'Kartmin*]. (Referred to in this chapter as the "*Qartmin Trilogy*". The copy referred to is that of Dr Andrew Palmer, in which he compared versions of the manuscript found in the British Library and the Istanbul Syriac Library. This manuscript can be found as a microfiche in Dr. Andrew Palmer's book, *Monk and Mason on the Tigris Frontier*, Cambridge: Cambridge University Press.

St. Gabriel and Religious Freedom in Turkey

By Gus H. Bilarakis

Congressman Gus Bilirakis has represented portions of Florida's Tampa Bay area since 2007. A member of the House Foreign Affairs Committee, Rep. Bilirakis has been a strong supporter of religious freedom around the globe and is a member of the International Religious Freedom Caucus. As co-chair of the Hellenic Caucus, Rep. Bilirakis introduced a resolution calling on the government of Turkey to facilitate the reopening of the Ecumenical Patriarchate's Theological School of Halki without condition or further delay and has cosponsored legislation seeking to preserve religious freedom worldwide.

In 1971, the Turkish government forced the closure of the Halki seminary, the primary theological school of the Eastern Orthodox Church's Ecumenical Patriarchate of Constantinople. In the more than forty years since the forced closure, there has been sustained international pressure on the Turkish government to allow the seminary to reopen. Some of the most vocal support for Halki has come from the government of the United States, including Congress and the executive branch. Presidents Bill Clinton, George W. Bush, and Barack Obama have all called for the reopening of the seminary, noting its importance for religious freedom in a country that has been reluctant to afford rights to its beleaguered religious minorities. In December 2011, the Hellenic Caucus on the 112th Congress introduced H. Res. 506 calling for the immediate reopening of Halki.[1]

Almost a thousand miles away, in the Tur Abdin region of the south-eastern Turkish province of Mardin, a battle for a different monastery is being waged and is no less deserving of our attention. The ancient monastery of Mor (Saint) Gabriel in Midyat is highly revered among Syriac Orthodox Christians, serving as both a physical and spiritual centre for a Syriac population that has been driven from its ancestral homeland over the past century and now exists overwhelmingly in Diaspora. Since 1997, the Syriac Orthodox Church has been engaged in a multi-front fight to save the monastery: both the Turkish government and neighbouring Kurdish tribes have sued the church to seize significant portions of the monastery's land. As the unresolved land disputes wear on, the Syriac Orthodox Church's efforts to retain one of its cultural and spiritual centres has become symbolic of the struggle of religious minorities in Turkey for basic civil rights.

Indigenous to south-eastern Turkey, Syriac Christians have fallen victim to

---

[1] HR 506, 112th Congress.

Mor Gabriel monastery, hallway in front of main church. (From the book by Y. Bilge)

Turkey's suffocating restrictions on religious freedom and been pushed out of their homeland. The dwindling population –numbering less than 25,000 in Turkey, with around 3,000 in the south-eastern region – is now dwarfed by a Diaspora in the hundreds of thousands which has fled to countries where it may practice its faith in peace.[2] Syriac Christians (including Protestant, Orthodox, and Catholic Christians) are also referred to as Arameans and share their ancient heritage with Chaldeans, Assyrians, Maronites, and Melkites. The roots of these people stretch all the way back to the dawn of Christianity; their ancestral language is Aramaic, the language of Jesus and his contemporaries. St. Gabriel Monastery serves as a constant reminder of the Syriacs' ancient ties to this land: it was built in 397 A.D., less than a century after Constantine embraced Christianity, and houses a relic of its seventh century abbot together with several other saints.[3]

Despite their millennia-old presence in modern-day Turkey, Syriac Christians of all denominations are not recognized as a minority community in Turkey. Instead, Syriacs reside in a religious no-man's land: they are not a formally designated religious minority with the associated rights, and they are not part of the Muslim majority with those associated religious rights. As such, Syriacs are essentially deprived of the most basic civil rights.[4]

The Turkish government utilizes the 1923 Lausanne Treaty as its basis for minority rights. In accordance with this treaty, three minority groups – Armenian Orthodox Christians, Greek Orthodox Christians, and Jews – are legally recognized as religious minorities. These minorities are allowed to run schools, educate their communities in their faiths, and use their native languages. Although the treaty makes reference to the rights of other "non-Muslim" minority groups, these groups have never been afforded specific rights; religious institutions of any minority, including Armenians, Greeks, and Jews, do not possess legal personality and are not recognized by the state. For Syriac Christians, this means that they cannot use their buildings for educational purposes or teach their children in their native language; the last Syriac school in Turkey was closed in 1938.[5] Syriac Christians must register their religious groups as foundations or associations that are tightly regulated by the Turkish government's Directorate of Foundations,

---

[2] US Department of State, 2011.
[3] For more information on the history of the Mor Gabriel monastery, see Brock's article in this book.
[4] Syrian Universal Alliance, 2012.
[5] Higgins, 2009.

thereby severely restricting their rights, particularly as related to the maintenance and acquisition of property.[6]

Given these restrictions, it is not surprising that so many Syriac Christians have emigrated from Turkey. They have been haunted by a history of devastation, escalating dramatically in the last century. Syriacs were the victims of massacres coinciding with the mass killings of Armenian and Greek Christians leading up to Turkish independence in 1923, and the Syriac Orthodox Patriarch was expelled to Syria shortly thereafter. As the violent conflict between Kurdish rebels and the Turkish government escalated in the southeast during the 1970s and 1980s, Syriacs were caught in the crossfire. The government perceived them as disloyal citizens who were possibly aiding the Kurds, while the Kurds subjected Syriacs to intimidation and violent attacks.[7] With no defence against either side of the conflict, Syriacs fled their ancestral homeland en masse.[8] The town of Midyat, close to the St. Gabriel Monastery, was once almost entirely Christian; there are now less than 120 Christian families in a population of 60,000.[9] Widespread Turkish nationalist sentiment has cast aspersions on non-Muslim minorities, particularly in Southeastern Turkey, where Christian populations have traditionally been centred. On a mountainside between the city of Mardin and St. Gabriel Monastery in Midyat, nationalists carved the famous saying of Mustafa Kemal Ataturk, "How happy is the one who says 'I am a Turk'".[10] Although some Syriacs – particularly those who found financial success in Europe – have returned to the region, a string of more than 60 unsolved murders throughout the 1990s and 2000s exemplified the persecution and intimidation felt by the community, most notably on the local level as land disputes have accelerated. The most significant of these disputes is that of St. Gabriel Monastery.

For more than 1,600 years, St. Gabriel Monastery has served as a focal point of faith and community for the indigenous Christian community of southeastern Turkey. Now, it is the target of five lawsuits which seek to seize land from the monastery on the claims that it is illegally occupied by the Syriac Orthodox Church.[11] Three of the lawsuits come from arms of the Turkish government, including the Treasury and the Forestry and Waterworks Ministry, and two have

---

[6] For more information on the the Turkish foundation laws, see Onder's article in this book.
[7] For more information on the consequences of the Kurdish conflict for the Syriacs, see Makko's article in this book.
[8] Oehring, 2010 and Jenkins, 2010.
[9] Higgins.
[10] Aykol, 2010.
[11] For more information on the monastery's trials, see Oran's article in this book.

been brought by local villages. The complexity of the cases illustrates the convoluted nature of Turkish law as related to religious minorities, foundations, and property. As the Syriac Orthodox Church does not have legal personality, it cannot own or transfer property and thus has been unable to register the property which the monastery has occupied (and paid taxes on) for centuries. So when local Midyat officials began preparing a land registry, they informed the monastery that much of its land was actually state-owned forest: under a 1956 law, any land that remains agriculturally fallow for 20 years becomes "forest," and forest cannot be privately owned. At the same time, two neighbouring Kurdish villages, Eglence and Yayvantepe, claimed portions of the monastery's property as their own. These villages are reportedly dominated by the Çelebi tribe – rumoured to have participated in massacres of Christians in 1915 and a source of fighters for a state-run anti-PKK militia – and have been the subject of tension with the monastery in the past.[12] In early 2011, Turkish courts decided in favour of the state in both of the cases brought against the monastery by the Forestry and Waterworks Ministry; after losing appeals at the Supreme Court in Ankara, the St. Gabriel Monastery foundation took the cases to the European Court of Human Rights, where they are currently pending.[13] Despite the reformed 2008 law on Foundations, as well as a decree in August 2011 that promised to return seized properties to religious minorities, the situation for the Syriac Orthodox Church and the St. Gabriel Monastery is unchanged.

Though the monastery has yet to feel any legal repercussions from the five lawsuits, the monastery and the Syriac Christian community have felt the impact in a number of ways. After being largely driven from the country, the few remaining Syriacs feel targeted anew. Many perceive the barrage of lawsuits that seek to drastically diminish the territory of a symbolic Christian icon as an attempt to rid the region of its last Christians – by both the Turkish state and civilians. During trials related to the land disputes, Syriac Christians have been accused of proselytism and "illegal religious activities," which is a very serious accusation in a country where non-Muslims (and Christians in particular) are routinely characterized as threats to national security.[14] In one of many complaints filed against the monastery by local Muslim villagers, one man called on prosecutors to remember Mehmed the Conqueror and his vow to "cut off the head of anybody who cuts down even a branch from my forest". Opponents of the monastery have posited that it is built upon the remnants of a mosque, a claim that is sure to rile local Mus-

---

[12] *Economist*, 2010.
[13] Syriac Universal Alliance, p. 12.
[14] Ceyhan, 2008.

lims but patently false given the establishment of the monastery almost 250 years before the advent of Islam. There have been numerous cases of physical violence against Syriacs, including lay people and religious figures. In 2009, Father Yusuf Akbulut of the Church of the Virgin Mary in Diyarbakir was threatened with violence in retaliation for the Swiss minaret ban. Father Akbulut is the same priest who was arrested in 2000 and charged with inciting religious hatred for stating that he believed Syriacs, Armenians, and Greeks were the victims of genocide; after international pressure, including from the government of the United States, he was released. In 2010, a man from a village near St. Gabriel set fire to monastery crops and surrounding land in retaliation for the ongoing land dispute.[15] Rather than being protected by the state, Syriacs have found themselves the victims of state-sponsored demonization of their community. For example, in 2011, the Turkish Ministry of Education issued a 10th grade history textbook which includes a lesson about Syriacs in which they are depicted as traitors, rebels, and agents of the West.[16] State officials deny that they are anything but accommodating to Syriac Christians, pointing to the fact that they have even approved the construction of a new Syriac church outside Istanbul – as long as it abides by Turkish property laws and is built on property possessed by the foundation.

Incidents such as these have amplified the unease and sense of siege in which Syriac Christians in Turkey live. The continuing struggle to hold on to the 1,600 year-old monastery that serves as a centre of faith and community is only one battle for this population. The last year has seen a series of telling incidents between Syriacs and the state: a number of Syriacs have petitioned to legally change their names from the Turkish surnames they were required to adopt under the Surname Law of 1934, seeking to reclaim surnames which reflect their Syriac ancestry. Turkish courts have rejected these requests because Turkish citizens are barred from adopting "foreign" surnames. Such decisions reaffirm the state-sponsored view that minorities are still considered foreigners – as reflected by the fact that matters concerning religious minorities are handled by the Foreign Ministry. As long as Turkey continues to treat its religious minorities as strangers in their ancestral homelands and deprive them of the basic right of religious freedom, the United States and countries around the world will continue to pressure the Turkish government to abide by international human rights standards.

Note: Sarah Schlesinger of the Becket Fund for Religious Liberty contributed to this chapter.

---

[15] Ibid.
[16] Ibid.

References

112th United States Congress, House Resolution 506: Calling upon the Government of Turkey to facilitate the reopening of the Ecumenical Patriarchate's Theological School of Halki without condition or further delay (2011). Retrieved 9 April 2012 from http://www.govtrack.us/congress/bills/112/hres506.

Associated Press, "Turkish Court Tries Assyrian Priest for Backing Armenians" (21 December 2000). Available at http://www.atour.com/~aahgn/news/20001221m.html.

Assyrian International News Agency, "Text of U.S. Congressional Letter on Fr. Yusuf Akbulut" (22 December 2000). Available at http://www.atour.com/~aahgn/news/20001222a.html.

Aykol, Mustafa, "Revisiting Jihad in the New Turkish Republic" in *Hurriyet Daily News* (30 March 2010). Available at http://www.hurriyetdailynews.com/default.aspx?pageid=438&n=revisiting-jihad-in-the-new-turkish-republic-2010-03-30.

Ceyhan, Güzide, "Turkey: One year after Malatya murders, time to address the causes" in *Forum 18 News Service* (15 April 2008). Available at http://www.forum18.org/Archive.php?article_id=1115.

Economist, "Wooing Christians" (2 December 2010). Available at http://www.economist.com/node/17632939.

Higgins, Andrew, "Defending the Faith" in *Wall Street Journal* (9 May 2009). Available at http://online.wsj.com/article/SB123638477632658147.html.

Jenkins, Gareth, "Non-Muslim Minorities in Turkey: Progress and Challenges on the Road to EU Accession" in *Turkish Policy Quarterly* (28 June 2010). Available at http://www.turkishpolicy.com/images/stories/2004-01-evasivecrescent/TPQ2004-1-jenkins.pdf.

Oehring, Otmar, "Turkey: Syriac Orthodox Land – All people are equal, but some are less equal than others?" *Forum 18 News Service* (9 November 2010). Available at http://www.forum18.org/Archive.php?article_id=1508.

Oehring, Otmar, "Turkey: Hopes for 2009 Disappointed" in *Forum 18 News Service* (22 October 2009). Available at http://www.forum18.org/Archive.php?article_id=1365.

Syriac Universal Alliance, *Recommendations for Implementation of the International Covenant on Civil and Political Rights: TURKEY* (Report to the United Nations Headquarters in New York City, Office of the United Nations High Commissioner for Human Rights, Human Rights Committee, 104th session, 12–30 March 2012). Available at http://www2.ohchr.org/english/bodies/hrc/docs/ngos/SyriacUniversa_Turkey_HRC104.pdf.

United States Department of State, "Turkey" in *2010 Report on International Religious Freedom (July-December)*, 13 September 13. Available at http://www.state.gov/j/drl/rls/irf/2010_5/168343.htm.

Mor Gabriel: A Symbol of how the Turkish State Deals with its Religious Minorities

An overview of German and European political initiatives in support of the Monastery

By Ute Granold

Ute Granold, Member of the German Bundestag, is Deputy Chair of the Human Rights Working Group of the CDU/CSU parliamentary group in the German Bundestag. She is also the spokesperson of the Stephanuskreis set up by the CDU/CSU parliamentary group to campaign on behalf of persecuted Christians and religious freedom.

As the chapters of this book have demonstrated, the survival of the Monastery of Mor Gabriel and its community is under threat. Fears have arisen that, as a result of the lawsuits which have been ongoing for years, the monastery could be seized and deconsecrated. This would spell the end of a liturgical and monastic tradition which has been preserved for more than 1,600 years. Because the Monastery is an important centre for the cultivation of the Syriac Aramaic liturgical and vernacular language, and is a vital institution for preserving the cultural heritage of the Syriac Orthodox community, this would jeopardize the continued existence of Syriac Orthodox Christian culture as a whole.

Since the various lawsuits began in 2008, we have been following developments at the Monastery of Mor Gabriel very closely and with great concern in Germany and in many other EU countries. Delegations from the Monastery have visited Berlin regularly – most recently in April 2011 – to report on the situation. Members of the German Bundestag have also visited Turkey to gain an impression of what is happening and to advocate for the monastery in talks with representatives of the Turkish government. For my parliamentary group, the CDU/CSU, in particular, supporting the Monastery of Mor Gabriel is a key aspect of our global engagement for religious freedom. Volker Kauder, the Chairman of our parliamentary group, and Deputy Chairman Johannes Singhammer were among those who visited Turkey in mid-2010. I myself have underlined my personal support with two visits to the Monastery in 2009 and 2011. And on 19 March 2011, a group of 19 EU ambassadors based in Ankara visited the Monastery as a signal of the widespread solidarity with Mor Gabriel which exists throughout the EU.

Regrettably, these initiatives have yet to achieve any substantial improvement in the situation.

Mor Gabriel monastery, inner court (From the book by Y. Bilge)

The ongoing lawsuits are being monitored very closely in the EU, with representatives of the Member States' embassies regularly observing the proceedings. After the announcement of the judgment in the dispute with the State Treasury, EU countries agreed on diplomatic demarches which were delivered by the Head of the EU Delegation in Ankara in March 2011. Deputy Prime Minister Arınç gave his assurances, in this context, that the Turkish Government is committed to achieving a practical and pragmatic solution. He talked about the option of the Turkish Government leasing the land back to the Monastery on a long-term basis free of charge if the final judgment is not in its favour. However, this arrangement is rejected by the Monastery itself, which points out that it has owned the land on which it stands for hundreds of years.

Rallying the public in Europe in support of Mor Gabriel is vital. It is essential to counter the Turkish Government's stalling tactics and ensure that interest in the Monastery's fate does not decline by constantly drawing the public's attention to the case. Together with parliamentary group colleagues, I take every opportunity to remind the plenary of the German Bundestag about the situation in Turkey – in debates on human rights policy, on religious freedom or on the progress made in EU accession negotiations with Turkey, for example. In addition, the CDU/CSU, SPD and FDP parliamentary groups came together to express their support for the Monastery by tabling a joint motion, entitled "Ensuring protection for the Monastery of Mor Gabriel", on 6 May 2009. The following year, the CDU/CSU and FDP tabled a motion on religious freedom ("Protecting religious freedom worldwide", 30 June 2010) which voiced criticism of Turkey's shortcomings in this area and reiterated the call for an end to discrimination against religious minorities in Turkey. The Metropolitan and other representatives of the Monastery have thanked politicians and the churches in Germany for their solidarity on numerous occasions.[1]

For the future, networking between the European initiatives in support of the Monastery needs to be further improved. A good example is the Joint Declaration against the Persecution of Christians adopted by the CDU/CSU parliamentary group and the ÖVP Parliamentary Club following a meeting in the German Bundestag on 26 October 2011. In this Declaration, the German and Austrian partners turn the spotlight on the situation in Turkey and criticize the curtailment of religious freedom in that country with reference to the example of Mor Gabriel.

Unfortunately, hopes that Turkey will make efforts to move towards full respect for religious freedom and protect and preserve religious diversity and the country's rich cultural heritage have not been fulfilled. Today, there are fewer than 100,000 Christians of all dominations living in Turkey. The figure has been steadily decreasing over recent years. Instead of seeing this small minority as an enrichment for Turkey and offering them special protection and support as Turkish citizens, the Turkish state is continuing to put their churches and religious institutions under extreme pressure. Restrictive legislation which strongly intervenes in individual religious life poses a major threat to the survival of the Christian communities.

Despite some minor progress in recent years, religious freedom in Turkey is still subject to severe constraints. The way in which the Turkish state deals with its non-Muslim minorities falls short of European Union standards. For years, the European Union's progress reports have repeatedly highlighted the same shortcomings. Muslim religious instruction is mandatory for all schoolchildren, religious minorities are not permitted to train young clergy, and the Christian churches are prohibited from teaching their liturgical languages. Religious affiliation is noted

---

[1] In June 2012 both, the German Bundestag and the Dutch Tweede Kamer held a parliamentary debate on the situation of Mor Gabriel monastery and the Syriacs in Turkey. The document handed in at the Dutch Parliament can be found in the appendix.

in personal documents, opening the way for numerous forms of discrimination in daily life. Individuals can now apply to have this entry amended (or to leave it blank), which has the same effect. Non-Muslims are frequently the target of violence, as are their places of worship.[2]

The Monastery of Mor Gabriel has thus become a symbol of how the Turkish state deals with its religious minorities, as well as a benchmark of Turkey's willingness to continue along the road towards democratic statehood and the rule of law. Full respect for human rights and fulfilment of the Copenhagen criteria are basic prerequisites in qualifying for EU accession.

In Germany, we will therefore continue to work with the other EU countries and urge the Turkish Government to provide long-term guarantees that safeguard the survival and future of the Monastery of Mor Gabriel and to ensure that the Syriac Orthodox minority in Turkey can exercise their rights under the European Convention on Human Rights, which are clearly spelled out in the accession partnership with Turkey. Together with our European partners, we will also continue to urge the Turkish Government to comply fully with its obligations towards religious minorities under Article 18 of the International Covenant on Civil and Political Rights and Article 9 of the European Convention on Human Rights and provide safeguards so that in accordance with other international conventions too, non-Muslim religious minorities acquire legal personality and can fully exercise their rights as recognised minorities. We will also focus more intensively on the gaps in religious freedom in Turkey in the context of our relations with Turkey. We also expect the European Commission to comment in detail on this issue in the progress report and to insist, in the current accession negotiations, that Turkey demonstrates that it is making substantial progress in this area.

---

[2] For more information on this topic, see Pastoor's article in this book.

United for the Sake of the Mor Gabriel Monastery

By Naures Atto

Dr. Naures Atto has obtained her doctoral degree from Leiden University. Her dissertation is about the identity discourses of Assyrians/Syriacs in the European Diaspora. Atto is Mellon Postdoctoral Fellow in World Christianities at Cambridge University (UK) and is founder and board member of the Inanna Foundation.

The purpose of this report is to inform the reader of the alarming concerns ... Mor Gabriel Monastery is currently facing. The great injustice that may occur within the following weeks demands an immediate attention and satisfactory response by Turkish authorities to ensure that real estate rightfully owned by Mor Gabriel Monastery is not illegally occupied and acquired by locals surrounding the monastery.

Archbishop Timotheos Samuel Aktas, 2008

Years after Archbishop Samuel wrote his *Report on the Imminent Problems Facing the Syriac Monastery of St. Gabriel in Midyat* (2008), the lawsuits against the Monastery continue, with no positive results in sight. Although it is not the first time that *Suryoye*[1] in Tur Abdin[2] have found themselves in such alarming circumstances, this time it concerns one of their main institutions, and not merely as a religious centre. What exactly is at stake here? In 2008 the Mor Gabriel Monastery was confronted with two threats to its position: the occupation of its land by neighbouring villagers and the act by the Turkish State in laying claim to, and acquiring forest land from, the Monastery which it proceeded to register in the name of the Treasury.[3] Exacerbating the situation, several allegations were levelled against the

---

[1] The emic name *Suryoye* is used here in a sense synonymous with Syriacs, Assyrians, Arameans and Assyrians/Syriacs. In this article, the term Suryoye refers more specifically to the members of the Syriac Orthodox Church.

[2] Tur Abdin is a geographical area in South-East Turkey where many of the Suryoye who migrated to Europe had been living in the last century. Tur Abdin means 'mountain of the servants [of God]', a reference to the monastic life in this region in the early centuries of Christianity. See Palmer, 2010.

[3] The report discusses how the legal proceedings of surrounding Kurdish villages against the cadastral survey of Mor Gabriel Monastery has resulted in:

"[T]he grossly erroneous decision made by *Midyat Cadastre Directorate*, the legal real estate of Mor Gabriel Monastery shall now unjustifiably and unfairly be registered under Eğlence and Yayvantepe village names thereafter. Consequently, the villagers of the Eğlence and Yayvantepe shall enjoy the right to dispose of Mor Gabriel Monastery's real estate, which Mor Gabriel

Monastery, which led to court hearings.[4] On 26 January 2011 the Turkish Supreme Court expropriated 24 hectares of land from the Mor Gabriel Monastery and appropriated it to the State. In a report presented by Archbishop Samuel on the occasion of the 20th anniversary of the Solidarity Group of Tur Abdin/North Iraq on 24 February 2012, the archbishop made reference to the main court cases that are currently ongoing, three of which have been taken to the Supreme Court in Ankara, and indicated that the case against Kuryakos Ergün (president of the Mor Gabriel Monastery Community Foundation) is still underway at the local court in Midyat.

It is noteworthy that, in the wake of Archbishop Samuel's report in 2008, several *ad hoc* solidarity committees had been established and a multitude of events had been voluntarily initiated. An important characteristic of these events has been their united character. Prominent among them, Aktion Mor Gabriel managed to mobilize a broad platform which even included opposing Suryoye political groups.[5] Taking its place alongside the autonomy project in Iraq and the quest for recognition of the Seyfo (genocide) by Turkey, the case of the Mor Gabriel Monastery has now achieved the status of one of the most debated issues affecting the Suryoye in Turkey. Nevertheless, neither of these two other issues has thus

---

    Monastery had legally and rightfully held for in excess of 1600 years. This illegal act blatantly violates the right to property of Mor Gabriel Monastery's Community Foundation secured under both national law and European Convention on Human Rights and its protocols ... "

[4] Submitted on 20 and 27 August 2008 to the Midyat Public Prosecution Office. The Mor Gabriel Monastery Community Foundation has been accused of: occupying forest land without having permission to do so; conducting missionary activities through children of unknown identity between the ages of 10–12; the Mor Gabriel Monastery building owned by the Community Foundation is a historical museum and therefore required to have permission for prayer; children enjoy a religious education in the Monastery and anti-Turkish activities are carried out; the Community Foundation acts in contravention to Unity of Education Law; monks and metropolitans of the monastery are attempting to destroy national unity and incite people to insurgency; the Community Foundation receives funds from dubious sources; and the bank accounts of the Community Foundation should be confiscated.

[5] Aktion Mor Gabriel was specifically founded for this aim on the initiative of the Syriac Orthodox diocese in Germany in cooperation with four secular Assyrian/Syriac organizations in Germany – symbolizing the inclusion of the broad and divergent ideas present in everyday life, but united in Aktion Mor Gabriel. This cooperation is the result of a gathering organised by Mor Julius Hanna Aydin, Archbishop of the Syriac Orthodox Church in Germany, 30 November 2008. It resulted in the foundation of Aktion Mor Gabriel based on cooperation between: the Archdiocese of the Syriac Orthodox Churches in Germany, Dachverband der Entwicklungsvereine Tur Abdin (DETA); the European Syriac Union (ESU); the Föderation Suryoye Deutschland (HSA); and Zentralverband der Assyrischen Vereinigungen in Deutschland (ZAVD).

far received as much attention during a single activity as the Berlin demonstration that was organised to save the Mor Gabriel Monastery from extinction.

On 25 January 2009, approximately 19,000 Suryoye walked the demonstration from the Berliner Dom to the Brandenburger Gate to show their solidarity with the Mor Gabriel Monastery in Tur Abdin. Thousands of Suryoye raised their voices and made themselves heard: chants such as "Peace for Mor Gabriel! Peace for Tur Abdin! Freedom for the Suryoye!", as well as slogans in Suryoyo[6] and German were shouted, punctuated by the ululation (helholo) by women. Different generations, many of them born and raised in Germany, were joined by a great number of clergy bearing banners and carrying placards (most of them in German) with such texts as: "Ihr habt uns schon genug weggenommen!" and "GESTERN Hagia Sophia, HEUTE Kloster Mor Gabriel! MORGEN Kölner Dom?"[7] Young people waved the Assyrian and Aramean flags high or wore them wrapped around their bodies. At times they stared directly into cameras on hand to capture the event, shook hands demonstratively, smiled and continued walking in the demonstration. Today, 25 January 2009 is different in several ways, it seems. No matter what their ideological adherence, Suryoye from the "four corners of Europe", but particularly from Germany, gathered in Berlin to make their voices heard on a matter that is very dear to their hearts: the survival of the Mor Gabriel Monastery in Tur Abdin. The discursive field of the demonstration has not been limited to Berlin. Throughout the entire process of organising the demonstration, Suryoye around the world were informed and prepared through the media and local institutions.

Prior to the demonstration, Aktion Mor Gabriel broadcasted short films on the satellite TV channels[8] Suroyo TV and Suryoyo Sat and films were uploaded on YouTube, in which Suryoye were summoned in their mother tongue to participate in the demonstration. In these film clips, to the sound of hymns and accompanied by images of the Mor Gabriel Monastery, a man or woman appears who states: "I am the daughter/son of Mor Gabriel".[9] In order to address different generations and genders, a different person appears in each of the three versions of this same message (a young female cashier, a car mechanic and a housewife). This is

---

[6] Here, 'Suryoyo' is used to refer to the spoken mother tongue, 'Surayt'. In the Diaspora, it is also referred to as 'Turoyo'.
[7] English translation: "You have taken enough from us already!" and "YESTERDAY Hagia Sophia, TODAY Mor Gabriel Monastery, TOMORROW Kölner Dom?"
[8] These two TV Channels are based in Södertälje, Sweden, and broadcast to 82 countries.
[9] See for example: http://www.youtube.com/watch?v=g-y5fYGHbKo&feature=related (viewed March 2009).

followed by a voice-over addressing the people watching in Suryoyo: "You are also a son of Mor Gabriel. Stand up and raise your voice for your Monastery and your Homeland. Come to the demonstration in Berlin for the sake of the Mor Gabriel Monastery on 25 January!" On the evening of 25 January, both Suryoyo TV and Suryoyo SAT devoted live programmes to the demonstration. The broadcasts gave Suryoye around the world the opportunity to call in and to express their views about the entire campaign.

Remnants of the collapsed Mor Elio monastery in the Tur Izlo region within Tur Abdin. (H. Oberkampf)

Why have Suryoye worldwide shown their support for the demonstration? How is it that Aktion Mor Gabriel managed to organize the biggest event in the history of Suryoye in Europe to fight for the survival of a fourth-century monastery with approximately seventy inhabitants in a remote region of Turkey? In his alarming report in 2008, Archbishop Samuel voiced the fear of Suryoye around the world that, in the long run, this first land occupation of the Monastery will end in the expropriation of the monastery from the Syriac Orthodox Community. This fear of the expropriation of the monastery is also frequently expressed in YouTube films, in programmes on the community's TV channels and among individuals when they discuss similar cases of land disputes and the occupation of other churches in recent times. Highly conscious of the past, they base their fear on their historical experiences of similar cases. One central answer heard among Suryoye when discussing the importance of Mor Gabriel refers to its historicity (with a foundation that dates back to the year 397 A.D.) and its continued importance for Suryoye as a centre today.[10] This aspect is also mentioned in the report by the Archbishop:

The Mor Gabriel Monastery has been of significant importance for the Syriac Church throughout history: a torch continuously flaming both for Syriacs in Tur Abdin and for those in the Syriac Diaspora for the last 40 years. In recent years the Mor Gabriel Monastery has been taking an active role in attending to the social problems of the Syriacs in Turkey. With the ever dwindling population of Syriacs in Turkey, and increasing problems, this has only heightened the importance of Mor Gabriel as a focus point.

For many who grew up in Tur Abdin, this relationship is not only symbolic, as indicated by Archbishop Samuel. As a spiritual and cultural centre of the people, the monastery has indeed played a central role in the lives of individuals[11]. The majority of Suryoye who lived in Turkey and who knew Syriac had studied at either the Mor Gabriel Monastery or at the Zaferan Monastery.[12] As a result most of today's clergy and deacons in the Diaspora were educated in these historical centres of education. Father Kenan Bardanho (Germany), for example, addressed Suryoye in their mother tongue on YouTube in an effort to express the importance of the Mor Gabriel Monastery – first to himself as an individual and second to Suryoye as a people – in order to mobilize them to participate in the Berlin Demonstration by stating:[13]

I am the son of Mor Gabriel, I am a neighbour of the Mor Gabriel Monastery from the village of Kefferbe, I am a priest of [educated in] Mor Gabriel Monastery. I grew up nurtured and cared for by the Mor Gabriel Monastery. I am proud of the Mor Gabriel Monastery and I thank the Amo SuryoyoChristians for whom this blessed Monastery is as one of the main arteries of their heart. Wherever we are we bow to this blessed Mor

---

[10] In the Ottoman Empire the monastery acquired the status of a non-Muslim Community Foundation with the right to exist as a religious or charitable organization.
[11] For more information on the history and importance of Mor Gabriel, see Brock's article in this book.
[12] Earlier Syriac names for this monastery were 'Dayro d-Kurkmo' and 'Dayro d-Mor Hananyo'.
[13] See www.youtube.com/watch?v=7zD70bcA-oA.

Gabriel Monastery; a pearl, the light of Suryoyutho.[14] We bow to the tombs of the Saints; [Mor Gabriel Monastery] which has been home to Saints, Patriarchs, bishops, martyrs [here: people who have been killed for their religious beliefs]; any Suryoyo has someone who is buried in that holy sand of Mor Gabriel.

Today while we are in the Diaspora[15] we hear that there are people who want to occupy the land and woods of Mor Gabriel. But no matter how far distanced we are from it, we shall defend it. The Mor Gabriel Monastery is a symbol of the Amo Suryoyo, a symbol and sign that the Amo Suryoyo has land, important monuments, one of which is the Mor Gabriel Monastery. It surprises us that a country such as Turkey, that demands the rights of Turks all over the world, and that at the same time does not know that the Amo Suryoyo who have been living there already for more than 1,600[16] years and starts lawsuits against them after 1,600 years. This confuses us very much and this shows to what extent these leaders [of Turkey] do not know the history of the Amo Suryoyo. We call for the conscience and justice of the people; part of them are the Kurds: they should put their hand on their conscience.... The Mor Gabriel Monastery never did anything to harm Turkey, the Kurds or any other peoples living there.... It is very shameful that if this request [lawsuits against the Monastery] is conducted on behalf of a religion then this religion is meaningless if it hates individuals and a people who is blessed and with no sin. If these individuals request it on behalf of a nation, then this concerns an oppressive nation. No matter what, we stand up against this request. Therefore we ask them, "put your hand on your conscience". The Mor Gabriel Monastery belongs to the Suryoye!

In his appeal, Father Kenan pointed out the central role that the Monastery has played in both the individual and collective life of Suryoye. Father Kenan refers to it with striking metaphors: "arteries of their hearts", "a pearl" and "the light of Suryoyutho". He resorts to history when he refers literally to the graves of the highest clerics who lie buried in the Monastery and in their company he includes the martyrs (Suryoye who have been killed for their religious beliefs). In this religious discourse, he stresses the symbolic importance of the Monastery to Suryoye as *Christians*. The Monastery of Mor Gabriel has assumed a double symbolic function in their history: utterly essential to the roots of their Christianity and to the roots of their people in the geographical area of Tur Abdin. As a monastery replete with its own distinct history, Mor Gabriel is one of the last two main Syriac Orthodox monasteries which have continued to be inhabited in Tur Abdin up to the present-day. People who have migrated from Tur Abdin over the last few decades still think of Mor Gabriel as one of their principal 'collective homes'. The

---

[14] *Suryoyutho* can be translated as "Suryoye way of life", and is intended to include culture, religion and more.
[15] In Suryoyo, Father Bardanho used the term 'nukhroyutho', which means 'foreign lands' and which is also used in a sense synonymous to 'Diaspora' and 'abroad'.
[16] Here, 1,600 years is a reference to date the foundation of the monastery (397 A.D.).

strong relationship with this Monastery is aptly summed up in the slogan devised for the support campaign launched by Aktion Mor Gabriel: "I am a daughter/son of Mor Gabriel". This link implies the closest link in a family relationship – the most central and important social network among Suryoye.

View on the recently re-occupied monastery of Mor Augin from above. The mountains mark the end of geographic Anatolia to the south, with a view on the wide-stretched plains of Syria's northeast. (M. Tozman)

In the second paragraph Father Kenan refers to the symbolic function of Mor Gabriel as a monument and its role in relation to the connection to its geography: to own Mor Gabriel means to remain connected to the land it is built on, to the 'athro'. He then makes an attempt at a public negotiation by directing himself to the Turkish authorities and the concerned Kurdish villagers with the appeal to be conscientious and just, implying that they are not. Addressing the Turkish authorities indirectly, he questions and criticizes the way the authorities have dealt with the issue concerned here – both at religious and political level.

As Father Kenan already indicates, for the ordinary people as well, Mor Gabriel functions as a home with a broad meaning. As one of the last remaining centres of the Suryoye, it has functioned as the pride of the people. It means that they still depend on it as an institution – be it religiously, socio-culturally or politically. This function has often been intertwined. The hope in times of crises was based on spiritual sources. And the presence of Mor Gabriel has been instrumental in this. Especially after the 1980s, during the heightened political crisis in the region, Archbishop Samuel did many efforts to keep the Suryoye in Tur Abdin. Those who have continued to live there would perhaps not have done so if the Mor Gabriel Monastery would no longer be there. And the former villagers who have returned from Europe to the village of Kafro and rebuilt it, would perhaps not have done so if Mor Gabriel would no longer be there.[17] The Monastery is the hope for the people's future – whatever this may mean – in Tur 'Abdin.

What is feared if Mor Gabriel Monastery were to be lost? Both in the memorandum of Aktion Mor Gabriel (which was presented at the demonstration) and in the speeches of the speakers at the demonstration, a link is made between the loss of Mor Gabriel and the end of Syriac Christianity in Turkey. It stands to reason that Mor Gabriel is considered to represent an important symbolic centre for Christianity. On another level, Mor Gabriel also embodies the roots of the Suryoye in their homeland. Among groups of people such as the Suryoye, who have never ceased to express their wish to continue to survive as a people or to maintain their distinct collective identity (especially for those living in the Diaspora), the connection to the homeland is of the utmost importance. Despite this fact, the older generation who grew up in Tur Abdin commonly refers to their position in the homeland as that of 'yasire' (hostages). It is common among the Suryoye to refer to the European Diaspora as a sea into which they will eventually be absorbed and disappear as a people.[18] Consequently, in the threat to the Mor Gabriel Monastery, they foresee their existence as a people being menaced: they fear that the last remaining Suryoye lingering in the homeland will also be forced to flee and seek refuge in the Diaspora. Their overriding fear is that it will be easier for people to assimilate if they are deprived of their relationship with their historical artefacts in the homeland. In other words, the Mor Gabriel Monastery functions as a symbol in the conscious development of a myth of survival. The older generation refers to their current position in the Diaspora (far removed from their homeland) using the metaphor of orphans (yatume). If Mor Gabriel were be lost to the 'others', they fear they will be permanently cut off from Tur Abdin (which is considered to be the very heart and hearth of their homeland), as one

---

[17] For more information on the returning Suryoye to Kafro, see Oberkampf's article in this book.
[18] Atto, 2011.

of their main community centres will have been swallowed up. When that day dawns, the orphans will no longer be able to say who their parents are and where their roots lie. To illustrate the significance of the Monastery to the Suryoye, in a letter by the Solidarity Committee for Mor Gabriel (Sweden) which was sent to the Turkish authorities and Swedish political parties, this committee compared the function of Mor Gabriel for the Suryoye with that of Jerusalem for the Jews and Christians and that of Mecca for the Muslims. The loss of Mor Gabriel would mean an unequivocal amputation from what they perceive to be their ancestral homeland. Bereft of this relationship, Suryoye would lose hope, as it would lead to yet another great dislocation in their lives, bringing them closer to what they refer to in terms of 'death throes' (u nfoso da raghle). At that moment, the hope of the continuation of their existence as a distinct people will have been irrevocably snatched from them. In short, to be cut off from the 'athro' (homeland) both physically (because of living in the Diaspora) and symbolically (by ceding their ancient Monastery to the 'others') will place them in a situation in which they feel that they will be staring extinction as a people in the face.

In the struggle of the Suryoye for the survival of Mor Gabriel there are two aims: they want to remedy their condition as hostages (yasire) in Turkey and heal their condition of being orphans (yatume) in the Diaspora, through their survival as a distinct people. Consequently, the battle for the existence of Mor Gabriel is the outward and visible sign of their struggle for their very existence as a people, which has also been galvanized in the field of discursivity through the 'name debate'.[19] This dual struggle for survival in Tur Abdin and in the Diaspora culminated on 25 January 2009 in the attempt of Suryoye to organize a united event to combat the perceived threat to their existence. The Archbishop of Germany, Mor Julius Hanna Aydin, overwhelmed by the huge number of people who gathered in the Pariser Platz, said in his speech: "Today marks the birthday of the 'Amo Suryoyo' (Suryoye people)" – referring to and putting into words the strength of unity the audience felt that day. A commonly recurring word of appreciation for the unified organized event by Aktion Mor Gabriel was continuously heard in the Suryoye media in the weeks that followed. As Father Kenan (who addresses people on YouTube is therefore by no means an exception) has said:

All our parties, for the first time ever in their history in Europe since we were scattered in the [D]iaspora, have joined hands regardless of names and parties. They have demonstrated that the more we are torn by internal disagreements, the more the enemy lurking outside will deny us our rights and will have no pity on us. Therefore, I call once again on

---

[19] Atto, 2011.

our people in these [various] parties: to unite the Suryoyo name and to reach an agreement to come together, to leave behind the names [name conflict], to leave behind the [personal] gains and chairs [positions]; to organize! This [disunity] will not lead us anywhere. For the sake of this people, for their rights, for the rights of the Mor Gabriel Monastery in Tur Abdin, for our brothers in Iraq, Syria and Lebanon and wherever they are oppressed in the world. Unite![20]

To summarise, the strong cohesion revealed in the Berlin demonstration contrasts with the situation prevalent during the last fifty years of settlement in Europe when Suryoye individuals and groups have been at loggerheads with each other competing for hegemony over the group. The case of Mor Gabriel Monastery has also revealed that even people who have never been to this Monastery can imagine, express and experience a close link with it. Words matter. The claim "I am the daughter/son of Mor Gabriel" is without doubt a discursive practice in terms of identification, representation and taking a stand in order to defend the monastery. This common point of departure is the reason the case of Mor Gabriel has been so widely embraced and why it has become a common demand. And last but not least, the external threat posed by 'others' is an essential dimension in the definition and identification of 'us'; when the chain of the 'others' is blurred, the identification of the chain of 'us' also becomes ambiguous. The emigration of Suryoye to Western countries has resulted in an identification crisis.[21] Although Suryoye left their homeland and established themselves in Western countries several decades ago, they have continued to perceive the majority populations in the Middle East as the main external threat to their existence, as if they are still living in their historical homeland. Given this situation, the threat to Mor Gabriel has recalled a historical fear for the 'others'; in other words, the experiences with the 'others' are remembered in the collective memory of the people. Consequently, this perception of threat caused a stronger need for 'internal unity' and thus internal differences were bridged.

References

Aktas, T.S. *Report on the Imminent Problems Facing The Syriac Monastery of St. Gabriel in Midyad* (2008), Turkey: Mor Gabriel Monastery.
Aktas, T.S., "Report about the Current Situation in Turabdin", Presentation on the occasion of the 20th anniversary of the solidarity group of Turabdin/North Iraq.

---

[20] My translation of the original in Suryoyo. Available at: www.youtube.com/watch?v=7zD70bcA-oA.
[21] Atto, 2011.

Retrieved 20 March 2012 from: www.nordirak-turabdin.de/2012/02/28/der-aktuelle-bericht-uber-die-situation-im-turabdin-24-02-2012-erzbischof-mor-timotheos-samuel-aktas/.

Aktion Mor Gabriel (website). Retrieved 20 March 2012 from: www.aktionmorgabriel.de/.

Atto, N., *Hostages in the Homeland, Orphans in the Diaspora: Identity Discourses among the Assyrian/Syriac Elites in the European Diaspora* (2011), Leiden: Leiden University Press.

Bardanho, K., Speech for Aktion Mor Gabriel. Retrieved 18 January 2009 from: www.youtube.com/watch?v=7zD70bcA-oA.

Ninjos de Dios, "Mor Gabriel", (2009). Retrieved 5 March 2009 from: www.youtube.com/watch?v=EJo_wgQrOCg.

Palmer, A., *Monk and Mason on the Tigris frontier: The early history of Tur Abdin* (1990), Cambridge: Cambridge University Press.

Palmer, A., "La Montagne aux LXX monastères: La géographie monastique de Tur Abdin", in Jullien, F. (Ed.), *Le monachisme syriaque, Études syriaques* 7(2010), Paris: Geuthner.

Interview with Sébastien de Courtois

Dr. Sébastien de Courtois (1974) graduated as lawyer in 1997. After a first trip to Tur Abdin in 1998 he wrote his dissertation (The Forgotten Genocide 1895–1915, the last Arameans) on the history of the Syriacs in the Ottoman Empire at the École Pratique des Hautes Études (Sorbonne-Paris). Since that time he has regularly been travelling to Turkey and the land of the Syriacs between Urfa and the border of the Tigris. He lives in Paris and Istanbul where he works as a journalist for the radio (France Culture), press correspondent and as an author. His academic focus is on Christian minorities in Turkey and the Middle East. Moreover, he leads some projects of restoration of ancient monuments with the collaboration of the World Fund Monuments.

Mr de Courtois, you recently spent several weeks travelling through the Tur Abdin region as part of your PhD research. What was your impression of the current situation of the Syriacs in south eastern Turkey?

I took my first trip to eastern Turkey in the spring of 1998. At that time Tur Abdin was still a remote part of Turkey, and I felt as if I were still travelling during the Ottoman times, far from Istanbul and the crossroads of the Middle East. As you know, the closest bordering countries are Syria and Iraq. Iran is not too far away either, if you consider the possibility of travelling over the high Hâkkari mountains. I was travelling in the direction of Anatolia together with a friend of mine, and we wanted to take a walk around Lake Van to view the Armenian churches in the area. By chance, a map-reading error and boarding the wrong bus led to our discovery of the monasteries and villages of Tur Abdin. I was not expecting such a surprise. As far as I knew, there were no more Christians living in this part of Turkey. I was wrong.

You have been travelling in Tur Abdin since 1998. What changes have you perceived in the region in that time?

The current situation of the Christian (Syriac, or Süryani) population seems to be improving – I'm talking in terms of fear of attacks and other social improvements. The situation in 2012 bears little resemblance to what I experienced in Tur Abdin in 1998. At that time, all of the people that I met, with the exception of a tiny fraction of them, told me that their only hope would be to leave the country and start a new life in Europe, America or Australia. That was very sad. It was certainly the end of a long and glorious history. Aramaic would no longer be spoken in northern Mesopotamia! Once the last of the grandparents had passed away, there would be no one remaining in those beautiful villages and the churches would fall apart. Again, I was wrong.

After several years I decided to come back to take photographs of what I believed to be the last remnants of human archaeology. I also published a book in France, *Les derniers Araméens, le peuple oublié de Jésus (Tur Abdin)*. By that time I had started my career as an attorney and I then returned to my university, *the Sorbonne*, to study the history of the final years of the Ottoman Empire. My PhD dissertation was published in 2002, and focussed on the Aramean massacres (or *Sayfo*), specifically the terrible years of 1915 and 1917. It was the first extensive work on the subject.

Elderly Syriac women praying in the church of Mor Izozoel in Kfarze (Altıntaş). (S. de Courtois)

Security in the region has improved since the capture of PKK leader Abdullah Öcalan. The Turkish Army has also stopped the illegal actions against villagers and Kurdish people. The Turkish Hezbollah has been dismantled – or at least were asked to be more discrete – as they were responsible for a rash of killings targeting the Christian community. During the nineties, more than 40 Syriac people were assassinated. Several people told me that 60 families could leave a village from one day to the next due to the overwhelming sense of fear and insecurity. And that, of course, was precisely the point: to scare the Syriac out of their homes so that the local Kurdish people could take over the houses, villages and property. This conflict must be placed in the context of the fight between the Turkish army and the Kurdish PKK groups – the Christians were stuck in the middle and had practically been taken hostage. The message was: "You leave or you die."

Since 2005, I have seen some Christian families returning to Tur Abdin. Some villages are thriving once again. At first many of them were returning for the holidays, but gradually some of them decided to try a new settlement – building new houses and resettling their ancestral lands. Two or three 'new' villages have been built close to where the old one. I must say that I am greatly in favour of conserving used stones. I believe that it is very important for each village or church to maintain its original appearance. The past is a patrimony that should be respected, not destroyed or disfigured by overly modern elements. Concrete is the enemy! The future of these resettlements depends upon economic viability and security for the coming decade. I believe that days of being forced through desperation to leave have ended. More Syriac people living abroad should consider returning to their home lands, at least to keep the link alive with the local culture and traditions. It is important that the Diaspora not create an artificial homeland in their dreams. Tur Abdin is as real as the stones of Mar Gabriel.

Mor Gabriel was one of the places you visited when you went to Tur Abdin. How are the people there coping with the judgements handed down in January and February in which they were expropriated by the Turkish government? The chair of the monastery's foundation, Kuryakos Ergün, will go on trial in December for the alleged illegal construction of the monastery's wall on state land[1] Have you spoken to him about these reproaches?

Mar Gabriel is a very important place in Tur Abdin. I would even say that it's a kind of political and spiritual centre for the region. All of this is thanks to Mar Gabriel's central figure, His Eminence Samuel Aktas. I can say with confidence that, without him and his constant strength, Tur Abdin would not be the same. In 1998 Mar Gabriel was a citadel lost in a desert. Now in contrast it is a living centre for the Syriac people. Students are coming for the summer season and visitors are travelling from all parts of Turkey and all around the world. The sense of hospitality is intact, even in the face of so much litigation.

The legal issue initiated by the Turkish government is particularly shameful. The issue reflects badly on the country itself – more and more Turkish citizens, pro-democracy activists and journalists oppose this manner of dealing with reli-

---

[1] This interview was held in November 2011. The trials against Kuryakos Ergün have repeatedly been postponed with no verdict at the time this book was finished.

gious minorities – and is a tremendous waste of time and energy for the religious authorities. The bishop's hair has gone completely white! All of the concerns are about the monastery's future and not about the development of the region or spiritual activities!

I am following the case. The government is asking the monastery to destroy the wall, which was built in 2005. At the time it was built, the wall was intended to protect the monastery's land against incursions by hostile outsiders. The monastery has owned those lands since the 5th century! How is it possible that it is now left to local Kurdish villagers owned by feudal masters now part of the leading party – the AKP – to decide on the matter? It's nonsense. The bishop, Samuel Aktas, tells of the day when a judge who had come from Mardin to visit the monastery turned and asked him where the mosque was. A great deal of scurrilous gossip is being spread by a few local residents, the more fanatic of whom even claim that the monastery is trying to convert young Muslims to Christianity. Which is of course an abject lie.

So in a way you have technical arguments presented from the tax office that you can argue against with lawyers, and on the other side you have to fight the public rumour. The Süryani community is not alone in Turkey now. The Prime Minister, Tayyip Erdogan, said several times that he will try to help the monastery, but personally speaking I don't trust him at all, he wants to change Turkey in a deeper Islamic state and there is no way that he cares about Christians except to please the European Community. I am living in Turkey since 2008.

You noted in your book* The forgotten Genocide*(2004) that "Arabs, Turks and Kurds have all viewed the monasteries as their favourite targets" (p. 282). In this light, how do you judge the overall situation and its implications for the remaining Syriacs in Tur Abdin?

Tur Abdin is a miracle due solely to the strength of its people throughout history. Indeed, the riches of the churches have always been the subject of envy and looting. We in Europe tend to paint Kurdish people as victims, but that is not really true, particularly if you consider the fact that Kurdish tribes were involved in the mass killings of Christians in the declining years of the Ottoman Empire. We must also make a distinction among the Kurds, as well: some families or clans were very close with Syriacs or Armenians and aided them during the massacres perpetrated during the First World War.

What do you know about the general expropriation of Christian land by the Turkish government and Kurdish villagers?

The situation regarding Christian lands is very complicated and varies from one village to the next. I know that in one or two villages, Syriac families have had to pay Kurdish families to get back their own house. Christians have a reputation of being rich because they are living in Europe. It is not a question of politics, but rather a question of money... But the Turkish justice system has returned the rights to a family, as well. It's never a matter of black and white...

Deserted monastery of Mor Yuhanon Tayoyo, built on the cliff of Mount Izlo. (M. Tozman)

What are your views of the minority rights regime under the current AKP government in light of, for example, the restitution decree announced by Erdogan in August?

This decree is a very important step. Some people say that it's not going far enough. The Catholic Church for instance, which is a large landholder, is not involved in the decree. Erdogan is a master of propaganda and media manipulation. We are still awaiting the first restitution. The Syriac Church should be united in this matter with the Chaldeans (who share a background in the Syriac language), the Greeks and Armenians. I'm not sure that they all think alike. There's also strong opposition in the Syriac community between people from towns such as Mardin and people from the villages. The two groups don't share the same view of history. The villagers are more deeply rooted in the region.

Will you remain committed to the region and its people in future?

Tur Abdin is still a vibrant region. The sombre predictions for the area have all been dispelled! There are still much to study in Tur Abdin: there is work for archaeologists, epigraphists, philologists, historians and so on. I am currently planning to work only on certain villages and to study the daily life there. I want to understand the structure of the Syriac family and society from an anthropological perspective. Relations with the Muslim neighbours are also very important to understand, as it is a condition for a better life in the region for Christians. I myself am quite optimistic about the future of Tur Abdin.

Thank you very much for your efforts and your help!

Appendix 1: Initiative Policy Document[1]

By Dr. P.H. Omtzigt

Member of Parliament

Christian Democratic Appeal (CDA)

THE ALARMING SITUATION OF THE MONASTERY OF MOR GABRIEL AND THE ARAMAIC-SPEAKING CHRISTIANS IN TURKEY – THE SYRIACS

1. Introduction[2]

In Turkey, Christian minorities often have a difficult position, socially, politically and economically. The expropriation of one of the oldest Christian monasteries in the world, the Syriac Orthodox Monastery of Mor Gabriel, which was built in 397 AD in the southeast of Turkey, is a typical example of this precarious situation and deserves special attention.

We have to bring up the question whether religious minorities are being sufficiently protected by the authorities in contemporary Turkey and whether this essential aspect of human rights should be subject to a more emphatic dialogue.

This Initiative Policy Document contains a summary of the situation and five recommendations to the government of the Netherlands to commit itself to the cause of religious freedom, not only in an abstract sense, but in this concrete case as well.

---

[1] This Initiative Policy Document was submitted to the Dutch Parliament on March 9, 2012 and received the document number 33195.

The Committee on International Relations of the Dutch Parliament has accepted this Initiative Policy Document on March 15, 2012 and has voted in favour of a debate. Moreover, the Committee has asked the Foreign Minister, prof. dr. U. Rosenthal, to react to the five recommendations made in the document.

After the Parliament has received the Foreign Minister's written statement, a debate on the subject took place on 20 June 2012. The political parties discussed the document with the Foreign Minister and its submitter, dr. Pieter Omtzigt and handed in several motions. Two of these motions demanded that the Mor Gabriel case should be put on the agendas of the Council of Ministers of the European Union and the Committee of Ministers of the Council of Europe. Both motions were accepted by the Dutch Parliament on 5 July 2012.

[2] This paper is the result of research carried out by Markus Tozman.

2. The importance of the Monastery of Mor Gabriel

The Monastery of Mor Gabriel was officially founded in 397 AD, but had been built a couple of decades earlier. In 397, the principal church of the monastery was founded with the support of the Byzantine Emperor Anastasias I. This church is still in use.

This makes the monastery 400 years older than the oldest monastery of Mount Athos in Greece, and one and a half century older than the monastery of Saint Catherine on Mount Sinai.

The current premises of the monastery still include parts dating back to the first centuries of its existence, such as the 17 metres high "Dome of Theodora", which dates from the 6th century, a gift from Byzantine Empress Theodora, the wife of Emperor Justinianus I. Another very special relic of paramount importance to art historians, is a beautiful mosaic from the 6th century. It decorates the apse of the principal church and is one of the most precious undamaged Byzantine mosaics from that period.

Through the centuries, the monastery was attacked and plundered by Persians, Arabs, Mongols, Kurds and Turks, yet the monastery, which housed hundreds of monks in its heyday, managed to maintain its leading role in the Syriac-Orthodox church and continues to be one of the spiritual centres of Eastern Christianity.

Saints like Philoxenus of Mabbug, Simeon of Kartmin and Abbot Gabriel, after whom the monastery was named, lived within the walls of the monastery. They are buried in the catacombs (built in 449), together with many other saints and more than 10,000 believers. The library of the monastery once was among the most important libraries of Eastern Christianity. Unfortunately, due to plundering and wars, the monastery contains much fewer volumes today. However, several European Museums, such as the British Museum, still display books from the Mor Gabriel collection.

Despite the fact that until the late 1990s, large parts of the Christian population emigrated from the surrounding villages to Europe, the importance of the monastery has increased significantly. Many members of the clergy of the worldwide Syriac Orthodox church were educated at Mor Gabriel. Even monks from Kerala (South-India), where the largest community of the Syriac Orthodox church lives, are sometimes sent to Mor Gabriel to receive their education. For the Syriac Orthodox church, which goes back to the Apostolic See of Antioch, the monastery is of paramount importance. The history of this denomination goes straight back to the Apostle Peter. Closure of this monastery as a centre would have disastrous consequences for the worldwide church community. It is not for nothing that the monastery is called the "second Jerusalem" of the Syriacs – the name of the Aramaic-speaking community.[3]

3. The structure of this Initiative Policy Document:

The first chapter contains a brief survey of the decline of the Christian community in Turkey over the past century, which caused many monasteries and churches to disappear. This brief overview is followed by two chapters about the legal position of Christians in Turkey and the cases brought against the monastery. The next chapter deals with other issues at stake and the international response to the Mor Gabriel case. Fortunately, there are some positive developments in Turkey, which deserve attention. The last section contains five recommendations.

4. Historical background: development of the Christian community in Turkey

Turkey plays a key role in Christianity and in the Holy Bible. This is where many saints and Church Fathers came from. Besides, for almost 1000 years, Asia Minor was part of the Christian Byzantine Empire. However, Christians constitute a decreasing part of the Turkish population. At the outset of the 20th century, as much as 20 % of the Turkish people were Christians. By today, this percentage has fallen to a mere 0,15 %[4]. In the course of a century, Turkey has changed from a multi-religious society into a mono-religious society. Old traces of Christianity, but also of other religious minorities in Turkey, threaten to be wiped out.

The table below shows that the number of Christians in Turkey has rapidly decreased over the past century during certain episodes:

Year	1914	1927	1945	1955	1965	1991	2005
Muslims	12,941	13,290	18,511	23,810	31,139	56,860	71,997
Greeks	1,594	110	104	87	76	8	3
Armenians	1,204	77	60	60	64	67	50
Other Christians	176	71	38	62	74	50	45
Jews	128	82	77	46	38	20	23

---

[3] This information is based on an article written by Brock, S. (2012) The Monastery of Mor Gabriel: a historical overview, and its wider significance today. It is to be published in the course of 2012.

[4] Icduygu, A., Toktas, S., & B.A. Soner. (2008). The politics of population in a nation-building process: emigration of non-Muslims from Turkey. Ethnic and Racial Studies, 31 (2), 358–389. (Other writers arrive at different and often higher estimates of the number of Christians).

Year	1914	1927	1945	1955	1965	1991	2005
Total non-Muslim	3,102	340	279	255	252	145	121
Total	16,034	13,630	18,790	24,065	31,391	57,005	72,120
Percentage non-Muslims	19,3	2,5	1,5	1,1	0,8	0,2	0,15

Table 1: Muslim/non-Muslim communities 1914–2005 in thousands[5]

5. Legal and political position of Christians in Turkey

The protection of minorities in Turkey is laid down in the Treaty of Lausanne from 1923, which is the revised peace treaty for Turkey after the lost World War I. It states that only non-Islamic communities are treated as minorities. This means that the Kurds or the Alevites are not recognised as minorities.[6] All non-Islamic religious communities should have this status, though. However, the Turkish government only recognizes Armenians, Greeks and Jews under the Treaty of Lausanne, and no other minorities.

According to the treaty, the "Lausanne-minorities" enjoy certain rights, including the right to use their own language, equal political and civil rights, the right to establish religious, educational and social welfare institutions as well as the right of freedom of religion, travel and migration.[7] In actual practice, problems still occur. The legal battle over the Greek-Orthodox seminary in the Isle of Halki is probably the most well known example of this. In 1971 the Turkish authorities closed the seminary, because a new law laid down that only the government was authorised to manage institutions of higher education. The seminary remains closed.

According to the Turkish government, the Syriacs, Roman-Catholics, Protestants and other Christian communities do not have a legal status and do not exist

---

[5] Aus Politik und Zeitgeschichte: Religiöse Minderheiten im Islam, 26/2008, Bundeszentrale für politische Bildung, p. 24. The figures for 2005 come from Icduygu, A., Toktas, S., & B.A. Soner. (2008). The politics of population in a nation-building process: emigration of non-Muslims from Turkey. Ethnic and Racial Studies, 31 (2), 358–389.

[6] Treaty of Lausanne, 1923, Sections 37–45.

[7] Toktas, S, & Aras, B. (2010). The EU and Minority Rights in Turkey. Political Science Quarterly, 124 (4), 697–720.

de jure in Turkey.[8, 9] This makes their legal position even more difficult. Formally, the Syriacs are not allowed to provide education in Aramaic, nor are they allowed to practice their (church) traditions in public. Moreover, religious buildings and lands are being expropriated and occupied by the government or their Kurd neighbours.[10] Their centuries-old churches and monasteries cannot be restored, because restoration often requires permits, which are not granted by the authorities.[11] The cases against the Monastery of Mor Gabriel in southeast Turkey, founded in 397 AD and one of the oldest monasteries in the world, are a symbol of this. The cases are described below.

6. The cases against the Monastery of Mor Gabriel

In the process of harmonization with European standards, the land registration and cadastre system of Turkey turned out to be obsolete. The introduction of a new system was decided on in 2004. The World Bank has been funding the project since 2008.[12]

The new land surveying methods have provided the authorities and the Kurdish neighbours of the Syriacs with the opportunity to expropriate the monastery in a legal way. In 2008, five lawsuits were brought against the monastery. They are described in the following.

The striking thing here is that government bodies take legal action on church property. In many countries that would be considered outrageous. It is curious that the Turkish State does this, especially now that it has taken the positive step of returning other religious property it had expropriated in the past. It is also curious that if the state loses a case like this, it will take it on to a higher court.

Apart from the State, the Kurds from the neighbouring villages also brought a charge against the monastery, accusing it of sending out 10-year old children as missionaries, together with the abbot and the monks, in order to undermine the integrity of the Turkish State. They also claim that the monastery is built on the

---

[8] EU Policy Department External Policies. (2008). Religious Freedom in Turkey: Situation of Religious Minorities, pp. 1–2 and p. 8.
[9] The Dutch Minister of Foreign Affairs, Mr Rosenthal, has confirmed this in reply to written Parliamentary questions (758, 2011/2012).
[10] Oberkampf, H. (2011). Ohne Rechte keine Zukunft. Erlangen: Verlag für Mission und Ökumene.
[11] European Commission against Racism and Intolerance. (2011). Report on Turkey, p. 32. Strasbourg: Directorate General of Human Rights and Legal Affairs.
[12] World Bank. (2010). Turkey Land Registration and Cadastre Modernization, www.worldbank.org.

premises of an earlier demolished mosque (The monastery was founded 200 years before the rise of Islam).[13]

1. The first case was initiated by the government. The claim is that the monastery uses parcels of land that are State property. However, the monastery possesses certificates of title and other documents confirming that the monastery has paid taxes for the land parcels in question since the early 20th century.
   The monastery won the case in first instance, but then the State appealed. In June 2012 the supreme court of Turkey decided in favour of the State, causing the monastery to lose 244.000m^2 of land.
2. The second case involves 276.000m^2 of land owned by the monastery, which the authorities (in this case the Turkish forestry commission) have defined as woodland. In Turkey woods and rivers cannot be private property, so parcels of woodland automatically became State property. However, the monastery possesses certificates of title for these parcels, too, and has paid taxes since the creation of the Turkish Republic. The trees have been planted on what once was very bare land, as old photographs prove.[14] The monastery went to court over this expropriation, but lost this case also in the supreme court, resulting in the loss of another 276,000m^2 of land in January 2011.
3. The third case is closely connected to the second one. The outer wall of the monastery, which has been there for several centuries, is built for two-thirds on parcels the government has defined as woodland. This means that the wall illegally stands on land of the government and therefore must be pulled down. This would deprive the monastery of its natural protection. Kuryakus Ergün, the president of the monastery foundation, is held liable for this. The case against him is still in progress and might lead to his being jailed.
4. & 5. The fourth and fifth cases were brought against the monastery by its Kurdish neighbours. Three villages used the cadastral survey to change the administrative boundaries of the monastery, established in 1930, to their advantage. Due to this boundary adjustment, the monastery was to lose land again. The monastery lodged an appeal against this and produced evidence of ownership (certificates of title and evidence of taxes paid). The monastery won this case too, in first instance. Again, the opposite parties lodged an appeal, but the court has not yet rendered a decision.

---

[13] Süddeutsche Zeitung. (24.12.2008). Trutzburg am Rande der Christenheit.
[14] For a clear description of how expropriation works and which legal fallacies are used, see: Oran, B. (2011). Turkish Foreign Policy 1919–2006, facts and analyses with documents, Utah: University of Utah Press.

Appendix 1: Initiative Policy Document on the Mor Gabriel Monastery

In the second cases the monastery has already lodged an appeal with the European Court of Human Rights in Strasbourg. In the first case, the appeal to the European Court of Human Rights is being prepared.[15]

7. The impact of these cases on other conflicts

Cadastral conflicts are not limited to Mor Gabriel. Hardly any Christian village or monastery has escaped form being affected by these measures. In a press release of 28 September 2011, the Syriac Universal Alliance made mention of over 10 million square metres of land expropriated by the government.[16] As early as in 2006, the bishops of the last two Syriac Orthodox bishoprics in the south-eastern part of the country submitted an official notice of objection to the expropriation of their churches to the president of the human rights committee of the Grand National Assembly of Turkey, Mehmet Elkatmis. They also made mention of the dilemma that they cannot defend themselves because they do not have legal personality.[17] The problems the Monastery of Mor Gabriel faces with its property is of paramount importance for the whole Aramaic-speaking community and their cultural heritage.

Moreover, there are problems concerning the buildings, which cause uncertainty to the inmates of the Monastery of Mor Gabriel. The monastery has been granted the status of a protected building ("sit alani"), which means that no restorations can be carried out without prior permission. Necessary repair works cannot be carried out without permission either. It is often pointed out that such permission is never granted by the government. For instance, the mosaic of the principal church of Mor Gabriel, a relic from the 6th century, badly needs restoration, but permission for this has not yet been given. Other monasteries and churches of the Syriacs face the same problems and may not be renovated, whereas chances are high that these centuries-old buildings, witnesses of a once rich Byzantine and Christian culture in Anatolia, may collapse. Therefore, the conclusion can be drawn that the government does not make any effort to ac-

---

[15] The sources of the description of the legal cases are several newspaper articles, a publication by the monastery titled "Report on Mor (Saint) Gabriel Monastery's Legal Problems", an extensive interview with delegates of the Mor Gabriel Monastery (07.10.2010) by M.K. Tozman (University of Maastricht) and an article written by Baskin Oran, Prof. emer. of International Relations (University of Ankara) with the title "Reconciled by Mor Gabriel".

[16] Syriac Universal Alliance. Arab Spring Must Protect Native Minorities in the Middle East. Retrieved 12.12.2011: http://www.sua-ngo.org/node/1353.

[17] Ersuch um Schutz für die syrischen Christen und für ihr kulturelles Erbe in der Türkei. (2006). Retrieved 12.12.11 from: http://huyodo.com/index.php?p=cheats&action=displaycheat&system=56&area=1&cheatid=466.

tively protect the cultural heritage of this minority.[18] In the case of the Mor Yaqub monastery, the authorities threatened to pull down recently restored parts, because no prior permission had been given for restoring them.[19]

8. Positive developments

However, there are also positive developments in Turkey with regard to the situation of minorities, which have to be mentioned. For instance, a committee has been set up, with representatives from all political parties, who will start preparing a new constitution in 2012. This means that the Kurdish party BDP can also take part in the decision-making. Representatives from minority groups, NGOs and other social interest groups will be involved. This offers a great opportunity to the Turkish government and the other parties to change their policy on minorities. Moreover, for the first time in 50 years, a Christian was elected MP, for Erol Dora (BDP). This is something that would have been totally unthinkable 20 years ago.

9. Final remarks: international action and follow-up

Several European countries have come into action for the protection of the Monastery of Mor Gabriel: Belgium[20], Switzerland[21], Germany[22], the Council of Europe[23], the European Parliament[24] and the European Commission[25], to mention only a few examples.

In October 2011 a delegation from the German Bundestag paid a visit to the monastery. The Archbishop and the people of Mor Gabriel described the situ-

---

[18] An incomplete list (limited to the region of Mardin) of churches and monasteries falling under "the preservation of monuments and historic buildings" can be found on this webpage http://www.mardinkulturturizm.gov.tr/belge/1-60907/kiliseler---manastirlar.html.

[19] Interview by M.K. Tozman (University of Maastricht) with delegates from the monastery 07.10.2010.

[20] Proposition de résolution concernant la protection de la communauté chrétienne en Irak, au Proche-Orient et au Moyen-Orient. Retrieved 13.12.2011: http://www.senaat.be/crv/5-31.html#_Toc299458943

[21] Turquie, Minorité Araméenne spoliée. Retrieved 13.12.2011: http://www.parlament.ch/F/Suche/Pages/geschaefte.aspx?gesch_id=20115410.

[22] Deutscher Bundestag: Schutz des Klosters Mor Gabriel sicherstellen. 16. Wahlperiode, 06.05.2009, Drucksache 16/12866.

[23] Parliamentary Assembly of the Council of Europe, resolution 1704 (2010, adopted), 19.6. and 19.7.

[24] European Parliament resolution (9 March 2011) on Turkey's 2010 progress report.

[25] European Commission. Turkey 2011 Progress Report. 12.10.2011.

Appendix 1: Initiative Policy Document on the Mor Gabriel Monastery

ation as "unbearable" and fear that Christianity may disappear from the entire region without active support from Europe.[26] The community of the monastery stands with its back against the wall. Of the more than 100.000 Syriacs who lived on Turkish soil in the early 20th century[27], a mere 13,000 remain in Turkey today.[28] (By way of comparison: in the Dutch region of Twente live more than 15,000 Aramaic-speaking Christians[29]). In Germany, the Christian Democratic Party CDU is considering whether a debate on the issue may be held in the Bundestag. Volker Kauder, leader of the CDU group, goes as far as linking the possible accession of Turkey to the European Union to the Mor Gabriel case.[30]

If Mor Gabriel is to lose all its land, this will have an enormous impact on the monastery, which will probably not survive. Mor Gabriel is the most important monastery of the Syriacs in Turkey and the only monastery in Turkey where boys are schooled in Syriac Orthodox liturgy, although not officially. Should the monastery be forced to close its door, this would mark the end of the remaining Syriacs and their religion and culture in Turkey. The clergy training will disappear. The Syriacs will lose their leaders and their cultural and religious centre. A very valuable cultural heritage would get lost. Therefore, the monastery is very symbolic for the future prospects of Christians in Turkey.

Apart from its significance for Christianity, the monastery is an example of the rich cultural heritage of Turkey, which is falling into disrepair in a large number of places. This cultural heritage is of great value for Europe as well. The cultures on Turkish territory were crossroads between East and West. Should they disappear, Europe would lose a pillar of its own history. It was precisely in what is now Turkey that the apostle Paul, one of the major saints of Christianity, established the first communities of faith. By applying for membership of the European Union, Turkey clearly made a turn towards its European history. That is why Turkey should commit itself to the preservation of the European-Christian

---

[26] Talk with Ute Granold, member of the German Bundestag and president of the Stephanuskreis, a cluster that has committed itself to the cause of persecuted Christians worldwide.
[27] De Courtois, S. (2004). The forgotten Genocide: Eastern Christians, the last Arameans. New Jersey: Gorgias Press.
[28] Thomsen, J. (2007). The Assyrians/Syriacs of Turkey. A forgotten people. Malmö University: School of International Migration and Ethnic Relations.
[29] Strümper, W. Gevargis, H. (publishers). Die Syrisch-orthodoxe Kirche in der Zeit. Paderborn: Bonifatius.
[30] Focus Nachrichtenmagazin. Die Türkei fühlt sich diskriminiert. Retrieved 16.12.2012: http://www.focus.de/politik/ausland/eu-beitritt-die-tuerkei-fuehlt-sich-diskriminiert_aid_603647.html.

culture. To put it in the words of Professor Dr Sebastian Brock, the worldwide leading expert in Syriac Studies:

"It has only been in the last half century that ecumenical dialogue between the Syrian Orthodox Church and the other Churches, Eastern Orthodox, Catholic and Reformed, has taken place, and this has led to a growing realisation among the other Churches, that the Syrian Orthodox Church, and the Syriac tradition in general, represents a hitherto very largely forgotten strand of Christian tradition that has much to offer to the other Churches, all of which have an essentially European background. Seeing that the Monastery of Mor Gabriel preserves this specifically Syriac aspect of Christian tradition in a pre-eminent way, its welfare is obviously a matter of very wide concern."[31]

10. Recommendations

The Christian Democratic Appeal promotes religious freedom, both in the Netherlands and in the Near East, and is dedicated to the preservation of the Monastery of Mor Gabriel and other religious and cultural heritage sites.

Two democracies, which both have signed and ratified the European Convention on Human Rights, should not only pay lip service to religious freedom, but also put it into practice. That is what they ought to confront each other about. The Turkish government talks to the German and Dutch governments about immigration and integration policy, and makes use of the religious freedom in these countries. It sends imams to the Netherlands, who are paid by the Turkish State. Given their friendly relations, the Netherlands and Turkey should talk to each other about the way in which both countries deal with minority groups and cultural heritage. The monasteries and churches of Turkey not only belong to the cultural heritage of Turkey itself, but also to the cultures that partly shaped the Dutch and European identity. That makes preservation of this cultural heritage of paramount importance for the Netherlands, Europe and the world. It is not done to expropriate property of churches and monasteries. This must be the clear position of the Netherlands when taking action. In the past, the Dutch government has said it will follow the case of the Monastery of Mor with apprehension.

The Dutch government can pursue its policy as follows:

1. Turkey preserves the Monastery of Mor Gabriel and its surrounding lands in their original size and nominates the whole site for Unesco world heritage sta-

---

[31] Brock, S. (2012). *The Monastery of Mor Gabriel: a historical overview, and its wider significance today* in the chapter by Sebastian Broch in this book.

Appendix 1: Initiative Policy Document on the Mor Gabriel Monastery

tus. Like other mosques and churches on the list, the monastery remains in use as a place of worship.
2. As part of the celebration of 400 years of contact between the Netherlands and Turkey, both countries organize a joint high-ranking visit to the Monastery of Mor Gabriel.
3. The Netherlands puts the case of the Monastery of Mor Gabriel and its rights on the agenda of the Council of Ministers of the Council of Europe, in reply to Resolution 1704/2010 not having been implemented, and asks Turkey to draft at least an answer to the request for improvements.
4. The Netherlands puts the case of the Monastery of Mor Gabriel, its rights and the expropriated lands on the agenda of the Council of Ministers of the European Union, in reply to the new foundations act, which does grant new rights to "Lausanne"-minorities, but not to the Syriac-Orthodox community.
5. The Dutch government writes a formal note to the Court in Strasbourg in support of the cases brought by the Monastery of Mor Gabriel and for the protection of religious property.

Appendix 2: The Disappeared Documents from St. Gabriel Monastery's Case File[1]

By Baskin Oran

Translation from Turkish original by Abdulmesih BarAbraham

1. **On court decision, a portion of the lands belonging to the historic Syriac Monastery of St. Gabriel has been seized by the State Treasury. This is apparently based on a mysterious "disappearance" of some essential documents from the case file submitted by the Monastery to the Court of Cassation.**

I have recently received surprising information which obliges me to revise an article that I had just written. I am referring to an article appearing on the front page of Radikal (June 16, 2012), reporting that parts of the lands of St. Gabriel's ancient monastery would redound to Treasury, pursuant to the ruling of Turkey's Supreme Court of Cassation (Yargıtay Hukuk Genel Kurulu, "YHGK").

This judicial decision appears to rest on the mysterious "disappearance" of some essential documents from the case file. These documents had previously been submitted to the court by the authorities of the monastery! Let me begin by summarizing the history of this affair, along with pertinent dates and references.

2. The Rationale for the decision of the Supreme Court of Cassation

On January 29, 2009 the Treasury of the Turkish Republic initiated a lawsuit in Midyat's Cadastral Court (hereinafter: "Midyat"), against the Foundation of St. Gabriel. The Treasury wants the transfer a total of 244 dönüm [approx. 80 acres] of land registered to the Foundation. Midyat examines the documents, conducts an on-site survey, and on June 24, 2009 it issues an extremely detailed decision rejecting the Treasury's lawsuit (base nr: 2009/11, decision nr. 2009/28).

The Treasury appeals. Chamber 20 of the Court of Cassation (hereafter: Chamber 20) overturns the decision on December 7, 2010 and orders the transfer of the land to the Treasury (base nr. 2010/13416, decision nr. 15347).

---

[1] The article appeared in the Turkish daily Radikal's Sunday supplement Radikal-2 on June 24, 2012: http://www.radikal.com.tr/Radikal.aspx?aType=RadikalEklerDetayV3&ArticleID=1092244&CategoryID=42

The decision of the appellate court is explained as follows: "Under Article 14 of the Cadastral Law, in the absence of a registered deed, where the petitioning party seeks to register ownership based on a de facto possession of 20 years or more, the registration cannot exceed an area greater than 100 dönüms. In the present case a land area of 244 dönüms was registered, which is well in excess of the maximum authorized by law."

But in the same way that the [Quranic] Surat An-Nisa 43 says "do not approach prayer," has its continuation that says: "...if you are drunk", similarly Article 14 of the Cadastral Law which states "cannot exceed 100 donum", has its own continuation. The Article specifies that "notwithstanding the designated limit [i.e., 100 dönüms], an area exceeding this may be registered upon submission of documentary evidence." Such proof includes "tax records up to December 31,1981 or to earlier dates." In accordance with the Land Registry Law, the monastery has regularly payed these taxes dating back to September 1,1937, after having formally claimed this land in its (famous) Declaration of 1936. As Midyat could verify this, it decides in favour of the Monastery (and later insists twice in its decision, see below).

I know it is not possible, but I first thought that for one reason or the other Chamber 20 neglected to take into consideration the continuation of Article 14. Yet, the situation proved to be totally different. In its decision dated December 7, 2010 the Chamber says: "1) It is claimed that taxes have been paid since 1937, but no tax record related to this land has been presented; 2) It is claimed that a notification was made in 1936 to the General Directorate of Foundations, but related documents were not submitted."

3. There is something odd about it ...

I have inquired more than once of the monastic authorities on this point, and they persistently state: "We submitted the tax records from the very outset.The Declaration of 1936 was requested by Midyat directly from the General Directorate of Foundations. Clearly, Midyat 's decision in our favour pointed to these very documents as the basis of its ruling. What's more, we specifically added these documents to the investigation records and to rest of the evidence. But somehow, these records seemed to have disapeared from the file."

I go on asking: "When did you notice this?" The monastic authorities say: "As the decision was reversed and the file was sent back to Midyat. When we studied the decision and looked at the file, we realized that our documents were not there." I ask further: "Did you immediately inform anybody about that?" They add: "As the Midyat court insisted on its decision, we have just written this in capital letters in our request to the Chamber 20 so that it corrects its decision. In addition, we have appended these documents once again. But the position of the Chamber did not change." I then asked for, and received, a copy of the request to change the decision. I can confirm, that all they say is true.

Well, what does the Chamber 20 of Court of Appeals say in its refusal dated June 28, 2011? Two sentences only: "The matters referred to in the petition asking to correct the decision were already brought up before. Our Chamber answered them in accordance with procedures and legislation." (base nr. 2011/3720, decision nr. 2011/8237).

As mentioned above, Midyat affirms its initial decision (October 10, 2011; base nr. 2011/38, decision nr. 2011/87). The Treasury appeals again. Now the file has to go to the General Assembly of the Court of Cassation. This latter says the last word on June 13, 2012: Midyat's decision voided. Midyat has to obey. 244 dönüms of land to be transferred to the Treasury.

4. Deep thoughts on the issue

I am at a loss to understand all these. Clearly, some answers are called for:

1. Midyat evaluated the documents in question and decided in favor of St. Gabriel. and part of the evidence for its decision were the tax records in question. However, the Court of Cassation did not consider these tax records, and it decided in favour of the Treasury because it says they [the documents] are not in the file. Okay, when did they disappear from the file? How did they disappear? Who took them?
2. Even if we assume these documents had disappeared en route to the Supreme Court, the authorities of the monastery sent yet another copy of those [documents] along with their appeal to correct the decision. Did the second set disappear as well? This stretches credulity.
3. The AKP government initiated reforms related to non-Muslims which was unprecedented, and it has engendered the enmity of some conservatives. But is the government not aware that its own Treasury is repeatedly filing appeals in this legal case? Isn't the Treasury an agency of the government?
4. This juridical process has been the zenith of pressures endured by St. Gabriel over the years Since it is involving religious rights, the matter has been followed abroad with great interest, more than it is followed by Turkish civil society. The reverberation of the final decision has not been kind to Turkey's image. The latest news from the Internet notes: "The German Federal Parlia-

ment protests with respect to St. Gabriel" (http://www.dw.de/dw/article/0,1602 8337,00.html).

5. As a result of this ill-adviced situation, the Court of Cassation has been badly hurt too. It is burdened with a sullied record in the past: The very same Assembly General of the very same Court of Cassation had said on May 8, 1974: "Juridical persons created by non-Turkish real persons cannot acquire immovable property." (base nr. 1971/2–820, decision nr. 1974/505). This decision was not referring to foreigners. It was referring to the governing Board of the Balikli Greek Hospital Foundation in Istanbul who's all members were Turkish citizens, of course. Simply, they were not regarded as "Turks" because they were not Muslims.

At the time, I wrote a lot about this great shame. But it happened to be forgotten in the turmoil of the Cold War period. Now, I don't think that such a strange thing as "disappearing documents" from a file of the Court of Cassation will be forgotten in the conjuncture of today. It will have serious consequences.

Foto Index

Sébastien de Courtois & Douchan Novakovic. These picture were taken from "Les Derniers Araméens, Le peuple oublié de Jésus", La Table Ronde, Paris, 2004, which has been translated and published in Turkey under the title: "Süryanliler", Yapi Kredi Yayanlari, Istanbul, 2011:
– p. 8: *The Annunciation of Archangel Gabriel to the Mother of God; image from a Syriac Bible,* Deir El-Zaafaran, 1250, Collection Leroy, EPHE, Paris, S. de Courtois.
– p. 22: *Mount Izlo from the South, where first ermits came from Egypt and Syria.*
– p. 34: *A group of Süryanis after the church service in the village of Bsorino.*
– p. 42: *Children receiving classes in syriac, village of Midun.*
– p. 58: *Church service during the Holy Week in Midyat. The Archbishop of Tur Abdin Samuel Aktas, together with now deceased Monk Yaqub, Deacon Isa Gares and several acolytes.*
– p. 90: *Image of a "sislo" bell symbolizing cherubim; they are used during the Eucharist service.*
– p. 160: *Singing in a hymn book (Fenqitho) during church service.*
– p. 168: *Tomb of Mor Yaqub from Nisibis.*
– p. 244: *Elderly Syriac women praying in the church of Mor Izozoel in Kfarze (Altıntaş).*

Horst Oberkampf. These pictures were taken from Oberkampf, H., "Ohne Recht keine Zukunft – Die Syrischen Christen des Turabdin im Südosten der Türkei" (2011):
– p. 10: *The monastery of Mor Malke in Tur Abdin with monk Yeshu.*
– p. 38: *Mor Gabriel's outer wall. Parts of it will have to be demolished after the judgement by the Turkish court, expropriation lands of the monastery.*
– p. 86: *Close up of the church of Mor Had Bshabo in Inwardo (Gülgöze). During the genocide it was successfully used as fortress against Kurdish and Turkish attacks. The village offered shelter for Syriacs from all over the Tur Abdin region.*
– p. 93: *The Church of Mor Quryaqus in Anhel (Yemişli).*
– p. 123: *Kafro (Tahtayto) with its new built houses in the background.*
– p. 136: *Two Syrian Orthodox priests and a Malfono (Syriac and liturgical teacher) in Tur Abdin.*

Foto Index

- p. 187: *View on Mor Gabriel and parts of its outer wall.*
- p. 234: *Remnants of the collapsed Mor Elio monastery in the Tur Izlo region within Tur Abdin.*

Yakup Bilge (From his book "Mor Gabriel Manastırı: 1600 Yıllık Gelenek"), Mehmet Süer, Gabriel Gülten:
- *Cover page: Acolytes in Mor Gabriel celebrating a Mass following the ancient rites of the Syrian Orthodox church.*
- p. 83: *Image and calligraphy of the last supper from an old, handwritten Syriac Bible.*
- p. 114: *Lit candles in the Mor Gabriel monastery.*
- p. 131: *Archbishop Samuel Aktaş is reading an old Syriac Bible.*
- p. 165: *The Patriarch of the Syrian Orthodox church Ignatius Afrem I in the centre (1933–1957) and bishop Iavanis Afrem Bilgic of Tur Abdin (1952–1982) who had his Seat in the Mor Gabriel monastery (front row, first right) together with other bishops, monks and priests.*
- p. 183: *Acolytes in Mor Gabriel celebrating a Mass following the ancient rites of the Syrian Orthodox church.*
- p. 196: *A picture of Archbishop Samuel Aktas, the monks, teachers and pupils of Mor Gabriel monastery.*
- p. 202: *Acolytes in Mor Gabriel singing hymns in Aramaic, the language Jesus Christ and his disciples used.*
- p. 204: *Footprint of the Mor Gabriel monastery, ground floor (without the outer wall and its surrounding lands).*
- p. 206: *Snow in Mor Gabriel monastery.*
- p. 210: *Dome of Theodora, part of the Mor Gabriel monastery; built in the 6th century by Theodora the wife of Byzantine Emperor Justinian I, the Great.*
- p. 214: *The Syrian Orthodox Church Patriach, Mor Ignatius Zakka I (second from right), and accompanying delegation visited Prime Minister Recep Tayyip Erdoğan (first from right) on 30 March 2011, at which time they communicated the problems they were experiencing with the Treasury. The Patriarch informed the Prime Minister that the entire Syriac community was carefully following the progress of the property dispute.*
- p. 216: *In order to inform state officials of the disagreements between the Monastery of St. Gabriel and the Treasury with respect to the surrounding land claims, the Patriarch of the Syriac Church, Mor Ignatius Zakka Iwas I (fourth from the left), together with accompanying delegation, visited the President of Turkey Abdullah Gül (center) on 31 March 2011.*

Foto Index

- p. 220: *Mor Gabriel monastery, hallway in front of main church.*
- p. 228: *Mor Gabriel monastery, inner court.*

Markus Tozman:
- *Cover page: Mor Gabriel monastery: main church from the outside.*
- p. 18: *The village of Kafro Eleito (Arica). Until the 80s it was still inhabited by Syriacs and Kurds. Today, there are no Syriac families left.*
- p. 19: *View on the church Mor Had Bshabo in Ciwardo (Gülgöze), one of the few centres of successful resistance of the Syriacs against the genocide.*
- p. 28: *Collapsed monastery of Mor Abhay close to the abandoned village of Beth Man'im. Tradition goes that the monastery had 365 rooms, for each day of the year one.*
- p. 30: *"Önce Vatan" – "(My) fatherland first". Nationalistic dictums in Turkish public to stir nationalist sentiments. This picture was taken close to Midyat.*
- p. 49: *A Syriac Bible with a cover made of gold and silver. The Syriacs are well known for their fine goldsmithery.*
- p. 55: *Apse of the church Mor Dodo in Basibrin (Haberli).*
- p. 61: *View on the Monastery Church of the Holy Virgin of Hah, with its foundation going back as far as the first century, one of the oldest churches in Tur Abdin. Tradition goes that the Three Wise Men founded it after they had given their presents to Jesus Christ in Bethlehem.*
- p. 66: *Christian graveyard at Mor Abrohom monastery in Midyat. This graveyard and other Christian tombs have frequently been defiled during the 80s and 90s.*
- p. 69: *Sunset above Tur Abdin, close to Mor Yaqub monastery.*
- p. 79: *The old Christian commercial main street of Midyat; once a thriving place of business, Today only abandoned stores remain.*
- p. 105: *Syriac village in Tur Abdin.*
- p. 108: *The old church of Mor Afrem in Bote (Bardakci), now state property; it was used as refuge during the genocide. The majority of the Christian inhabitants were massacred nevertheless.*
- p. 127: *Syriac village of Chrabe Mishka (Dagici) within Tur Izlo; some of its former habitants have rebuild their old houses and are planning to return for good.*
- p. 148: *One of the Christian villages in Tur Abdin severely hit by state expropriations of land.*
- p. 150: *Monastery of Mor Augin from below; received a preservation order by the state, too.*

Foto Index

- p. 152: *Apse of the church of the Holy Virgin of Hah; the church has been put under preservation order.*
- p. 173: *Mor Gabriel monastery; main church from the outside.*
- p. 237: *View on the recently re-occupied monastery of Mor Augin from above. The mountains mark the end of geographic Anatolia to the south, with a view on the wide-stretched plains of Syria's north-east.*
- p. 247: *Deserted monastery of Mor Yuhanon Tayoyo, built on the cliff of Mount Izlo.*

Mor Gabriel Monastery:
- p. 102: *Aramaic Estrangelo carved in stone.*
- p. 111: *View on Mor Gabriel's main church at night.*
- p. 143: *The monastery of Mor Gabriel with some of its lands; Mor Gabriel has severely been hit by consequences of the cadastral registration of its lands.*
- p. 176: *Mosaic above the monastery's main church apse from the 6th century.*
- p. 192: *The main church of the Mor Gabriel monastery.*